Evangelicals
and the Early Church

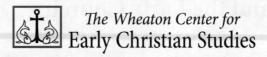

The Wheaton Center for
Early Christian Studies

The Wheaton Center for Early Christian Studies supports the mission
of Wheaton College by fostering systematic study in the fields of Patristics
and early Christian literature, and by engaging in sustained teaching,
research, and publications related to the early Church.

Evangelicals and the Early Church

Recovery • Reform • Renewal

Edited by
GEORGE KALANTZIS
and ANDREW TOOLEY

CASCADE *Books* • Eugene, Oregon

EVANGELICALS AND THE EARLY CHURCH
Recovery • Reform • Renewal

Cascade Books
An Imprint of Wipf and Stock Publishers
199 W. 8th Ave., Suite 3
Eugene, OR 97401

www.wipfandstock.com

ISBN 13: 978-1-61097-459-2

Cataloging-in-Publication data:

Evangelicals and the early church : recovery • reform • renewal / edited by George Kalantzis and Andrew Tooley.

xiv + 274 p. ; 23 cm. Includes bibliographical references and indexes.

ISBN 13: 978-1-61097-459-2

1. Church history. 2. Church. 3. Evangelicalism. I. Title. II. George Kalantzis. III. Andrew Tooley.

BR165 E9 2012

To

Drs. Frank and Julie Papatheofanis

whose vision and sacrifice made
The Wheaton Center for Early Christian Studies possible

Contents

Epilogue: The *Radical•*ness of the Evangelical Faith
—*George Kalantzis, Wheaton College* ◆ 242

Contributors

JEFFREY W. BARBEAU (PhD, Marquette University) is Associate Professor of Theology at Wheaton College. He is the author of *Coleridge, the Bible, and Religion* (2008), and editor of *Coleridge's Assertion of Religion: Essays on the Opus Maximum* (2006).

D. JEFFREY BINGHAM (PhD, Dallas Theological Seminary) is Department Chair and Professor of Theological Studies at Dallas Theological Seminary. He is the author of *Irenaeus' Use of Matthew's Gospel in Adversus Haereses* (1997), the *Pocket History of the Church* (2002), as well as many articles and essays on early Christianity. He serves as the general editor of the Brill monograph series, *The Bible in Ancient Christianity*, and was the editor of *The Routledge Companion to Early Christian Thought* (2010).

GERALD L. BRAY (LittD, University of Paris-Sorbonne) is Research Professor of Divinity at Beeson Divinity School and Director of Research for the Latimer Trust. He is a prolific writer and has authored or edited numerous books including a number of volumes in the Ancient Christian Commentary on Scripture, Ancient Christian Doctrine, Ancient Christian Texts, as well as the forthcoming systematic theology *God is Love* (2012). He is also the editor of the Anglican journal *Churchman*.

ELESHA COFFMAN (PhD, Duke University) is Assistant Professor of History at Waynesburg University, and, in 2011–2012, a visiting fellow at the Center for the Study of Religion at Princeton University.

EVERETT FERGUSON (PhD, Harvard University) is Distinguished Scholar in Residence at Abilene Christian University, where he taught for thirty-six years. He served as president of the North American Patristics Society and is the recipient of its Distinguished Service Award as well as a former member of the Council of the American Society of Church

History and of the Council of the Association Internationale d'Études Patristiques. He is the author of numerous books on early Christianity including, *Baptism in the Early Church* (2009), *Backgrounds of Early Christianity* (1989, 1993, 2003), and *Church History*, vol. 1 (2005), and served as editor of the *Encyclopedia of Christianity* (1997, 1999).

MICHAEL W. GRAVES (PhD, Hebrew Union College) is Associate Professor of Old Testament at Wheaton College. He is the author of *Jerome's Hebrew Philology* (2007) and the forthcoming *Jerome's Commentary on Jeremiah* in the Ancient Christian Texts (2012).

CHRISTOPHER A. HALL (PhD, Drew University) is chancellor of Eastern University, and dean of Palmer Theological Seminary. He is the author and editor of a number of books including *Ancient Christian Commentary on Scripture: The Gospel of Mark* (with Thomas C. Oden, 1998) *Reading the Scripture with the Fathers* (1998), *Learning Theology with the Church Fathers* (2002), and *Worshiping with the Church Fathers* (2009).

DARRYL G. HART (PhD, Johns Hopkins University) is visiting professor of history at Hillsdale College. He is the author and editor of many books on American religion, including *The Lost Soul of American Protestantism* (2002), *Deconstructing Evangelicalism* (2004), and *From Billy Graham to Sarah Palin: Evangelicals and the Betrayal of American Conservatism* (2011). Hart serves on the board of directors at the Institute for the Study of American Evangelicals at Wheaton College.

KEITH L. JOHNSON (PhD, Princeton Theological Seminary) is Assistant Professor of Theology at Wheaton College. He is the author of *Karl Barth and the Analogia Entis* (2010) and the forthcoming *Thinking After God: The Method and Practice of Theology* (2013).

GEORGE KALANTZIS (PhD, Northwestern University) is Associate Professor of Theology at Wheaton College, where he also directs of The Wheaton Center for Early Christian Studies. He has written extensively on Alexandrian and Antiochene theology and hermeneutics, and on the intersection of theology and ethics. His books include, *Theodore of Mopsuestia: Commentary on John* (2004), *The Sovereignty of God Debate* (with D. Stephen Long, 2009), *Life in the Spirit: Spiritual Formation in Theological Perspective* (with Jeffrey P. Greenman, 2010), and the forthcoming *Caesar and the Lamb: Early Christian Attitudes on War and Military Service* (2012).

TIMOTHY LARSEN (PhD, University of Stirling) is McManis Professor of Christian Thought at Wheaton College. He is a Fellow of the Royal Historical Society, and in 2012 he will also be a Visiting Fellow in History, All Souls College, Oxford. He has authored and edited a number of books, including *Contested Christianity: The Political and Social Contexts of Victorian Theology*, (2004), *Crisis of Doubt: Honest Faith in Nineteenth-Century England* (2009) and most recently, *A People of One Book: The Bible and the Victorians* (2011).

BRYAN LITFIN (PhD, University of Virginia) is Professor of Theology at Moody Bible Institute. He is the author of *Getting to Know the Church Fathers: An Evangelical Introduction* (2007), as well as three adventure novels.

D. STEPHEN LONG (PhD, Duke University) is professor of Systematic Theology at Marquette University. He has authored and edited over a dozen books including, *Divine Economy: Theology and the Market* (2000), *The Goodness of God: Theology, Church and Social Order*, (2001), *Speaking of God: Theology, Truth and Language* (2008) and *Hebrews: Belief: A Theological Commentary on the Bible* (2011).

SCOT MCKNIGHT (PhD, Nottingham University) is the Karl A. Olsson Professor in Religious Studies at North Park University. He is the author of more than thirty books, including the award-winning *The Jesus Creed: Loving God, Loving Others* (2004). His most recent book is *The King Jesus Gospel* (2011).

DAVID NEFF (MDiv, Andrews University) is editor in chief of *Christianity Today*. He serves on the board of the Robert E. Webber Institute for Worship Studies and the executive committee of the National Association of Evangelicals.

DOUGLAS A. SWEENEY (PhD, Vanderbilt University) is Professor of Church History and the History of Christian Thought at Trinity Evangelical Divinity School, where he also directs the Henry Center and Jonathan Edwards Center. A former editor of The Works of Jonathan Edwards, Yale Divinity School, he has written a number of books about the history of Christianity, American religious history, and theology, including *The American Evangelical Story: A History of the Movement* (2005) and *Jonathan Edwards and the Ministry of the Word: A Model of Faith and Thought* (2009).

ANDREW TOOLEY (PhD, Candidate, University of Stirling) served as the project director at the Institute for the Study of American Evangelicals at Wheaton College from 2008 to 2011. His research focuses on the intersection between religion and culture in the nineteenth-century transatlantic world.

DANIEL J. TREIER (PhD, Trinity Evangelical Divinity School) is Associate Professor of Theology at Wheaton College. He has authored and edited a number of books, articles, and essays, including, *Virtue and the Voice of God: Toward Theology as Wisdom* (2006), *Introducing Theological Interpretation of Scripture* (2008), and *Proverbs and Ecclesiastes* (2011) in the Brazos Theological Commentary on the Bible.

ROBERT LOUIS WILKEN (PhD, University of Chicago) is the William R. Kenan, Jr. Professor of the History of Christianity Emeritus at the University of Virginia and the Rev. Robert J. Randall Professor in Christian Culture at Providence College (2011–2012). He serves as chairman of the board for the St. Anselm Institute for Catholic Thought and the Institute on Religion and Public Life and is a member of the board of Ave Maria University. Wilken has also served as president of the American Academy of Religion and the North American Patristic Society and is an elected fellow of the American Academy of Arts and Sciences. A prolific writer, Wilken is the author of numerous books, articles and essays on early Christianity, including *Isaiah,* (2007), *The Spirit of Early Christian Thought: Seeking the Face of God* (2003), and *On the Cosmic Mystery of Jesus Christ* (2003).

Introduction

George Kalantzis *and* Andrew Tooley

I N HIS BOOK *The Life of Reason* (1905) the Spanish American philosopher George Santayana famously remarked that "those who cannot remember the past are condemned to repeat it."[1] With this sentiment in mind this book offers an historical as well as custodial function. It reminds readers of the lost treasures in their own ecclesiastical backyard, illuminating how they were lost and why we need to recover them, before offering a few suggestions on how this might be done; and it educates would-be historians on the difficulties of interpreting the past, explaining why careful attention to the cultural contexts in which ancient doctrines were developed is so vitally important when appropriating age-old truths for present religious purposes. Finally, it offers a general plea for evangelicals to continue their thoughtful explorations of, and conversations about, the apostolic and patristic periods of Christian history.

The essays in this book originated as a year-long discussion that celebrated the inauguration of The Wheaton Center for Early Christian Studies in the fall of 2009, culminating in a conference held in the spring of 2010 at Wheaton College that was an intentional collaboration between The Wheaton Center for Early Christian Studies and the Institute for the Study of American Evangelicals. The discussion was organized around the conviction that despite a growing body of literature on, and increased interest in, the early church over the last thirty years, most evangelicals continue to be largely unaware of the historical connectedness between the earlier periods of Christian history and their own more

---

1. Santayana, *Life of Reason*, 284.

1

contemporary ecclesiastical and theological heritage, as well as of the many resources the early church can provide the contemporary church.[2]

The prologue to this book is the inaugural address of The Wheaton Center for Early Christian Studies, delivered by the noted historian Robert Louis Wilken, who reminded us that "the great accomplishment of the church fathers was to provide a unified interpretation of the Scriptures centered on the triune God." Wilken continued in his charge to Christians of the twenty-first century—including evangelicals—to dig deeply into the history of the church and see the love for Christ that is diachronically present in our common story, and to recognize that the church fathers offer a way of reading Scriptures that leads us more deeply in the sacred texts. Wilken closed with these words, which serve as the impetus for the discussion that follows in the rest of this book: "My prayer is that as the church fathers have been the teachers of many other Christians in previous centuries they will also become the teachers of evangelical Christians."

The first part of this book, then, examines the relationship of evangelicalism to the early church. In chapter 1 Christopher Hall flags a number of reasons why evangelicals are inattentive to the ancient church before proposing several ways in which this problem might be remedied. He reminds readers that the impulse for immediate intellectual and spiritual gratification must be replaced with a patient and thorough analysis of the past. Jeffrey Barbeau, in chapter 2, examines the extent to which one prominent eighteenth-century evangelical valued and appropriated the writings of the early church. Meticulous historical study, Barbeau concludes, played a central role in the development of Wesley's thought. In the response that follows D. Stephen Long provides five reasons as to why evangelicals should study the church fathers and explains why they would be well served to take instruction from Wesley's reading of the early church.

A third chapter by Darryl Hart explores the interests of two nineteenth-century figures, John Williamson Nevin and Philip Schaff, who sought theological renewal within American evangelicalism through the appropriation of the ancient Christian past. Through this study of Mercersburg Theology, as it came to be known, Hart cautions contemporary evangelicals about the potential pitfalls that await them

---

2. See, for example, Husbands and Greenman, eds., *Ancient Faith for the Church's Future*; also Greenman and Kalantzis, eds., *Life in the Spirit*.

when they attempt to garner insights from the past for use by present communities. Douglas Sweeney responds with a criticism followed by several clarifying questions, which, when taken together, suggest that a greater understanding of Nevin and Schaff's discontent with nineteenth-century confessional Protestantism would serve contemporary evangelicalism well. Elesha Coffman rounds out the last chapter of part 1 by providing an overview of, and response to, the 1977 *Chicago Call*, which urged evangelicals to recover a more catholic and historically informed Christian faith. An autobiographical response by David Neff, who experienced the immediate effects of the *Chicago Call* in his own spiritual life, follows Coffman's essay.

The second part of the book offers various proposals for the ways in which evangelicals might recover a healthy relationship with the early church. Everett Ferguson's plenary address begins this section with several prefatory remarks on the supremacy of Scripture before embarking on a journey that highlights the benefits of and dangers to avoid when studying the ancient past. A sixth chapter by Scot McKnight examines the present need for authority in contemporary evangelicalism and provides suggestions on how a recovery of ancient creeds, and a distillation of the insights of the ancient church through popular and scholarly works, might fill this void. Daniel Treier responds with a general agreement while suggesting the need for more careful attention to, for instance, how these creeds might function in various evangelical communities. D. Jeffrey Bingham begins chapter 7 with a diagnosis that evangelicalism is in jeopardy. He continues with an overview of the way in which a baptismal catechesis mode of thought helped instruct and enrich Irenaeus's Christian faith, and ends by commending this rule of faith as a lens through which the Scriptures and all of life might be interpreted, thereby aiding contemporary evangelical spirituality in its renewal efforts. A response by Bryan Litfin questions whether Bingham's vision of biblical catechesis might create more problems than solutions for evangelicalism in the twenty-first century.

Any book on evangelicals and the early church would be incomplete without a chapter dedicated to the reading, interpretation, and application of the Bible. Michael Graves tackles this task in chapter 8 with a discussion of how the early church read the Bible, suggesting a place for tradition in contemporary readings of Scripture, and pointing out several strengths and limitations of using tradition to guide the interpretation of Scripture. Timothy Larsen responds by echoing the sentiment that greater attention to the rule of faith is needed when interpreting Scripture, and highlights the powerful influence the church fathers have had in guiding his own spiritual life. A ninth chapter by Gerald Bray explores the nature of evangelicalism and the complex relationship that exists between evangelicals and Catholic and Eastern Orthodox Christians. Bray concludes by offering a definition of the church and the ways in which evangelicals are the true heirs of the early church. A response by Keith Johnson addresses several key elements of Bray's definition of the church and suggests that evangelicals might not be as catholic or orthodox as some would hope. The book concludes with an epilogue by George Kalantzis in which he addresses a few lingering questions and argues for the *radical•*ness (from *radic*, meaning "rootedness") of the evangelical faith. Kalantzis closes our discussion with a warning about the dangers of an idiomatic, ahistorical evangelicalism, followed by several practical suggestions for a successful evangelical engagement with the Great Tradition.

While encouraging the need for a greater understanding of all periods of the Christian past, this book's aim is to advance the notion that contemporary evangelicalism would do well to strengthen its religious moorings in the ancient church. The benefits to be gained by such realignment, as several of these essays demonstrate, are enormous. The shared hope of these authors is that this book will further the discussion about the ancient tradition and the reforming role it might play within contemporary evangelicalism. While all writing here are concerned with the ways in which the insights of the early church can aid the present, they are acutely aware that an accurate understanding of the social, political, and theological contexts out of which these ideas emerged must inform any attempts at application. Only through a serious engagement with the early church fathers on their own terms can one hope to avoid the pitfalls and mistakes so common to scholars who wish to elucidate the past. In this endeavor the authors align themselves with the sixteenth-century Reformers and seek, as they did, to restore the ancient catholicity of the church.

In order to facilitate the reader to enter with us into this discussion about history, trajectories, and, ultimately, identity formation, we thought it necessary to provide a brief summary of the developments that helped shape the discussion of evangelicals and their engagement with the early church over the last half century.

Evangelicals Seeking Historical Understanding

In the post-World War II era, at Wheaton College and later Northern Baptist Seminary, professor Robert Webber was one of the first to offer a sustained polemic for why evangelicalism would benefit from a robust exploration of the patristic period. For many evangelical Christians his *Common Roots* (1978) was a clarion call to wisely recover that which had been lost through, most recently, the pervasive theology and cultural ideology of the fundamentalist movement. Webber's quest for evangelicalism's ancient roots led him to author several additional books that passionately promoted evangelical engagement with the early church while questioning the hegemonic role modernity held over the contemporary church.[3]

Robert Webber's discovery of and abiding interest in the past coincided with the larger evangelical reengagement with politics, the academy, and popular culture. Shortly after Jimmy Carter was elected to the presidency of the United States, he made a comment about being a born-again Christian. This claim encouraged *Newsweek* magazine to declare 1976 the "Year of the Evangelical" and sparked a sustained curiosity about evangelicalism by the media elite. In the 1980s evangelicals witnessed the rise to prominence of the political Religious Right and a commercialization of Christian conservatism aided by the efforts of such public religious figures as Southern Baptist minister Jerry Falwell and TV evangelist Pat Robertson. During the Cold War period populist evangelicals developed a renewed interest in redeeming and restoring America to her supposedly Christian past. This interest helped fuel strident debates about evangelical identity and its historic roots. The spotlight was now on evangelicalism, but many Americans, protestant and secular alike, were scratching their heads over what exactly constituted an "evangelical."

The rise of evangelical historiography can be dated to the 1970s and early 80s when conservative protestant scholars began scrambling to define the evangelical movement. Which characteristics define an evangelical, they wondered, and to which historical moments can the roots of the movement be accurately traced? One book that emerged during this period was confidently titled *The Evangelicals: What They Believe, Who*

3. Webber, *Ancient-future Faith; Common Roots; Divine Embrace; Evangelicals on the Canterbury Trail; Younger Evangelicals*; Webber and Bloesch, eds., *Orthodox Evangelicals.*

They Are, Where They Are Changing (1975). It regarded evangelicalism as a relatively new development that arose out of the fundamentalist movement but had roots in the Reformation and the eighteenth-century revivals. As scholars increasingly devoted more research to the question of evangelical identity, a general consensus among religious historians began to take shape in the late 1980s, which concluded that evangelicalism was a product of the British, French, and American Enlightenments, eighteenth-century transatlantic revivals, and English Puritanism. As a transdenominational movement, evangelicalism emphasized the saving work of Christ on the cross, the Bible as the primary source of religious authority, conversion from a life of sin, and active involvement in spreading the gospel and working for social reform. Even while this thesis was gaining ground among religious historians, British historian Reginald Ward was challenging and revising its conclusions. Ward advocated instead that the intellectual roots of evangelicalism were as much, if not more, a product of seventeenth-century European Pietism as they were of the Enlightenments, eighteenth-century revivals, and Puritanism. Further revision by several historians has argued that a more accurate placement of evangelicalism's roots lay in the Reformation movements occurring across continental Europe and Britain.[4] Proponents of this view contend that the evangelical heritage in America overwhelmingly owes its thought and practice to the work of those venerable sixteenth- and seventeenth-century Reformers rather than the innovative religious thinkers from the great Age of Enlightenment. Still others contend that the evangelical faith is anchored in the ancient doctrines forged in the fires of the patristic period.[5]

This complex pedigree has allowed evangelicalism to be a creative and innovative force in the American religious marketplace. From George Whitefield's open-air preaching in the eighteenth century to Rob Bell's use of popular media to spread the gospel message, evangelicals have found opportunities to thrive among competing forms of Christianity. Yet one of the movement's greatest strengths has also been a considerable weakness. While evangelicals have played a significant role in shaping their environments, they have also been molded by their

4. Haykin, Stewart, and George, *Advent of Evangelicalism.*

5. For a summary and discussion of the nature and history of evangelicalism see "Defining and Locating Evangelicalism" in Larsen and Treier, *Cambridge Companion to Evangelical Theology,* 1–14.

surroundings and often unwittingly accommodated their beliefs to prevailing views and customs. A cursory search on evangelical attitudes towards, for example, divorce, economics, war, and foreign policy will reveal that evangelical views more often than not mirror those of most Americans. The evangelical tendency to prioritize the spirituality of an individual and her private interpretation of Scripture has led to heated debates about, among other things, the role of women in the church, when Christ will return, speaking in tongues, and homosexuality.

With these debates in mind, Robert Webber, Thomas Oden, and others set out in the 1980s to interpret Scripture intentionally with reference to what Christians believed in the past. They were convinced that the intellectual and spiritual climate within American evangelicalism had suffered in part because evangelicals were overlooking or ignoring this ancient tradition. What would happen, they wondered, if evangelicals began interpreting Scripture in ways the church fathers would approve? How might an interpretation of the Bible that valued rather than eschewed early Christian traditions provide a helpful corrective to various excesses and ideological neuroses that had crept into evangelicalism?

These questions and renewed interest in the early church did not escape the keen eye of one of evangelicalism's best and most well-known chroniclers. In 1978 Mark Noll wrote an article appearing in *Eternity* magazine entitled, "Evangelicals on the Canterbury Trail," which described the efforts of Webber and others to foster a greater historical consciousness. Answering the call to rediscover ancient roots was a difficult task to achieve for non-specialists, in large part because patristic writings were not easily accessible, especially for clergy seeking insight on a particular text or topic. Such an undertaking was also difficult because, as mentioned above, evangelicalism was undergoing an identity crisis and multiple voices within the movement were directing evangelicals to different solutions. In recent decades it has become easier to explore the ancient past with the steady publication (in print, compact disc, and on the Internet) of the Ancient Christian Commentary on Scripture (ACCS) series since the early 1990s, together with The Church's Bible series, edited by Robert L. Wilken, and the continued appearance of several scholarly monographs and popular books on the early church by evangelicals.

Other efforts that helped promote an interest in the early church were the engagement with contemporary Roman Catholics by several well-respected card-carrying evangelicals. Beginning in 1992, Chuck Colson, Timothy George, James Packer, and Richard Mouw among others began an ecumenical discussion with Roman Catholic Christians. The discussions culminated in a 1994 collaborative document entitled *Catholics and Evangelicals Together*. Among the many things affirmed by the group was a commitment to justification by faith alone. Further discussions by evangelicals with Eastern Orthodox Christians followed in subsequent years. The outcome of these discussions has been largely positive, with the various parties identifying one another as cobelligerents on a number of issues, from family and sexuality to patriotism and anticommunism.

Yet amidst these efforts an informed awareness of the ancient church and the benefits to be gained from the serious study of the Christian past remains elusive to most Protestant Christians. Why is this still a reality? Perhaps one reason for the continued inattentiveness to the early church is that the Christian past remains an uncertain and dangerous place in the perspective of many evangelicals. For those unfamiliar with the rhythms by which the Christian faith has developed over the centuries, diving into the interminable controversies of the patristic period, for instance, can produce nail-biting moments followed by serious doubts about accepted Christian truths. Still others have been conditioned to view much of Christian history through Martin Luther's pessimistic lenses, believing the story of Christendom contains great periods of decline, corruption, and apostasy. This view created a tendency within evangelicalism to connect the past with their present Christian faith by selecting Christian individuals whom their particular faith community has identified as orthodox. So, for example, such a community might trace their theological lineage from the apostle Paul in the first century, to the North African St. Augustine, to the Reformers of the sixteenth and seventeenth centuries, to Jonathan Edwards in colonial America and other revivalists of the eighteenth century, to Dwight Moody of the nineteenth, to Billy Graham of the twentieth, before arriving at their own convictions in the early twenty-first century. Such an approach is governed in part by an unhealthy fear of tradition and a misunderstanding of the church's legacy, perpetuating a belief that the church as it developed between the apostolic period and the Protestant Reformation was misguided and ultimately wrong in its expressions of the Christian faith.

A third reason why evangelicals have paid little attention to the early church is that evangelicalism has primarily been and currently is a populist rather than elitist movement. Evangelicals are overwhelmingly democratic and individualistic in their polity, and generally favor decisions made by intuition rather than informed scholarly consensus of opinion. Most of the early church, especially in the post-Constantine era, and European Christianity during the Middle Ages, does not reflect this style of faith. It is little wonder then that the Christian beliefs and practices of our forefathers can seem odd and even disagreeable when perceived from a twenty-first-century North American perspective.

Upon closer examination of twenty-first-century evangelical inattentiveness to the early church, it is also possible to trace most of their suspicions to the pervasive anti-Catholic mood dominating American Protestantism since the colonial period, and to the enduring legacy of the fundamentalist movement in the twentieth. Evangelicals have long expressed anti-Catholic sentiments. Throughout the nineteenth century, in the wake of much Catholic immigration, evangelicals created numerous organizations and societies to advance the antipopery cause and convert Catholics to the Protestant faith. During the early twentieth century, Catholics further cultivated their distinct religious identity by establishing parochial schools and their own hospitals and universities. These activities provoked a backlash from Protestant nativists who, in the mid twentieth century, feared that a resurgent Catholicism would transform America into a Catholic country. Thus, evangelicals regularly preached against papal authority, the Mass, and the veneration of saints. This anti-Catholic hostility, which subsided after World War II with the help of the reforming efforts of the Second Vatican Council and the election of President John F. Kennedy in the 1960s, continued through much of the century even as Protestants and Roman Catholics entered into numerous ecumenical discussions.

An additional formidable influence that has had a lasting effect on the psyche and theology of American evangelicalism from the decades surrounding 1914 to the present is the fundamentalist movement. Militant towards mainstream Protestantism, strict in their adherence to the (self-designated) fundamentals of the faith (the virgin birth, the inerrancy of Scripture, etc.), possessing a generally belligerent attitude, embracing positions as cultural isolationists, and supremely confident in their particular theological views, fundamentalists developed a specific brand of, and approach to, Christian theology that prioritized human reason while leaving little room for intellectual exploration. Although fundamentalists can be commended for their efforts to preserve the faith and their passion for spreading the gospel, they bequeathed a subculture that directly contributed to the intellectual and spiritual stagnation of American evangelicalism. A generalized and simplified rhetorical strategy for identifying the different paths taken by fundamentalists and liberals during the progressive era of American history contrasts their readings of the two greatest commandments mentioned in Mark's Gospel. It has been suggested that the fundamentalists prioritized the first commandment, "Love the Lord your God with all your heart, soul, and mind," while the liberals emphasized the second, "Love your neighbor as yourself," resulting in a withdrawal from popular culture and the life of the mind by fundamentalists and a withdrawal from orthodoxy by the liberals.

The Maturing of the Evangelical Mind: Evangelicalism at the Start of a New Century

In 2009, scholars, students, and interested laypersons gathered at Gordon College in Boston, Massachusetts, to reflect on Mark Noll's famous book *The Scandal of the Evangelical Mind* (1994). While agreeing that significant advances had occurred in the life of the evangelical mind over the last fifteen years, many concluded that such a scandal still existed and that populist and scholarly evangelicalism is still devoid of much serious thinking. Whether or not this observation is an accurate one is difficult to ascertain. What is clear, however, is that evangelicalism has significantly matured in the last two decades. Perhaps no one has shown this more clearly than sociologist and President of Gordon College D. Michael Lindsay in his book *Faith in the Halls of Power: How Evangelicals Joined the American Elite* (2008). Lindsay demonstrates that a new cosmopolitan evangelical has emerged, one who is more likely to have been converted to the evangelical faith as an adult and has thus avoided much of the evangelical kitsch subculture. This new breed of evangelical is more likely to have been educated at a top-tier university and nurtured in the Christian faith through one of evangelicalism's campus ministries than at a traditional Bible college. Lindsay also points out that evangelicals have significantly shaped mainstream academic discussions in, for example, the disciplines of history and philosophy, while making significant contributions to other areas of American life, from Wall Street to Hollywood.

As Mark Noll has recently observed, a new shape of world Christianity is afoot, and its entrepreneurial and individualistic impulses are remarkably similar to North American Christianity.[6] The reason for this fact is because much of the world is coming to resemble a modern society; and America, with its competitive market-oriented lifestyles, serves as the primary model. Churches in many countries around the world continue to send their young people to the United States for ministerial training, and a result is that many African and South American countries, for example, are embracing forms of the Christian faith that closely resemble North American Christianity. In this current religious climate the need is ever more pressing for an evangelical rapprochement with the ancient church.

The challenge remains for evangelicals to reject the fundamentalist-influenced sectarian tendencies still cascading across the evangelical landscape. Theological disagreement among evangelicals will surely persist, but the ancient church offers a faithful articulation of scriptural doctrine around which many can unite. In this way the ancient Christian tradition offers invaluable resources for present Christian communities and can serve not only as an authoritative, intellectually and spiritually rich voice in service of the Christian Scriptures and present Christian communities, but as a potentially stabilizing and corrective influence on certain unhappy tendencies within American evangelicalism.

George Kalantzis & Andrew Tooley
Lent 2011

6. Noll, *New Shape of World Christianity*.

Prologue

Going Deeper into the Bible

The Church Fathers as Interpreters

Robert Louis Wilken

University of Virginia

GREGORY THE GREAT, BISHOP of Rome in the year 600, once said that the "Word of God," by which he meant the Holy Scriptures, "exercises the understanding of the wise . . . and nurses the simple. . . . To some it speaks in the open day, to other it holds things in secret to lead them to loftier matters . . . It is, as it were, a kind of river . . . which is both shallow and deep, in which both the lamb may find a footing and the elephant float at large."[1]

These words appear in the introduction to Gregory's *Moralia*, his commentary on the book of Job, a verse-by-verse exposition of one of the most difficult and challenging books in the Bible. Though other early Christian writers had written on Job, Gregory's work surpasses all others in length and spiritual insight.

Gregory lived at a turning point in the church's history. He was at once a man of the medieval world yet he had been formed by the ancient Roman literary culture. He is sometimes called the last of the church fathers, and some accounts of the history of the early church bring their accounts to a close with his papacy. He is celebrated in Christian tradition as one of the four Latin *doctores ecclesiae*, teachers of the church, along with St. Ambrose, St. Jerome, and St. Augustine.

---

1. *Letter to Leander* 4, in Gregory I, *Morals of the Book of Job*. For the Latin text of the *Moralia* see Gregory I, *S. Gregorii Magni Moralia in Job*.

In common usage the term "church fathers" designates those Christian teachers who lived from the second to the seventh centuries, the period in the church's history after the books of the New Testament were written and before the beginning of the Middle Ages. It is a long time span, more than six centuries, and the company of thinkers is large and diverse, some from Greece and Asia Minor, others from Palestine and Egypt, North Africa (present day Algeria and Tunisia), Syria and Iraq, Italy and Spain. Some wrote in Latin, others in Greek, and others in Syriac, Coptic, Armenian, and other languages. Among them were luminaries such as Origen of Alexandria, Eusebius of Caesarea, Athanasius of Alexandria, Gregory of Nyssa, Basil of Caesarea, Ephraem the Syrian, Ambrose, Jerome, Augustine, Cyril of Alexandria, Maximus the Confessor, to name only the best known. And of course Gregory the Great.

The church fathers belong to an illustrious period in the history of Christianity, those early centuries when the new religion was setting down roots in the cities of the Roman Empire and beyond. They forged the language to express Christian belief clearly and precisely in creeds, oversaw the communal life of the Christian people—most were bishops—clarified and applied moral norms, explained and defended the faith to outsiders. In short they prepared the church for its great mission of transforming the ancient world and creating a new Christian civilization.

Because their writings were so formative in Christian history, they have been honored with the venerable title "fathers," a term that designates orthodox doctrine as well as a holy life. The phrase begins to appear in Christian writings in the third century, and by the fifth century it was widespread. In fact, the opening words of the famous decree at the Council of Chalcedon in 451—the council that gave us the christological formulation "two natures in one person"—are: "following then the holy fathers." In the hierarchy of authorities the church fathers rank second, the Sacred Scriptures being of course the primary authority.

As we look back on Christian history from the perspective of the early twenty-first century it is evident that Christians of many different traditions have come to recognize the church fathers as a precious inheritance of all Christians. If one thinks seriously about what Christians confess and teach, inevitably one will turn to their writings for instruction and illumination. After the New Testament there is no body of

Christian literature that makes a greater claim on us. This of course is why Wheaton College has founded a Center of Early Christian Studies—the first of its kind in an evangelical institution.

There was a time not too long that the only persons to study the church fathers in this country were Roman Catholics and Eastern Orthodox, and an occasional Episcopalian or Lutheran. But over the last two generations evangelicals have begun to read the church fathers and to learn from them. Most of my graduate students over the last ten years have been evangelicals.

To some that may come as a surprise, but one only need open a treatise of Augustine or Irenaeus or Athanasius to discover why. Their writings are spread through with citations from the Scriptures and their thinking is formed by the Bible's language and imagery. In studying the church fathers I have learned one must have an open Bible at hand. They knew the Scriptures intimately, quote passage after passage by heart, and their exposition of Christian teaching rests on a firm scriptural base.

The great accomplishment of the church fathers was to provide a unified interpretation of the Scriptures centered on the triune God. The Bible they sought to understand was a single book, and all its tributaries and rivulets flowed from the great river of God's revelation, the creation of the world, the history of Israel, the saving work of Christ, the beginning of the church, and the final vision of the heavenly city.

Someone might, however, say: the church fathers are interesting and significant historical figures. If one wishes to understand the history of Christianity they make up a significant chapter. They help us to understand the Christian doctrine of the Trinity and a term such as *homoousion*, of one substance with the Father, which appears in the Nicene Creed. Their writings explain why at the Council of Chalcedon the language of one person in two natures was adopted. But are they really helpful in reading and interpreting the Bible today? Isn't the Bible intelligible on its own terms to a person of faith? Doesn't it possess what theologians call perspicacity, clarity? And do we not have at our disposal the historical, philological, literary, and archaeological resources that biblical scholars have provided over the last two centuries?

A reasonable question that leads to the topic of my talk: going more deeply into the Scriptures. To give you a feel for how the church fathers go about interpreting the Bible let us consider their approach to three biblical passages: Isaiah 6, one of the beatitudes from the Sermon on the

Mount in the Gospel of Matthew, and an enigmatic text from the book of Job.

First Isaiah 6, in particular the opening words: "In the year that King Uzziah died I saw the Lord sitting upon a throne high and lifted up; and his train filled the temple." For most biblical commentators today biblical interpretation deals with historical, philological, and literary questions to which theological or spiritual comments may be appended. If one takes a commentary of Isaiah off the shelf in a library the interpretation focuses on the literary setting of the passage, its date, whether it is a "call" narrative, what kind of a vision is being depicted, whether Isaiah had an actual vision, where it took place, et al. When these questions are dealt with—and they are of course things a skilled interpreter wants to know—one may turn to the theological or spiritual meaning of the text.

If, however, one turns to the patristic commentaries, the theological and spiritual meaning of the text is at the center of interpretation. So in the case of Isaiah what stands out—in fact it leaps off the page—is the verb "see." For Isaiah said that he "*saw* the Lord." The first thing an interpreter will do then is cite other biblical texts with the word "see" with respect to God. For example God's word to Moses, "You cannot *see* my face; for no man shall *see* me and live" (Exod 33:20). Or the Gospel of John: "No one has ever *seen* God; the only Son who is in the bosom of the Father, he has made him known" (1:18). And especially 1 Timothy: "King of kings and Lord of lords who alone has immortality and dwells in unapproachable light, whom no man has ever *seen* or *can see*" (6:16).

My first point then is this: the church fathers read Isaiah 6 in light of the Bible as a whole. The focus is not on what Isaiah thought, but what the Scriptures teach. Second: the citation of other biblical texts allows the interpreter to pose questions that lead more deeply into the meaning of the text. How can Isaiah say that he "saw" the Lord when elsewhere the Scripture says that one *cannot* see God?

Jewish scholars had already seen the problem. As the ancient apocryphal text *The Martyrdom and Ascension of Isaiah* attests, Isaiah is said to have been martyred by the Jewish king Manasseh because he said, "I have seen God, and behold I am alive." As punishment for his blasphemy Manasseh had Isaiah sawn in half with a wooden saw, a historical detail that is mentioned in the Epistle to the Hebrews in the catalogue of heroes of faith: "others were sawn in two" (11:37).

Christian interpreters faced the same dilemma. "By what rule of interpretation," writes Augustine, "shall we prove that these statements that seem opposed and in conflict (e.g., Isaiah 6:1 and John 1:18) are not opposed and in conflict? For it is in no way possible that this authority of the Scriptures is not truthful." By nature God is invisible yet the truly devout person longs to see God not only as He appears when he wills, e.g., in historical events, but to gaze on God as he is. Did not Moses say, "If I have found favor before you, show yourself to me" (Exod 33:13). What does he mean, asks Augustine? "No one has ever grasped the fullness of God, not by the eyes of the body, not even by the mind itself. For it is one thing to see; it is another to grasp the whole by seeing. . . . To say, then, that no one has ever seen God . . . means that no one has seen the fullness of his divinity."[2]

John Chrysostom, the eloquent Christian preacher most of whose sermons are verse-by-verse commentaries on biblical books discerns the same problem in the passage from Isaiah 6 and comes to a similar conclusion: first he cites John 6:46, "No one has seen the Father except him who is sent from God; he has seen the Father," then asks, does Isaiah contradict what Jesus said? No, says John: "Christ was speaking about perceiving God fully, and no one has ever seen God in that way. . . . Only the Only-Begotten has seen the divine nature in all its splendor and beheld the essence of God. The prophet saw what he was capable of seeing. He did not see the essence of God, he saw the form that God had assumed when he lowered himself to the level human weakness could reach."[3]

A second example is Gregory of Nyssa's homily on the beatitude "Blessed are those who hunger and thirst for righteousness (or justice), for they shall be satisfied" (Matt 5:6). In this case Gregory focuses his interpretation on the term "righteousness" or "justice." The Greek term can be translated with either English word.[4]

First Gregory asks, "What is justice?" and gives a traditional philosophical answer. Justice is to give to each according to his due. But then he observes that there is a higher form of justice, not based on merit.

2. See Augustine, *Letter* 147.12–22.

3. A translation of Chrysostom's commentary on Isa 6:1 can be found in Wilken et al., *Isaiah Interpreted*.

4. English translation of *Homily* 8 on the Beatitudes can be found in Gregory of Nyssa, *Lord's Prayer*, 165–75.

This is the kind of justice we "desire," for the beatitude says, "blessed are those who hunger and thirst for justice." Here the homily takes a surprising turn as Gregory offers what he calls a "bolder interpretation." The Lord proposes to his followers that he himself is what they desire, for in 1 Corinthians we read, "he became for us wisdom from God, justice, sanctification and redemption" (1:30). By appealing to 1 Corinthians Gregory opens the beatitude to a christological interpretation. In his view it is speaking about desiring the living God, as the psalmist said, "My soul thirsts for God, for the living God" (Ps 42:2).

Gregory interprets the words of Jesus with the help of St. Paul in 1 Corinthians—a procedure, one might observe, that would be shunned by a modern interpreter. But if Scripture interprets Scripture his approach makes good sense. The consequence is that Gregory is able to transform the beatitude into an invitation not only to seek "justice" but the living God, or better, to find justice by knowing Christ, who is justice or righteousness himself. So Gregory concludes: the one who tastes the Lord "has received God into himself and is filled with him for whom he has thirsted and hungered. . . . He recognizes that his desire is fulfilled when he says, 'It is Christ who lives in me'" (Gal 2:20).

Finally, I return to Gregory the Great with a final example, his interpretation of Job 14:18–19, "But the mountain falls and crumbles away and the rock is removed from the place; the waters wear away the stones, the torrents wash away the soil of the earth little by little; so you will in like manner destroy man." The words come from Job's speech in response to the first discourse of Zophar. Job is lamenting how transient is the life of human beings. A tree will put forth branches like a young plant when it is watered, but when man breathes his last, he will not be roused from his sleep. In the same way a mountain crumbles and waters wear away stones.

To interpret this passage Gregory uses the technique of allegory. The term means "another sense," and it is used to designate a method of interpretation that discerns in the text a sense other than the plain meaning. St. Paul uses the term in Galatians in the well-known passage about Sarah and Hagar and their two sons, one born of a servant woman and the other a "free woman." "Now," writes Paul, "this is an allegory: these women are two covenants. One is from Mount Sinai, bearing children for slavery; she is Hagar. Now Hagar is Mount Sinai in Arabia; she corresponds to the present Jerusalem, for she is in slavery with her children. But the Jerusalem above is free, and she is our mother" (Gal 4:24–26).

For a long time allegory had fallen out of favor and was shunned by interpreters, but it is undergoing a revival. One reason is that allegory is used by New Testament authors to interpret the Old Testament. Besides the allegory of Sarah and Hagar, there is the passage in 1 Corinthians where St. Paul recounts the wandering of the Israelites in the desert and says that the rock from which they drank was Christ (10:1–6). Though the plain sense of the passage in Exodus (17:6; also Num 20:8–9) is that Moses struck the rock to bring forth water for the Israelites to drink, Paul finds another meaning. In Ephesians Paul cites the words from Genesis, "a man shall leave his father and mother and be joined to his wife," then says that this is a mystery, for "it refers to Christ and the church" (5:31–33).

Consider also Paul's citation of Psalm 19:4, "Their voice has gone out to all the earth, and their words to the ends of the world," in Romans 10. The psalmist was speaking about the heavens silently proclaiming the glory of God without words. But Paul takes the text to refer to the preaching of the apostles: "How beautiful are the feet of those who preach good news" (Rom 10:14–18). Here the other meaning seems to run against the plain meaning.

The first great biblical scholar, Origen of Alexandria, who lived in the early third century, noticed these passages and concluded that in them St. Paul was teaching Christians how to understand the Old Testament. That is he gave us a model that could be used to interpret other passages.[5] In other words, allegory does not have to be limited to those passages the writers of the New Testament allegorized.

Gregory the Great puts allegory to work to illumine the inner workings of the life of faith. In his understanding the passage from Job 18 is taken to describe two different kinds of temptations: those that come on suddenly like a mountain that falls, e.g., an avalanche, and temptations that come on gradually but are no less destructive, like rocks worn down slowly, "penetrating unobtrusively into the heart of man." To illustrate concretely what he means, he gives an example of each kind of temptation. For the first, the sudden crumbling of a mountain, he mentions David's desire for Bathsheba: David "slipped by a sudden fall while walking on the roof." As an example of the latter, the rock worn down slowly, he mentions king Solomon, who by his inconstancy in sensual matters was led to perfidy in spiritual things, as water wears away the stone.[6]

5. Origen, *Homily* 5.1 on Exodus.
6. Gregory I, *Moralia* 12.18.22–23.

After the similes of a mountain and a rock the text says, "in like manner you [God] will destroy man." The phrase "destroy man" leads Gregory to his central point, the "destruction" of man by temptation. To yield to temptation in spiritual matters, he says, is as destructive of human life as losing one's cattle and house is to one's well-being. The simile of the mountain that crumbles and the stones worn hollow refer not to material misfortunes, but to adversities of the inner life.

Allegory is useful primarily for the Old Testament. There are some places in the New Testament where it is fitting—the parable of the sower, the tree that did not bear fruit—but it is seldom needed in dealing with the Gospels or St. Paul. As a medieval writer put it, "the New Testament stands on its own as it is heard; it does not need allegory, it does not signify another Christ."[7] In the New Testament the subject of the Scripture, God's saving work in Christ, is explicit; but in the Old Testament it has to be found. In some cases the way is shown—1 Peter drawing on Isaiah 53 to interpret the suffering and death of Christ, or the bronze serpent on a staff from Numbers signifying raising up Christ on the cross in the Gospel of John—but in others it is the task of the interpreter to find Christ in the Old Testament. And there is no more trustworthy guide in this quest than those Christians who interpreted the Bible in the early centuries.

As my title suggests, the church fathers offer a way of reading the Scriptures that leads us more deeply into the sacred text. They recognized that books, even the books of the Scripture, do not bear their own significance. And they are unanimous in affirming that what gives the books meaning is Christ. "The purpose of the inspired Scripture," wrote Cyril of Alexandria, "is to present the mystery of Christ through a myriad of different kinds of things. Someone might liken the Scriptures to a glittering and magnificent city, having not one image of the king, but many, and publicly displayed in every corner of the city. . . . The aim of the Scripture is not to provide an account of the lives of the saints of old. Far from that. Rather its aim is to lead us in to the mystery of Christ . . . so that the word about him might become clear and truth."[8] The Bible is a book about God's revelation in Christ. Hence the interpreter must always see its history, its stories, its words within a frame of reference that includes Christ.

7. *Patrologia Latina* (hereafter, *PL*) 96:958d.

8. *Glaphyra on Numbers*, in *Patrologia Graeca* (hereafter, *PG*) 69:308c.

Under the tutelage of the church fathers, one learns to see things whole, to interpret individual texts in light of the central biblical narrative and the Christ confessed in the creeds and celebrated in the church's worship. When I was in seminary I had a good foundation in modern historical methods of biblical interpretation. And I thought I was well equipped to interpret and expound the Scriptures to others. But it was only as I took seriously the exegesis of the church fathers (which was uncommon fifty years ago) and read their biblical commentaries that I began to enter deeply into the language and idiom of the Bible. Paradoxically it was when I immersed myself in the old did I find myself discovering the new—things I never imagined would be there. And much to my delight I could say with Augustine, "In my needy life, Lord, my heart is much exercised by the pounding of the words of your holy Scripture."[9] I have learned that there is nothing more precious than a biblical word.

But there is something else the fathers have to teach us, and that is that the interpreter is a participant in the mystery the Scriptures convey. He is not a disinterested observer or voyeur. This can be illustrated by a story told about St. Antony, the monk of the Egyptian desert.

Once some visitors came to Antony and asked him for a good word. He told them that they should heed the Scriptures. When they pressed him for specifics he said they should follow the word of Jesus in Matthew: "If anyone strikes you on one cheek, turn to him the other also" (5:39). But they objected, "We can't do that!" So Antony tempered the exhortation. "If you can't do that, at least allow one cheek to be struck." Again they replied, "We cannot do that." So Antony revised the saying another time: "If you are not able to do that, at least do not return evil for evil." But again they protested. Realizing that it was futile to try and teach such folk how to understand the Bible, Antony instructed his disciples, "Take a little porridge" to them because "they are ill." And to the visitors he said, "If you cannot do this, or that, what can I do for you? What you need is prayers."[10] They showed that they did not understand the Scripture by not heeding what it says.

Or take another example from the wisdom of the desert fathers. Once a young monk went to visit Abba Silvanus to seek his counsel. When he saw the brothers working hard tilling their gardens, he quoted

9. Augustine, *Confessions* 12.1.1.

10. *PG* 65:84c.

the Scriptures "Do not labor for the food which perishes" (John 6:27) and "Mary has chosen the good portion" (Luke 10:42). Then Silvanus asked one of the brothers to give the visitor a book and take him to a cell where he could get on with his reading. When the ninth hour came, the visitor watched the door, expecting that someone would come to call him for dinner. When no one came he went to find Silvanus, and asked, "Have the brothers not eaten today?" The old man replied that they had. Annoyed at having been forgotten the visitor asked, "Why did you not call me?," to which Silvanus replied, "You are a spiritual man and do not need that kind of food. We, being carnal, want to eat, and that is why we work. But you have chosen the better portion and read the whole day long and do not need carnal food." When the brother heard these words he fell on his knees saying, "Forgive me, father." "Mary needs Martha. It is really thanks to Martha that Mary is praised."[11] The story suggests what is at stake in getting the meaning of a text wrong. It is not simply a matter of ideas; it has to do with the way one lives. The older monks showed him how the text was to be understood—living a life that is whole.

For the church fathers the Bible is a book about how to live in the knowledge of God and of oneself. God's Word is not something to be looked at but acted on. St. Bernard said it well: the interpreter must see himself in that which is said. It is not enough, observes Origen, to say, "'Christ was crucified'; one must say with St. Paul, 'I am crucified with Christ' (Gal 2:20). Likewise it is not enough to say, 'Christ is raised'; one who knows Christ says, 'We shall also live with him' (Rom 6:10)."[12] This is why St. Augustine said that anyone who "thinks he has understood the divine scriptures . . . but does not build up the double love of God and neighbor, has not succeeded in understanding them."[13]

There is of course much more in the church fathers than biblical interpretation. They wrote major works on Christian doctrine; they composed learned tomes in response to the critics of Christianity; they forged an understanding of the Christian moral life in terms of the virtues; they wrote extensively on prayer; and they have left us a veritable library of works on the spiritual life.

Some of you will remember the passage in St. Augustine's *Confessions* in which he said that when he read the treatise of Cicero entitled

11. *PG* 65:409.

12. Origen, *Against Celsus* 2:69.

13. Augustine, *On Christian Doctrine* 1.36.40.

Hortensius, a book dealing with wisdom, it "changed my feelings." He explains that the book did not give him a new perspective on wisdom or change his opinions; rather it moved him to love wisdom itself, to "hold fast to it," to "embrace it" and to take it to himself.[14] Wisdom, which he learned later was Christ, had lit a fire in his heart. Later in the *Confessions* Augustine, addressing God, says that his desire was "not to be more certain *about* you, but to be more stable *in* you."[15]

The church fathers teach us that the goal of human life is to know God and to be known by God, to delight in the face of God. The psalmist had written, "My heart has said to thee, I have sought thy face, O Lord, your face will I seek." Augustine comments, "This is magnificent. Nothing could be spoken more sublimely. For those who truly love will understand. What does the psalmist seek? To gaze upon the Lord's loveliness all the days of his life. His fear is that he should be deprived of what he loves. And what is that? What does he love? Thy face."[16]

Each period in Christian history makes its own unique contribution to Christian life. The church fathers, however, set in place a foundation that has proven to be enduring. Their writings are more than a stage in the development of Christian thought or an interesting chapter in the history of the interpretation of the Bible. Like an inexhaustible spring, faithful and true, they irrigate the Christian imagination with the life-giving water flowing from the biblical and spiritual resources of the faith. Today they are still our teachers.

My prayer is that as the church fathers have been the teachers of many other Christians in previous centuries they will also become the teachers of evangelical Christians. The inauguration of the Center for Early Christian Studies at Wheaton College is more than a promise—it is a sign that this has already begun to happen.

14. Augustine, *Confessions* 3.4.7.

15. Ibid., 8.1.1.

16. Augustine, Ps 26, *Exposition* 2.16.

PART ONE

Evangelicals and the Early Church:

A Movement in Search of Roots?

1

Evangelical Inattentiveness to Ancient Voices

An Overview, Explanation, and Proposal

CHRISTOPHER A. HALL

Eastern University

Possible Roadblocks to Engagement with Ancient Voices

I BEGIN BY INITIALLY DRAWING our attention to the general issue of inattentiveness, before focusing on the more specific question of "evangelical inattentiveness to ancient voices." Or put differently, to explore adequately our overarching theme, we must first examine three related topics: first, the nature of inattentiveness and attentiveness; second, "evangelical" characteristics that might engender inattentiveness to ancient perspectives; and third, the particular characteristics of "evangelical inattention" to ancient Christian viewpoints. Evangelical inattentiveness, for instance, may be quite different from a theologically liberal inattention, or, surprisingly, more similar than we might ever have imagined.

Ponder for a moment the last time someone said—probably impatiently or angrily—to you, "You're not paying attention." Ouch! Why weren't we listening? What may have caused our failure to pay attention? If we weren't listening to the other, whom were we listening to?

A number of possibilities present themselves. Perhaps we were *distracted* by an idea, issue, or concern that was occupying our attention and preventing us from effectively listening to our interlocutor. Our concentration was diverted or scattered.

In the context of this essay's topic, we could then ask, "Have evangelicals—some directly and some more indirectly or subconsciously—been distracted or diverted from ideas, themes, and practices that were extremely important to early Christians?" My response is "yes." If so, within a moment or two, we will need to explore the possible causes of our distraction.

Distraction, however, may not be the sole cause of our inattentiveness. Occasionally we fail to pay attention to others because we don't recognize the *relevance* of what we're hearing to our own life or situation. "What you're saying doesn't relate to me. I can't see how it applies." And so we discount the other's words as irrelevant or inapplicable. Irrelevance and *a perceived lack of importance* seem clearly linked. And so we ask, in relation to this essay's theme, "Why might evangelicals consider the history and theology of the early church as irrelevant, inapplicable, or unimportant for our life as Christ's apprentices and followers today?"

A third possibility for inattentiveness relates to the issue of error. For one reason or another, we judge another's perspective to be simply wrong. Our judgment, of course, may be correct or incorrect. Yet we are sure of one thing: the person speaking to us is dead wrong. When we reach this point—"you're clearly wrong and I'm right"—we stop listening.

The question, certainly, is whether the judgment we have made is correct. On what is it based? Are the sources or viewpoints we have relied on to make our judgment wise and reliable? Have we taken time to carefully sift through the evidence before making our decision?

Some evangelicals, for example, don't attend to ancient perspectives, largely represented in the writings of the church fathers, because they believe the fathers are profoundly mistaken and misleading. Some may be disturbed by the fathers' sacramental worldview. Others may be repelled by the tendency of at least some early Christians to interpret the Scripture allegorically.

A corollary problem to evangelical inattentiveness relates to the evangelical tendency to reject the whole because of error in the part.

Suspicions of particular perspectives or practices too easily lead to blanket rejections of the whole.

Both Michael Casey and Allan Bloom identify other key cognitive attitudes and behaviors—some of which I've already mentioned—as noteworthy roadblocks to attentiveness that we should also keep in mind as we examine evangelical inattentiveness to ancient sources. They include: judging too quickly that an argument or example is irrelevant; considering something trivial that is actually important; branding the initial inaccessibility of a text or its seeming irrelevance as boring; dismissing a text too quickly because we refuse to create space in our own cognitive framework or intellectual landscape for it, fearing that it will significantly challenge or rearrange dearly loved ideas or ways of framing reality, God, and so on; unconscious, ingrained resistance and intolerance for a different point of view, a resistance we project onto the text—in this case the voices of the ancient church—and then peremptorily dismiss.[1] For example, are there specific texts you—and I—have too quickly dismissed, not because they are not worth reading, but because, perhaps on a subconscious level, they have challenged us too deeply?

To be fair, though, evangelical inattentiveness to ancient voices may also be linked to what has been—until the last fifteen years or so—*the general inaccessibility of patristic sources* to evangelical theologians, pastors, and lay people. Many English translations of the church fathers— some produced in the nineteenth century—are wooden, flat, dry, and in some cases well-nigh unreadable. Try your hand at making sense of the English translation of Chrysostom's homilies on Matthew in the NPNF and my point will be clearly demonstrated.

The fathers' lively and bracing Greek and Latin—for most evangelical readers a linguistic reach at best—have too often been disserved by their translators. The sad result is the frustration, confusion, and disappointment of many eager to explore the world and thoughts of ancient Christians. "This text is so dry it's like drinking sand," readers may reply as they attempt to make their way through a stilted translation, and any desire to further explore the ancient church dries up. Happily, recent translation series of patristic texts such as Ancient Christian Commentary on Scripture and The Church's Bible now provide English bridges to the ancient Christian world through accessible, readable translations. Healthy sales to Orthodox, Roman Catholic, Anglican, and

1. Insights gleaned from Casey, *Sacred Reading*, 4–11.

evangelical audiences indicate both a growing desire in Christ's followers to appropriate ancient sources and the possibility that our inattentiveness has been significantly connected to a basic issue: you can't listen
well to someone you can't understand.

Yet a basic question remains: have we as evangelicals offered our
conversation partner—in this case, the ancient church—an attentive,
empathetic ear? Generally speaking, we have to respond, "no." Is our
inattentiveness related to a need for evangelicals to deepen their listening skills in general? Most assuredly yes. John Sanders—whom I have
debated publicly and in print on the issue of open theism—occasionally
commented to me on the poor listening skills of the evangelicals who opposed his position, demonstrated by what John viewed as a tendency to
name-call, employ guilt by association, highlight the weakest arguments
of their opponents, or portray tangential aspects of an argument as the
main point. John felt that Wolterstorff's Rule—formulated by Nicholas
Wolterstorff, formerly of Yale University—would aid evangelicals in
more empathetically and wisely listening to and engaging those with
whom they disagree. Consistent application of this rule would surely, I
think, help us understand and engage the early church more effectively.

> Thou must not take cheap shots. Thou must not sit in judgment
> until thou hast done thy best to understand. Thou must earn
> thy right to disagree. Thou must conduct thyself as if Plato or
> Augustine, Clement or Tertullian, were sitting across the table—
> the point being that it is much more difficult (I don't say impos-
> sible) to dishonor someone to his face.[2]

It is genuinely difficult to listen attentively, deeply, and fairly to
others, particularly when we feel those speaking to us are not trustworthy. We discount the value of what we are hearing—but not listening
to—because we don't trust the person or persons speaking. In the past
this person—or the group the person represents—may have hurt us or
misled others and we are reluctant to release the suspicion and mistrust
our pain and disillusion have engendered.

Our mistrust may quickly morph into *guilt by association*. Because
our interlocutor uses expressions or engages in practices similar to our
perceived enemies, we are reluctant to listen. If, for instance, we are
suspicious of Roman Catholics and their sacramental theology, we may

---

2. Quoted in Hall and Sanders, *Does God Have a Future?*, 192.

transfer our suspicions on to the early church because of the fathers' sacramental realism.

Lurking behind mistrust—invariably it seems to me—is fear of some kind: fear of becoming tainted, fear of slipping into unorthodox— or unevangelical—manners of thinking and living the Christian faith, fear of the unsettling discomfort cognitive dissonance produces, fear of change. "What," we ask ourselves softly, "if they're right and I'm wrong? How could I face the fact that I may have been mistaken for so many years? If I change my opinion, what will my students think? My peer group? My church? My family? My friends?"

Lack of attentiveness, then, is linked to a variety of factors: distraction, questions of perceived relevance or lack thereof, judgment calls as to value and importance, mistrust, guilt by association, and fear. Other aspects of inattentiveness may come to mind as we proceed to a closer examination of the specific question of evangelical inattentiveness to ancient voices.

My hope is that as we analyze more thoroughly why evangelicals have largely been inattentive to the ancient church, we can formulate cogent, coherent proposals for wisely and discerningly appropriating our ancient Christian heritage. Among other things, we can learn to overcome our lack of attention by developing new listening skills, skills that do not require us to abandon our evangelical heritage, but rather may actually enrich it as they enable us more effectively to enter and engage another's world.

The Evangelical Mind and Inattentiveness to Ancient Voices

I now proceed to a more focused and direct examination of evangelical inattentiveness to the ancient voices of the church. Are there particular characteristics of the evangelical mind and movement that might serve as predictors of evangelical inattentiveness to Christian exegesis, theology, and history before the time of the Reformation and—in the case of this essay—significant voices, themes, movements, and practices from the second to seventh centuries? Perhaps an autobiographical comment or two may prove helpful as we explore these questions together.

You're reading the thoughts of an old Jesus freak. During the time of the "Jesus Movement," a lively and powerful revival that rippled across college campuses from the late sixties to the late seventies, thousands of college students were drawn to the wonder of Jesus Christ. At the time I was a student at UCLA, and at the end of my sophomore year began attending Wednesday night meetings at the "Light and Power House," a fraternity house that had been transformed into an unaccredited Bible school. A group of ex-Campus Crusade leaders had founded the school and Hal Lindsey became the best-known teacher of the group, though not necessarily the most influential in students' lives.

The leaders of the Light and Power House possessed the gift of communicating the gospel to young people in a clear, accessible, exciting way. Since most of these teachers had come out of a Campus Crusade background, they had learned to package key tenets of the faith in a form that students with little church background could readily respond to in a matter of minutes, and many did.

We learned that God loved us and had a wonderful plan for our lives. Yet God was also righteous. Our sins necessarily—because of God's righteous character—separated us from God, a separation that would last eternally if not dealt with and overcome. Through the incarnation of God's Son and his death and resurrection, the alienation and separation between human beings and God had been miraculously overcome. God had done for us what we could never have done for ourselves. Through personal belief and trust in Christ—"accepting Christ as our savior"— our sins would be forgiven and the gift of eternal life become a present possession. Here, indeed, was good news that we could comprehend and embrace. And it remains so today.

It's difficult to describe the excitement we felt as new believers, many of us studying the Bible for the first time. Some of us had read the Bible before but had not understood it. For others it was an entirely new text. All of us—teachers and students alike—believed the Bible to be utterly unique, a divinely inspired and revealed book given to us by God to help us understand the gospel we had accepted and to aid us in explaining who Jesus was to other people. The Bible contained all we needed to know—plain and simple. Both our teachers and we ourselves were convinced that all we needed to understand the Bible was the text itself, a good Bible handbook, and a few good commentaries written by evangelical scholars.

My perspective toward biblical interpretation as a young evangelical believer—largely based on the model of my teachers' thoughts and practices—was not dissimilar to that of John L. Thompson, professor of historical theology and Reformed theology at Fuller Seminary in his younger days. Thompson writes:

> Back when I was a seminary student, I was deeply (and rightly) captivated by the Bible. I had a dozen binders for storing notes on the Bible, with a different color for each section of the Bible. I also had a color-coded scheme for marking the text of various gospels and epistles that I possessed—retyped, double-spaced, on punched paper. Problems of interpretation fascinated me, as did all the themes and theology of the Scriptures. As a budding minister, I thought the goal was to become a biblical scholar, and I looked forward to any course that would focus directly on the Bible. None of this enthusiasm, however, extended to courses in history. I was quite unexcited by the year's worth of church history I knew I would eventually have to take, and I kept postponing it. History was boring. Everyone knew that. Even the prospect of studying *church* history struck me as surely second best. Who would want to read the uninspired opinions of dead theologians *when you could go straight to the inspired word of God and figure it out for yourself?*[3]

Who indeed?

In my mind I recall the thrill of spending hours in the library of the Light and Power House. Certain titles are firmly etched in my memory: *Haley's Handbook to the Bible*, *Vine's Expository Dictionary*, *Cruden's Concordance to the Bible*, R. K. Harrison's huge *Introduction to the Old Testament*, Donald Guthrie's *New Testament Introduction*, Lewis S. Chafer's *Systematic Theology*. Chafer's volumes were the first systematic theology I had ever encountered and I read them with great interest.

Little did I know that Chafer's exegesis and theological methodology represented a stream of conservative theological reflection largely divorced from the broader church's history of biblical and theological interpretation. Mark Noll sheds helpful light on many of the texts I was reading as a young Jesus freak and the presuppositions underlying them. For conservative theologians such as Chafer, "the 'Bible alone' (in both senses of the term—as the *supreme* religious authority but also as the *only* hereditary authority) survived the assault on tradition that characterized" the heritage of the Enlightenment.[4]

---

3. Thompson, *Reading the Bible with the Dead*, 6. Emphasis added.

4. Noll, *Scandal of the Evangelical Mind*, 97.

Sola scriptura, a fundamental tenet of the Reformation's theological tradition, survived in thinkers such as Chafer, but in a mutated form. While Reformation worthies such as Luther and Calvin had immersed themselves in patristic sources, many nineteenth- and twentieth-century scholars—particularly in fundamentalist circles—had not. Rather, as Nathan Hatch observes, for many the Bible "very easily became . . . 'a book dropped from the skies for all sorts of men to use in their own way.'"[5]

Under the restorationist impulses surging across the nineteenth-century American religious landscape, the principle of *sola scriptura* merged with the aim of restoring the church to its first century New Testament purity. The church's traditional history of exegesis from the second century on was viewed with suspicion and largely ignored. Alexander Campbell, a leading light in the Restorationist movement, reflects this anti-traditional ethos: "I have endeavored to read the Scriptures as though no one had read them before me."[6]

Inductive Bible study became the order of the day, as in many ways it still is in evangelical circles. "The Scriptures admit of being studied and expounded upon the principles of the inductive method," James S. Lamar wrote in 1859 in his *Organon of Scripture, or, The Inductive Method of Biblical Interpretation*—the very hermeneutical method I was taught to employ by my teachers at the Light and Power House. Here was a method of biblical interpretation that seemed foolproof. As Lamar put it, "when thus interpreted [the Scriptures] speak to us in a voice as certain and unmistakable as the language of nature heard in the experiments and observations of science."[7]

Evangelicals are to be praised for the seriousness with which they take the study of the Bible and for the fruits of their exegesis. I continue to read evangelical commentaries and derive great benefit from doing so. So what's the problem? At least when viewed through the lens of more ancient perspectives, evangelical interpretation too often ignores the Holy Spirit's exegetical guidance of the church through the previous centuries; inductive Bible study indeed takes into account first century historical, cultural, and linguistic background and context, but then tends to leap inattentively across centuries of exegetical contributions.

5. Hatch, *Democratization of American Christianity*, quoted in Noll, *Scandal*, 97.

6. Cited in Noll, *Scandal*, 98.

7. Cited in ibid.

Fast-forward a few years to the early twentieth century, the time when Lewis Sperry Chafer was writing his systematic theology. Noll and others contend that Chafer, one of the great founding lights of Dallas Theological Seminary, clearly based his own dispensational approach to the Bible and systematic theology on the inductive, seemingly scientific approach to reading Scripture well. Note carefully Chafer's definition of systematic theology:

> Systematic Theology is the collecting, scientifically arranging, comparing, exhibiting, and defending of *all* facts from any and every source concerning God and his work. . . . The student of the Scriptures . . . will discover that God's great time-periods, characterized as they are by specific divine purposes, fall into a well-defined order. . . . God's program is as important to the theologian as the blueprint to the builder or the chart to the mariner. . . . Contemplation of the doctrine of human conduct belongs properly to a science which purports to discover, classify, and exhibit the great doctrines of the Bible. . . . [T]he science of interpretation [is] usually designated *hermeneutics*. . . . [L]ogical procedure and scientific method [are the key to hermeneutics].[8]

Hence, theology, in Chafer's estimation, is a science, similar to other sciences in its discovering, collecting, classifying, arranging, exhibiting, and defending of data, of "facts." "Logical procedure" and "scientific method" will inevitably, it seems, lead the unbiased theologian to discover and elucidate God's "great time-periods," "program," "blueprint." From Chafer's perspective, if we approach the biblical text unburdened by presuppositions and freed from tradition, we'll be able to interpret the Bible well. All one needs to do is induct the Scripture's meaning from the biblical data itself on the basis of established rules of interpretation.

Noll has observed a distinct self-confidence in Protestant fundamentalism—a self-confidence that has seeped into sectors of evangelicalism today—that borders "on hubris, manifested by an extreme antitraditionalism that casually discount[s] the possibility of wisdom from earlier generations."[9] He notes that Chafer considered his lack of formal theological training as actually an advantage, protecting him from past errors that might influence his own reading of the Bible. In

---

8. Chafer, *Systematic Theology*, 1:x, xiii (2nd and 32nd quotations), xix, xx, 115, 119; cited in Noll, *Scandal*, 128.

9. Noll, *Scandal*, 127.

Chafer's words, "The very fact that I did not study a prescribed course in theology made it possible for me to approach the subject with an unprejudiced mind and to be concerned only with what the Bible actually teaches."[10]

It is striking—indeed breathtaking—to observe the similarities in interpretive approach between conservatives such as Chafer and hermeneutical stances advocated by liberal theologians such as David Tracy. Tracy, like Chafer, warns of the dangers of reading the Bible through the lens of a traditional hermeneutic. "The traditional Christian theologian of whatever tradition," Tracy writes, "preached and practiced a morality of belief in and obedience to the tradition and a fundamental loyalty to the church community's beliefs. The modern historian and scientist—whether in natural or social sciences—preaches and practices an exactly contrary morality. For him, one cannot investigate a cognitive claim with intellectual integrity if one insists simultaneously that the claim is believable because tradition has believed it."[11]

The result of the modern, scientific approach in biblical studies and theology—one inherited from the Enlightenment's confidence in unshackled, autonomous reason—is a tendency for evangelicals and liberals to produce biblical exegesis and theology in a context (the university) and with a hermeneutical stance (Chafer and Tracy's autonomous inquiry) that ironically and unnecessarily divorces biblical studies and theology from the very religious community in which biblical and theological exploration and reflection should be rooted: Christ's body on earth, the church. As I think back on my experience reading in the library at the Light and Power House, I now realize more clearly how what I was doing—studying the Bible for the first time—was occurring in a context (a school with no ecclesiological ties) and with a methodology (autonomous study with a few selected guides at best) that at least partially reflected the perspectives of both a fundamentalist (Chafer) and a liberal (Tracy), though each theologian produced significantly different theological conclusions.

---

10. Cited in C. F. Lincoln, "Biographical Sketch of the Author," in Chafer, *Systematic Theology*, 8:5–6; cited in Noll, *Scandal*, 128.

11. Tracy, *Blessed Rage for Order*, 6.

Cultural Background and Context

We also must take into account the cultural background and context of evangelical life and thought if we are to understand and overcome our inattentiveness to the ancients. North Americans—including North American Christians—have a very short attention span. We are bred by our culture to expect immediate, accessible, and simple answers to questions or issues that by their intrinsic nature demand a slower, broader, and deeper analysis. Christians who have grown up in this cultural context frequently lack the patience—and often the training—to slowly, reflectively, painstakingly work our way through the intricacies of a sophisticated, theologically dense text. "Get to the point," we say to ourselves. If the point is not readily or easily apprehended, we are apt to move on to less demanding and often less rewarding teachers and texts. We surely are more comfortable and happy with sound bites than extended, complex discourse.[12]

Attentiveness to ancient voices demands a much different approach, one that involves both the methodology the student employs and the disposition of the student herself. Even when translated well, patristic texts are often complex, demanding, and occasionally tangled and grainy. They demand a paced, detailed, patient reading and do not readily yield their riches to readers who expect a rapid glance to tender the desired results. Ancient writers will often answer the questions we pose, but on their terms, within their own cultural, historical, and linguistic framework; not infrequently their perspectives will initially seem foreign, confusing, and even jarring. The ancients will frustrate our culture's quest for immediate spiritual or intellectual gratification by insisting that short-term, simplistic solutions to long-term problems ultimately break down. Ancient Christians insist that spiritual, theological, and biblical understanding does not appear overnight or in a vacuum. Instead, they are convinced that insight comes to those whose disposition and methodology for approaching the Bible—indeed God—have been shaped in a particular manner and context: prayer, worship, and communal reflection.[13]

Unlike most modern people—including evangelicals—ancient Christians led a more paced, reflective, less frenetic life. You will not

---

12. All insights from Casey, *Sacred Reading*, 4–11.

13. Ideas I have developed in Hall, *Reading Scripture with the Church Fathers*.

find early authors providing ten easy steps for spiritual fulfillment, nor evincing great sympathy for those who might find their writings difficult to grasp for the first time. Ancient Christians pondered the same vexing and wondrous problems, questions, and realities we face today in a modern, evangelical context—sin, evil, death, grief, Trinity, incarnation, redemption, creation, recreation—and firmly believed these issues demanded the attention of a mind and heart that had learned to be patient, to listen, to pray, to meditate, to worship, to be silent, to study.

From a patristic perspective, a holy, loving disposition is a *sine qua non* for those who would plumb the depths of the Bible. Both Athanasius and Gregory of Nazianzus are of one mind on this crucial point. Athanasius writes that

> the searching and right understanding of the Scriptures [demands] a good life and a pure soul. . . . One cannot possibly understand the teaching of the saints unless one has a pure mind and is trying to imitate their life. . . . Anyone who wants to look at sunlight naturally wipes his eye first, in order to make, at any rate, some approximation to the purity of that on which he looks; and a person wishing to see a city or country goes to the place in order to do so. Similarly, anyone who wishes to understand the mind of the sacred writers must first cleanse his own life, and approach the saints by copying their deeds. Thus united to them in fellowship of life, he will both understand the things revealed to them by God and, thenceforth escaping the judgment that threatens sinners in the judgment, will receive that which is laid up for the saints in the kingdom of heaven.[14]

Gregory of Nazianzus offers similar advice in his theological orations. Studying and speaking well about God does not belong to everyone, not "before every audience, nor at all times, nor on all points; but on certain occasions, and before certain persons, and within certain limits." Gregory insists that theological study "is permitted only to those who have been examined, and are past masters in meditation, and who have been previously purified in soul and body, or at the very least are being purified."[15] Neither Athanasius nor Gregory envisioned exegesis or theology as the academic activity of biblical scholars or theologians divorced from the life of the church or personal spiritual formation. Rather, the

14. Athanasius, *On the Incarnation*, 96.
15. Gregory of Nazianzus, "First Theological Oration," 129.

fathers believed, the best exegesis occurred within the community of the church. For the church fathers, the Scriptures have been given to the church; are read, preached, heard, and comprehended within the community of the church; and are safely interpreted only by those whose character is continually being formed by prayer, worship, meditation, self-examination, confession, and other means by which Christ's grace is communicated to his body. That is to say, the fathers argue that a divorce between personal character, Christian community, and the study of Scripture will be fatal for any attempt to understand the Bible. This holistic, communal approach is surely a methodology that warrants a closer investigation in our highly individualistic, autonomous evangelical culture.[16]

So, if we are to deepen our attentiveness to ancient voices—tuning our hearing to the wavelength of their speech, so to speak—we must learn to read more slowly and more communally. We must engage—or at least consider—both *the practices* and *the words* of the ancients if we are to understand their world and their teaching. We must read ancient texts at a pace the texts themselves demand, while simultaneously cultivating the dispositions access to the texts requires. This slow, paced reading will likely be difficult for us; we have grown up, as North Americans and as evangelicals, exposed to media that reduces the necessity for extended thought and meditation, scrutiny, and judgment. How different from the environment of ancient Christians, who faced fewer distractions and learned to listen, meditate, and remember as part of the basic rhythm of their ecclesial lives.

Ancient Christian Practices and Perspectives

Though the literacy rate among ancient Christians was around 10 percent—similar to that across the Roman Empire—most Christians had significant exposure to Scripture as they *heard* large chunks read during worship by trained readers. Early Christian texts had no spacing between words, so *lectors* within the church—readers who read the Scripture to the gathered Christian community—read the Scripture out loud, interpreting where breaks between words, sentences, and paragraphs should appear.[17]

16. The quotations from Athanasius and Gregory of Nazianzus are also found in Hall, *Reading Scripture*, 41–42.

17. These comments and the information that follows are indebted to Harry Y. Gamble's excellent *Books and Readers in the Early Church*, 203–5, 218–26.

Reading in the ancient world—Christian and otherwise, private and public—was largely auditory. Few ancient readers would have thought to use only their eyes in reading a text, though we encounter a few instances. Because so few could read texts on their own, Christians grew up hearing the Scripture read again and again, not in short snippets but extended sections. The ancients depended much more on their ears than on their eyes. The constant, auditory reading of Scripture served as a wonderful memory device for both illiterate and literate Christians. It would not have been uncommon for illiterate Christians to have significant sections of Scripture stored on the hard-drive of their minds, available for retrieval and contemplation.

John Chrysostom—a literate Christian like almost all pastors and bishops—spent at least two years in a cave above Antioch memorizing the entire Bible, no doubt by reciting passages over and over again. His memory work gave him a deep appreciation for reading slowly and meditatively, chewing on each word and phrase. In the future, Chrysostom would exhort his congregation to engage in the same process. "Therefore, if you wish you may have both Paul, and Peter, and John, and the whole chorus of the prophets conversing with you continually. For take the books of these blessed ones, and continually read them; their writings and they will be able to make you like the tent-maker's wife."[18]

I mention Chrysostom and his own spiritual formation—in this case the memorizing of texts by audibly repeating them—because the evangelical retrieval of ancient perspectives must involve more than an engagement with the thoughts of the church fathers on theological or biblical loci. We have to also be attentive to the communal and individual habit patterns that nurtured the insights and practices of ancient Christians and their leaders.

As I've said, slowing down and quieting down is not easy for North Americans, and not easy for evangelicals. If the authors we read do not quickly make their practical, exegetical, or theological point in an entertaining and immediately accessible fashion, we are prone to set them aside in our search for easily attained, immediate solutions. We want answers and we want them quickly. We have a hard time with ambiguity and theological complexity.

18. Chrysostom, *Hom. in Rom.* 30.4; translated and quoted in Mitchell, *Heavenly Trumpet*, 46.

Perhaps even more problematic is the evangelical tendency to be side-tracked onto peripheral theological issues, principally because we have not immersed ourselves in the initial centuries of the church's history, a time when Christians were forced to determine—in the context of worship, prayer, and heretical opposition—exactly what was the heart of the matter for the church as it proclaimed the gospel in word and deed.

Many evangelicals, for instance, have spent hours—indeed years—focusing on eschatological issues related to the millennium, the time of the tribulation, the timing of the rapture, and so on. This was my own experience as a young convert. Hal Lindsey, after all, authored *The Late Great Planet Earth*, a book the New York Times described as "the number one non-fiction bestseller" of the 70s. The book continues to sell today.

Yet the very same folks who can explain the details of the second coming frequently fall into familiar heresies when probed concerning the hypostatic union or the relationship between the Father, Son, and Holy Spirit. I would estimate that close to 95 percent of the students I quiz at Eastern on basic knowledge of the Trinity respond in terms of classical heresies. They are predictably Sabellian or tritheistic in their responses.

My description of my students' knowledge level—students who have grown up in evangelical homes and churches—is neither an exaggeration nor caricature and points to the desperate need to catechize evangelical young people and the broader evangelical community in the basics of the faith, essentials rooted in the teaching and practices of the ancient church. Unfortunately, what were once viewed as basics by protestant luminaries such as Luther and Calvin—elementary tenets of the faith all Christians were expected to understand—now too often are viewed as esoteric territory to be explored by theologians alone.

Of course, we would be misled or naïve to think that all ancient Christians followed Chrysostom's exhortation to a wiser, deeper reading of Scripture, a reordering of their priorities, and a firm "no" to the allurements and distractions ancient Greco-Roman culture offered. We chuckle to hear Chrysostom rebuking his congregation over their tendency to listen attentively to his sermon—often his audience would break into applause—and then scurry out of the church before the celebration of the Eucharist in order to catch a glimpse of their favorite charioteer at

a near-by stadium. Ancient Christians could be lazy, distracted, preoc-
cupied, undisciplined, and self-indulgent, just like us.

Origen, like Chrysostom, was troubled by the indifference of his
students to the private reading of Scripture. They, like us on some days,
could find the Bible to be dry, boring, and seemingly irrelevant. "[Origen's
students] complained of the *taedium verbi divini*—the irksomeness of
the private study of Scripture," in response to Origen's admonition to
read the Scriptures at home, for at least a few hours a day.[19] In response
Origen formulated a reading program of sorts, encouraging readers to
begin with accessible texts such as Esther, Judith, Tobit, or the Wisdom
of Solomon and then to move to the Gospels and Paul's epistles; harder,
less accessible books such as Leviticus or Numbers should be attempted
only when reading skills had been sharpened.[20]

We also find Chrysostom struggling to get his parishioners involved with regular Bible reading. In fact, he devotes an entire sermon
to the topic: "That the Private Reading of Scripture Is Useful" (*Hom. in
princip. Act.* 3). Chrysostom wants to get folks reading the Bible at home
and is clearly meeting resistance:

> I wish to ask one favor of you all, that each of you take in hand
> that section of the Gospels which is to be read among you on the
> first day of the week, or on the Sabbath, and before the day ar-
> rives that he sit down at home and read it through, and carefully
> consider its contents, and examine all its parts well, what is clear,
> what is obscure, what seems to be contradictory but is not really;
> and when you have tried, in a word, every point, then go to hear
> it read. (*Hom. in Joh.* 11.1)

Clearly, John is having a hard time convincing his congregation to take
his words seriously. "Who among you, if required, could recite one
Psalm or any other part of divine scriptures? No one" (*Hom. in Matt.*
2.9). Chrysostom has heard many excuses, some not at all dissimilar to
what we might hear today: "a lack of leisure, a lack of the books, a lack of
interest, even 'I am not a monk.'"[21]

> Which of you when at home takes some Christian book in hand,
> goes over its contents and searches the scriptures? None can say
> that he does, but with most we shall find draughts and dice, but

19. Gamble, *Books and Readers*, 232.

20. Ibid.

21. The Chrysostom material is found in ibid., 233.

books nowhere, except among the few. Even those few have the same dispositions as the many, for they tie up their books and keep them always put away in cases, and all their care is for the fineness of the parchments and the beauty of the letters, not for reading them.[22]

So, some things differ from our time and that of the fathers, and some remain the same. Should we be surprised?

A Specific Proposal

I now desire to make a specific proposal for increasing evangelical attentiveness to ancient voices. In short, evangelicals must make catechesis a fundamental priority, a catechesis that purposefully and discerningly draws on the riches of ancient Christian exegesis and the theology that blossomed from it. We are already seeing increasing attentiveness to ancient Christian sources in some evangelical schools and academic societies, an engagement and concentration that can be guided and empowered by societies such as The Wheaton Center for Early Christian Studies. This new evangelical attentiveness must begin with a clear awareness of our deep need for the nourishment the early Christian centuries offer us.

Catechesis, of course, requires skilled, knowledgeable catechists. Evangelical catechists must themselves be catechized in the riches of the faith, the heart of the matter, the dazzling theological substructure supporting the healthy, vital emphasis within evangelicalism on the evangelistic mandate, the preaching of the gospel to every person, across every culture and continent.

To acknowledge our need to be catechized is a humbling affair— a healthy and robust antidote to the pride that so often manifests itself in inattentiveness. It's hard to admit—especially for people who have already been theologically trained—that significant gaps remain in our biblical, theological, and spiritual formation. To become attentive, to be willing to be taught, to stop talking and start listening, is humbling indeed.

We will have to resist the temptation to flee back to more comfortable and familiar surroundings when cognitive dissonance strikes or a valued position is challenged. For a lengthy period—perhaps longer

22. Ibid., 233.

than we had imagined—we must accept the status of students, catechumens, struggling to enter, hear, and comprehend the strange, mysterious, wondrous world the early church offers to us as we cultivate the
theological, spiritual, and emotional patience to engage ancient perspectives honestly and receptively.

Our catechesis will entail time and effort. We must be convinced
that convergence between the world of evangelicals and the ancients is
possible and beneficial, and that a wise and discerning merging of hori-
zons is more than a pipe dream. Gradually, I think, evangelicals will feel
more at home as catechumens of the ancients. Trust will grow, and as
trust increases, learning will deepen. In time we may even earn the right
to criticize and reject ideas we simply can't buy.

The great temptation for the evangelical mind will be to criticize
too quickly, to reject the unfamiliar, to become angry or dismissive. The
arrogance and insensitivity our broader culture has perceived in our
evangelical community—at times fairly and at times unfairly—are apt
to appear as we seek to increase our attentiveness to our distant ecclesial
cousins. We do best to acknowledge—and confess when appropriate—
our own communal habit patterns, acknowledging our unique strengths
and admitting our weaknesses.

Some of these habit patterns will abet our entry into the world of
the ancients. Others will be obstacles. Our love for the Bible, for example, will immediately aid us in listening to the church fathers, for they
too loved and honored the Scripture as uniquely inspired and authoritative. On the other hand, our impatience with those who disagree with
us, our quick temper, our elevated self-estimation, our rush to judge before adequately understanding the position of our discussion partner—
characteristics that also occasionally appear in our ancient friends—can
undercut our endeavor to grow under their tutelage.

As we ponder the issue of catechesis, a significant question to reflect
upon is this: What are the specific steps we can take to deepen our evangelical self-awareness of our weaknesses and strengths, both corporately
and individually? A fundamental movement toward spiritual maturity is
this very movement from self-deception to self-awareness; the better we
understand ourselves as evangelicals the more effectively we can assume
the role of a receptive, engaged, and yes, discerning catechumen to an
ancient catechist. Consider the following questions: Are there theological underpinnings and appreciations already present in the evangelical

worldview that support a healthy attentiveness to ancient Christians? And are there particular evangelical roadblocks or resistances we may experience as we read and interact with ancient Christian authors? The answer to these two questions will be both similar and dissimilar for every person reading this essay.

A positive first step in answering these questions is to examine our own hermeneutical and theological pedigree. How has growing up in an evangelical context nurtured my relationship with Christ? How and what have my evangelical teachers taught me about the gospel? On what have they focused? What aspects might they have overlooked or underplayed? To query more broadly, what are the blind spots in the evangelical mind, the issues to which we remain unaware and yet were central concerns for Christians in the early centuries of the church's history? Individually, what do I need to know that I don't know? Where does my knowledge need to grow? What have I considered unimportant or too quickly dismissed as irrelevant? What are the gaps in my own evangelical theological education?

For instance, for many years—roughly 1973–1985—I had no idea how my early exposure to a particular evangelical perspective had shaped my responses to other Christians. Little did I realize that what I had been taught in my earliest years as a believer—what I might describe as a Reformed dispensationalism—represented only one stream in the broader Christian tradition, and a relatively minor one at that.

Many of you are aware of Tom Oden's journey into the evangelical world by way of the church fathers, a mirror image of the voyage I am encouraging evangelicals to take. Oden, for years embedded in the classical liberal tradition, was reawakened from his theological stupor—he had been anesthetized by what he describes as "modernity"—through the rebuke of Will Herberg, a Jewish philosopher at Drew University. It was Herberg who in no uncertain terms warned Oden that his overall understanding and theological perspective would remain grossly misshapen unless he supplemented his immersion in modern theological sources with a concentrated exposure to the world of the church fathers.

Oden moved toward the fathers from a liberal perspective. Evangelicals are called, I believe, to undertake a similar pilgrimage, but from the other end of the theological spectrum. To do so, they must be willing to listen, which at first may prove threatening and confusing. Yet if a theologian such as Oden, trapped in his idealization of the "new" and "innovative," can make such a journey, so can pilgrims traveling from much safer territory. To do so Oden had to hone his listening skills, as we evangelicals will also have to do. Oden writes:

> Then while reading Nemesius something clicked. I realized that I must listen intently, actively, without reservation. Listen in such a way that my whole life depended upon hearing. Listen in such a way that I could see telescopically beyond my modern myopia, to break through the walls of my modern prison, and actually hear voices from the past with different assumptions entirely about the world and time and human culture. Only then in my forties did I begin to become a theologian. Up to that time I had been teaching theology without having sufficiently met the patristic mentors who could teach me theology.[23]

Consider the phrases Oden employs to describe his attentive listening: "intently, actively, without reservation." Oden had accepted the position and status of a catechumen. He realized he needed to be catechized by ancient Christian masters—though he had already taught theology for many years—a "hermeneutical reversal" that still marks Oden today and has provided his interpretive north star for years. As a catechumen, he listened and listened and listened. From what did Oden's profound attentiveness beckon him? Myopia: biblical, theological, historical, and spiritual nearsightedness.

As Oden's liberal methodology and the theology it produced was myopic, so is our short-sighted evangelical conservatism. We attest key affirmations that without doubt are valid—the divine inspiration of the Bible and its accompanying unique authority for the church and the individual believer, the wonder of the forgiveness offered to us through a personal relationship with God through Christ, the absolute imperative to reach a lost world with the message of Christ's love and forgiveness regardless of the cost—but have needlessly cut ourselves off from ancient exegetical, theological, and spiritual resources that significantly support our assumptions, that can breathe into our sails as we navigate a world that desperately needs Christ. Just as Oden needed to learn to listen, so do we. Just as he was catechized, so must we be. Our ancient Christian friends are calling us back to school, but the classroom is not a university; it is the church, the church ancient, the church catholic in its universal sense.

23. I relate Oden's journey in some detail in Hall, *Reading Scripture*, 15–18.

The question then becomes this: will evangelicals be willing to develop the dispositions and skills that mark attentive, able catechumens? How can we learn to sup from the meal the ancients offer us, without developing indigestion? Is there a certain etiquette involved in overcoming inattentiveness to people more than willing to host us for a healthy repast?

Surely catechumens must be willing, as much as possible, to set aside their own prejudices, presumptions, and presuppositions as they sit down with their catechist. In a word, evangelicals who desire to learn from ancient teachers must adopt the posture of the attentive, listening student. How, then, can we learn to listen deeply to a Jerome, Chrysostom, Basil, Ambrose, or Augustine?

As I have already emphasized, we must guard against the penchant to prejudge texts that appear to fall outside our particular evangelical worldview, values, and experience. We will need to expand our vocabulary. We will have to work hard at developing theological empathy rather than resistance at the first appearance of a foreign expression or jarring idea.

Evangelical catechumens need not abandon their evangelical heritage as they listen to their ancient teachers nor should they do so. Rather, an engagement with early perspectives should lead to an expansion and deepening of the evangelical mind and heart, rather than an abandonment. As we come alongside older brothers and sisters in the faith and ask them to open their world to us, our own world will become larger and our biblical and theological awareness broaden. We will discern the value of matters we underestimated or discounted, ponder questions posed to us in a new way or perhaps for the first time, and struggle to understand how the world we have always known fits into an ancient world that appears both familiar and strange.

Some of us may experience cognitive dissonance, an intellectual unsettling, as we discover that cherished ideas and heartfelt beliefs are more recent, idiosyncratic, and superficial than we had ever imagined. Simultaneously, though, evangelicals will experience encouragement and excitement—encouragement as we discover many evangelical hallmarks as characteristic of our new, older teachers; excitement as we understand more fully the rhyme and reason of truths we had always held dear and affirmed strongly.

Our ancient catechists, though, will be demanding. Concentrated attentiveness to their teaching and the world from which it springs will be far from easy. Best to admit this from the beginning. Reading ancient texts—Christian or otherwise—can be difficult, frustrating, and threatening; not infrequently the fathers will challenge our values and cherished opinions.

Jerome, Chrysostom, and Augustine can be intimidating teachers. They have little patience or tolerance for lazy, inattentive students and refuse to dumb down their teaching. I can imagine Gregory of Nazianzus watching me as I read through one of his theological orations. I look up, puzzled at his line of thought, and he responds, "Read it again." "But I've already read it five times. You could have been a bit clearer, you know." "Who is the teacher here? Read it again." Or as Augustine might put it, *Repetitio studiorum mater est* ("Repetition is the mother of learning").

The fathers demand much and we grow in the demanding. Michael Casey, himself steeped in the thoughts of the church fathers, reminds us of a fundamental "principle that operates when we read the great works of antiquity. The texts that at first appear unattractive are often the ones that will most repay the effort to understand them."[24] Or, to turn to the insight of Allan Bloom, "The argument or example that seems irrelevant, trivial, or boring is precisely the one most likely to be the sign of what is outside of one's framework and which calls it into question."[25] Casey, rightly I think, insists that there "is an unconscious antagonism in us to anything that threatens our ingrained prejudices, and challenges us to grow. Because we are reluctant to admit our intolerance of a different viewpoint, we project the problem onto the text and proclaim, 'This is a hard saying and who can bear with it?' We blame the text for our unwillingness to receive."[26]

And so we must work hard to transform what may be initial unwillingness into willingness by honestly identifying our own resistances to ancient perspectives and what our resistances can teach us about ourselves. Casey offers wise coaching: "A much more creative way of dealing with difficult texts is to take our negative reaction as an indication that there may be an issue beneath the surface with which

24. Casey, *Guide to Living*, 4–5.

25. Bloom, "Study of Texts," 308.

26. Casey, *Guide to Living*, 13.

we must deal. So we return to the text, reading it very closely, word by word, and line by line."[27]

Lest we be confused, to listen well to an ancient perspective does not demand naïve, unquestioning acceptance. Yet how will we know if we have listened well and earned the right to question the teaching of our catechist? Imagine Augustine sitting in your living room, arguing vociferously for his understanding of the church as a *permixta ecclesia*, a mixed society of genuine and pseudo-believers that only God can distinguish in the midst of this present evil age. You come from a holiness tradition and are much more apt to agree with Cyprian that the church is called by Christ to be his holy body on earth, visibly separate and distinct from its surrounding society. And so you find yourself bristling at Augustine's teaching, longing for him to stop talking so you can rebut his position point by point. Finally Augustine stops speaking. He knows you're agitated and angry, eager to argue your case. But he is the master, the teacher, the catechist. "And so you disagree with me?" "Yes, on a number of points," you respond, and begin what you believe will be a robust rebuttal. "Hold on one minute," Augustine interjects. "You have yet to earn the right to disagree. First, explain my position point by point. Attempt to convince me of my own position. If I find you have understood it and can explain it convincingly to me, I will welcome your disagreement. If not, we will repeat the lesson once again." Again Alan Bloom is helpful: "The hardest thing of all is the simplest to formulate: every word must be understood. It is hard because the eye tends to skip over just those things which are most shocking or most call into question our way of looking at things."[28] Or, to stick with the listening metaphor, we tend to stop listening at the very junctures of an argument we find most challenging and with which we most disagree.

Happily, some evangelicals—though probably not the majority—increasingly realize that no Christian, past or present, comes to the Bible, a theological text, a different ecclesial community, or the ancient Christian world "cold, as it were, but each [has] been exposed to the Christian message and to forms of Christian life before being 'reformed' by the text of Scripture."[29]

---

27. Ibid.

28. Bloom, "Study of Texts," 308, quoted in ibid.

29. Brown, "Proclamation and Preservation," 78.

As we understand who we are as evangelicals—thankful for our strengths and acknowledging our weaknesses—let me suggest a few concrete steps evangelicals can begin to take, with the help of societies such as The Wheaton Center for Early Christian Studies or the Center for Early African Christianity at Eastern University—to overcome our inattentiveness to ancient sources and to facilitate our understanding of the exegetical and theological world of the fathers.

We would do well to consider the early church's rule of faith and early Christian creeds as springboards for the creation of a curriculum for catechists and catechumens of the ancient church. As the ancient church pondered and performed the gospel—especially within the context of communal worship—it formulated a rule of faith, a sort of shorthand summary of the heart of the Christian message to help its members understand the core of Christian belief and to interpret the meaning of the Bible well. Think of the rule of faith as a catechetical map that guided the Christian community and protected it from veering away from the truth revealed in Christ.

The church fathers possessed a finely tuned awareness of the tendency of individual believers, especially those young in the faith, to attach themselves to minor themes and peripheral matters. By way of contrast, the rule was christological in its heart and core, specifically because it was shaped by the worship of the church, itself profoundly christological. This christological center helped to bridle the novice's tendency to be infatuated with the exotic or esoteric—think of the ink and paper evangelicals have spent on the timing of the rapture—rather than exploring the Trinitarian and incarnational depth at the heart of the gospel.

In the summary of the faith represented by the rule, the church focused on the nonnegotiables, those truths that all Christians must believe if they are to validly claim and bear the name of Christ. Here, then, is a gift of the early church to the evangelical world—one that in a more developed form we find in the creeds promulgated at Nicaea, Constantinople, and Chalcedon.

I would argue that even noncreedal churches such as Baptists and independent Bible folks would benefit from the catechetical opportunities offered by a thorough grounding in each affirmation of the Nicene Creed. For here we have the heart of the gospel—its riches affirmed line by line. Those evangelicals uncomfortable with creedal statements could still employ the creed as a catechetical framework for their engagement with the early church, using its statements as gateways into the thoughts of early Christian writers on a variety of subjects. The creedal scaffolding of this catechetical reading program, though, would ensure that we drive in the center of the road, avoiding the temptation to explore prematurely inviting and alluring byways.

To change metaphors, the Nicene Creed can serve as a springboard for evangelicals back into the rhyme and reason of the gospel as understood by our ancient brothers and sisters. For this creed—in its fullest form given to us at Constantinople in 381—coupled to that of Chalcedon from 451, delineates and emphasizes the heart of the apostles' understanding of the gospel, the very truths that almost all evangelicals affirm yet struggle to understand and explain.

For instance, we affirm the deity of the Father, Son, and Holy Spirit, but in our reliance on the Bible alone—*scriptura nuda* rather than *sola scriptura*—we often attempt to explain the triune nature of God solely on the basis of biblical testimony. By doing so, we inevitably reinvent the wheel, but too often with missing or cracked spokes. Not infrequently we fall into the very heresies the church rejected after much toil, tribulation, and yes, spilled blood. Our inattentiveness to ancient sources undercuts our ability to mine the riches of the Scripture well, with the unhappy result that poorly catechized evangelical teachers produce poorly catechized students.

To remedy this unfortunate situation—one that we have seen is based on a wide variety of factors—we begin with a specific aim: the deepening of the evangelical mind and heart through a thorough exposure to ancient voices. The means of doing so? First, we purposely cultivate the dispositions that will enable us to empathetically, receptively, and discerningly enter the world of early Christianity, specifically by assuming the role of a catechumen. Second, we use the creeds of Nicaea and Chalcedon as the catechetical scaffolding for our own catechesis and that of those we teach, whether our ecclesial background be creedal or not. Third, we as evangelicals explore together the patristic texts—and the reasoning behind them—that support the creeds. And, as we explore the writings of these early Christian leaders and authors, we will be inevitably led to the Bible itself, for patristic thinking is largely commentary on the Scripture. Finally, we take what we have learned from our ancient teachers and assume the role of catechists for our own students, building sturdy, lasting bridges between the ancient world that has nourished us and the challenging world of the twenty-first century.

2

John Wesley and the Early Church

History, Antiquity, and the Spirit of God

JEFFREY W. BARBEAU

Wheaton College

"... it being their one desire and design to be downright *Bible Christians*—taking their Bible, as interpreted by the primitive Church and our own, for their whole and sole rule."

—John Wesley, *A Short History of Methodism*[1]

EARLY METHODISTS SOUGHT, ABOVE all things, to be *Bible Christians*. At least from the time of Wesley's arrival at Oxford, the study of early Christian writers was part of his avid reading practices.[2] The Oxford "Holy Club" that began the Methodist movement was itself an effort to replicate the spirituality of primitive Christianity: small bands of common fellowship, regular prayer and sacramental observance, and social works modeled on the earliest apostolic witness. Wesley's later mission to Georgia in 1735, where he continued to study early Christian writings, reflects his interest in inculcating ancient Christian faith and practice among a people he regarded with naïve idealism, while cherishing their apparently unsullied belief systems:

1. In *Works of John Wesley* (1984), 9:368. Hereafter simply *Works*, with the year of the edition in parentheses. All editions listed in the bibliography under Wesley.

2. For a review of Wesley's reading habits, see Tolar Burton, "Appendix B: John Wesley's Book Inventory."

> I hope to learn the true sense of the gospel of Christ by preach-
> ing it to the heathens. They have no comments to construe away
> the text, no vain philosophy to corrupt it, no luxurious, sensual,
> covetous, ambitious expounders to soften its unpleasing truths,
> to reconcile earthly-mindedness and faith, the Spirit of Christ
> and the spirit of the world. . . . They are as little children, humble,
> willing to learn, and eager to do the will of God.[3]

Wesley's complex and dramatic failure in Georgia, however, does not appear to have diminished his interest in antiquity. Subsequent historical
writings, polemical treatises, and abridgments of early Christian theologians all point to Wesley's ongoing fascination with the early church.

Wesley's well-known appeal to Scripture still resonates with evangelicals today. But what about his devotion to the historical writings of
the church? Does the Bible "as interpreted by the primitive Church and
our own" still have a place as the "whole and sole rule" among evangelicals? In this essay, I explore Wesley's engagement with early church writings, explain his understanding of history and his rejection of "atheistic"
historiography, and clarify why Wesley regarded the early church as one
important demonstration of the continual work of God in every age of
the history of the church. I argue that Wesley's appeal to early Christian
resources reflects his eclecticism. Moreover, Wesley's use of antiquity
furthered two paramount aims: a programmatic interest in reviving the
Church of England through the reinstitution of early Christian practices
and, simultaneously, a conservative defense of Methodist thought and
practice against those who regarded Methodism as a heretical aberra-
tion in Christian history. Wesley's use of Christian antiquity reveals his
evangelical commitment to a wide range of spiritual resources found in
historic Christian faith and practice. Wesley's eclecticism can continue
to instruct Christians in the twenty-first century.

I.

Ever since Albert Outler's provocative "Introduction" to the widely-
published *John Wesley* (1964), Wesley scholars have been captivated
by his conspicuous interest in the history and theologies of the early
church.[4] Outler confidently proposed that John Wesley's earliest days in

3. Wesley, "Letter to the Revd. John Burton," in *Works* (1984), 25:16–25; cf.
Hammond, "John Wesley's Mindset."

4. On Outler's influential view of tradition in late twentieth-century United
Methodism, see Campbell, "Scripture and Tradition"; idem, "Albert C. Outler."

Oxford brought him into contact with *Eastern* theological voices: "In the thought and piety of the early Church he discovered what he thereafter regarded as the normative pattern of catholic Christianity."[5] For Outler, pseudo-Macarius (whom he identifies as Macarius the Egyptian),[6] Ephraem Syrus (c. 306–73), Clement of Alexandria (c. 150–c. 215), and other ancient Eastern thinkers merged with Wesley's heritage of Caroline Anglicanism. Eastern Christian thought saturated Wesley's theology with a dynamic vision of grace leading towards perfection, "of holiness as *disciplined* love [that] became fused in Wesley's mind with his own Anglican tradition of holiness as *aspiring* love, and thereafter was developed in what he regarded to the end as his own most distinctive doctrinal contribution."[7] Outler believed that the early influence of these thinkers placed Wesley's intellectual development directly in contact with some of the great minds of Eastern Christian theology.[8]

Outler's provocative claim endures. Wesley scholars ever since have attempted to clarify or expand on the notion that ancient church sources fundamentally influenced Wesley's theology. In my opinion, two pivotal studies—one historical and one systematic—have most dramatically shaped Outler's original claim. Ted Campbell's *John Wesley and Christian Antiquity: Religious Vision and Cultural Change* (1991), based on Campbell's dissertation at Southern Methodist University (1984), is a historical study that maintains that Wesley participated in a widespread and even commonplace interest in Christian antiquity during the period. Campbell claims that Wesley takes up both Eastern and Western early church theologians as programmatic resources for the evangelical

---

5. Outler, "Introduction," 9.

6. Outler devotes a long note to the problem of identifying Macarius. He ultimately relies on the views of Werner Jaeger in asserting a close connection between Macarius and Gregory of Nyssa: "What matters most in connection with Wesley is that in the writings of what he thought was 'Macarius the Egyptian,' he was actually in touch with Gregory of Nyssa, the greatest of all Eastern Christian teachers of the quest for perfection. Thus, in his early days, he drank deep of this Byzantine tradition of spirituality at its source and assimilated its conception of devotion as the *way* and perfection as the *goal* of the Christian life." Outler, *John Wesley*, 9n26. However, the Macarian homilies that Wesley includes in the *Christian Library* are more likely from a fourth- or fifth-century writer known alternately as pseudo-Macarius or (in all Arabic mss.) Simeon (see *Oxford Dictionary of the Christian Church* [1997], 1015–16).

7. Outler, *John Wesley*, 10.

8. On the mixed reception of Jaeger's work and Outler's subsequent claim, see Smith, "John Wesley's Growth."

revival of eighteenth-century Britain. Campbell hesitates, however, to identify the direct influence of any one thinker on Wesley (this "requires far more than simple comparisons between early Christian writers and his writings").[9] Although the paradigm for Christian thought and practice is found in Jesus Christ and the witness of the New Testament, "this religious ideal was 'realized' in post-canonical Christianity, especially in the ante-Nicene period, and thus he could call upon Christianity in the first three centuries as a vision for the renewal of 'true' Christianity."[10] Campbell, who recognizes that Wesley often read his ancient church sources in the many new editions and translations available in eighteenth-century England, concludes that Wesley relied upon the authority of early church writings in four contexts: (1) right *interpretations* of Scripture, (2) *illustrations* of biblically-proscribed practices and morality, (3) *suggestions* of right practice (though not proscribed by the Bible), and (4) *confirmations* of Methodist teachings and practice.[11] For Campbell, Wesley sought "genuine" Christianity in early church sources towards the programmatic renewal of the Church of England in the eighteenth century.

The second influential monograph related to Wesley and the early church is Randy Maddox's systematic study *Responsible Grace: John Wesley's Practical Theology* (1994). Maddox maintains that Wesley had more than a "casual" interest in the contemporary Anglican revival of patristic scholarship—especially Greek authors who had "receded from Western consciousness": Wesley "not only became aware of many of these Greek authors through his study, he seems to have imbibed a marked preference for them over the Latin writers!"[12] Recognizing the inherent difficulty of pinpointing Wesley's ancient church sources, Maddox explains that he has "been content simply to provide a counterpart to the many comparisons of Wesley to the various Western Christian traditions already available in Wesley scholarship."[13] Despite this goal, Maddox's

9. Campbell, *John Wesley and Christian Antiquity*, 3.

10. Ibid., 5.

11. Ibid., 110–11. Though not exhaustive, note the "Appendix 2: References to Ancient Christian Works in John Wesley's Works" (125–34).

12. Maddox, *Responsible Grace*, 22–23; cf. idem., "John Wesley and Eastern Orthodoxy."

13. Maddox, *Responsible Grace*, 24; cf. the role of Pietist and Protestant mystic sources (261 n. 43).

repeated assertions of Eastern themes in relationship to Wesleyan theology makes clear that he believes that Eastern theological influences were among the most significant factors in Wesley's apparent departure from Western models of the *ordo salutis*. Thus, to give one example, Maddox asserts that Adam's sin led to "inherited consequences" more than universal "punishment":

> Far from an aberration, this move illustrates the dynamic consistency in Wesley's theology. In retrospect, the most basic and consistent claims running throughout his reflection on inherited corruption resonate with the Eastern theme of *lost participation*: Humans are creaturely beings who can develop spiritual wholeness only through dynamic relationship with God's empowering grace.[14]

The work of redemption is, in line with Eastern theological models, an act of therapeutic healing from "Christ our Physician." Although offering an assessment of Wesley's practical theology, Maddox firmly relocates Wesley's theology in the traditions of Eastern thought. In effect, Maddox's work best supports a conservative reading of Methodist theology under Wesley: while Methodism may appear to be nothing more than an aberrant theological position within Western Christianity, it is actually rooted in ancient Christian sources.

These two studies are key parts of a broader conversation. Scholarship in the last twenty-five years has largely fallen into three primary categories, locating John Wesley's chief theological sources and interlocutors with (1) early Eastern church theologians, (2) early Western church theologians, or (3) High Church Anglican theologians as mediators of a range of ancient Christian traditions.[15]

Outler's original supposition, further substantiated by the works of Campbell and Maddox, led many scholars to associate Wesley's thought with the Eastern theological tradition.[16] Michael Christensen (1996),

14. Maddox, *Responsible Grace*, 81. Maddox is careful to recognize Western tendencies in Wesley's thinking, such as when discussing his retention of the *filioque* in the Articles of Religion, though even then he makes a case that "Wesley's deepest sympathies would lie with those who are seeking an alternative to the *filioque* in current debates" (137).

15. In the review of literature that follows, my aim is not to offer an exhaustive list so much as a one that adequately represents the varied strands of discussion. Several of the cited articles examine the relevant literature at various phases during recent decades.

16. Keefer, "John Wesley: Disciple of Early Christianity," describes Wesley's attitude

for example, explores the variety of poetic images Wesley encountered in pseudo-Marcarius and Ephraem Syrus.[17] Steve McCormick's work (1991) on Wesley and Chrysostom traces key familial influences on the young Wesley, maintains that the Eastern concept of *theosis* is the "organizing principle" of Wesley's *ordo saludis*, and asserts in Wesley a unique synthesis of Eastern and Roman Catholic traditions of grace and freedom.[18] Ted Campbell later revisited the Eastern roots of Wesley's theology by recalling the pressing question of Albert Outler amidst his dissertation work a decade earlier: "What, then, did Wesley find in ancient ascetic Christianity that he valued and passed along ('traditioned') to the Methodist people?"[19] Campbell's answer focuses on five legacies of Eastern Christian monasticism: (1) "the actual holiness he perceived in the ancient monks," (2) an "understanding of the religious life as the quest to restore the lost image of God," (3) a deepened understanding of "religious communion and communal discipline," (4) a use of "therapeutic imagery" drawn from ascetic literature, and (5) a vision of Christian perfection as the goal of sanctification.[20] More recently, J. Warren Smith (2003), recognizing the difficulties with Outler's belief that Wesley's "Macarius" could so closely be linked to Gregory of Nyssa, argues for a strong "family resemblance" between the two, especially on the matter of "the soul's eternal movement towards God's infinite being" (*epektasis*).[21] Finally, S. T. Kimbrough Jr. has edited two full volumes of Wesleyan-Orthodox consultations that reflect study and ecumenical dialogue on the links between Eastern theological traditions and Wesleyanism.[22] Each of these studies reflects the belief that when Wesley's theology departs from Augustinian concepts, he does so because he conserves the insights of early Eastern theological sources.

---

as one of *reviving* early Christianity more than *restoring* a primitive faith; restoration intimates a static view of the church and restorationist bodies can fall into a state of listlessness, too.

17. Christensen, "Theosis and Sanctification"; cf. Lee, "John Wesley and Early Eastern Spirituality"; idem, "Experiencing the Spirit."

18. McCormick, "Theosis in Chrysostom and Wesley."

19. Campbell, "Wesley's Use of the Church Fathers," 63.

20. Ibid., 63–66.

21. Smith, "John Wesley's Growth in Grace," 348ff.

22. Kimbrough, *Orthodox and Wesleyan Scriptural Understanding and Practice*; idem, *Orthodox and Wesleyan Spirituality*.

Other scholars continue to point to the direct influence of Western patristic works on John Wesley. Wesley's debt to Western theology remains the dominant scholarly assumption, since Wesley was raised, trained, and communicated within the Western tradition of the Church of England. In response to the increasingly vocal body of scholars who favor Eastern Christian influences, scholars such as Thomas Noble (2003) claim that Wesley actually preferred Augustine to Eastern sources and most consistently favors ante-Nicene Trinitarian thinkers with a predilection for the works of God over ontology.[23] John English (2005) similarly asserts that Augustine's influence is larger than many recognize and his ubiquitous influence on Wesley is difficult to categorize. English maintains that Wesley often cites Augustine approvingly, but at other times his views on predestination and perfection reveal an "independence of mind" and underscore a willingness to challenge his most influential opinions (such as the all too easy judgment of the early church heretic Pelagius).[24] Kenneth Collins (2007) characterizes the effort to link Wesley with Eastern sources as one among a number of misguided attempts to link Wesley with a singular, "preferred theological *tradition*": "though interesting and engaging, each one of these interpretations yet falters in failing to reckon with the diversity, the sheer 'otherness' of the panoply of elements—beyond the bounds of discrete theological traditions—that were actually factored into Wesley's practical theological reflections."[25] This scholarship certainly keeps Wesley firmly within the Western theological tradition, including its terminology and debates.

A third body of scholarship places the accent on possible mediating sources for Wesley's use of antiquity. Frank Baker's seminal *John Wesley and the Church of England* (1970) helped establish an important scholarly recognition of Wesley's place within the varieties of English church practices, and several recent works on Wesley and antiquity incorporate

23. Thomas A. Noble, "East and West"; cf. Im, "John Wesley's Theological Anthropology."

24. English, "References to St. Augustine." Note English's "Appendix" (20–24) where he lists quotes or paraphrases to Augustine in Wesley's works (and thereby "corrects or extends" Ted Campbell's list in *John Wesley and Christian Antiquity*, Appendix 2, cited above).

25. Collins argues for the kind of eclecticism that I find most compelling, but he risks making Wesley something of a demigod in the process (*Theology of John Wesley*, 4); cf. Collins's mixed response to Maddox's *Responsible Grace* in "State of Wesley Studies," esp. 14–22, 36–37.

Baker's insights.[26] David Bundy's (1991) work on the Alexandrian tradition is representative, since he not only traces Wesley's specific references to Alexandrian theologians such as Clement of Alexandria and Origen, but also highlights, for example, Wesley's reliance on Anthony Horneck's *The Happy Ascetic: or the Best Exercise* (1693).[27] Horneck (1641–1697), a leading figure in the English Restoration, also appears in Wesley's *Christian Library*. Bundy concludes that a comparison of the sources reveals that

> there are more correspondences between Clement and Horneck than between Clement and Wesley; and one could argue that Wesley appears to depend on Horneck's sequence of virtues and other emphases rather than on those of Clement. Horneck appears to have understood the integral theological and philosophical structures of the Alexandrian position better than Wesley did.[28]

Carter's (1995) analysis of Wesley's literary sources again places him within the sphere of English High Church and Non-Juror interest in Christian antiquity. Through readings in Horneck, William Cave, William Reeves, and Nathaniel Marshall, Wesley became acquainted with a rich patristic tradition taken up by English theologians wishing "to expose the laxness of the official church and to call the church's adherents to the primitive Christian character."[29] Similarly, Hammond's (2009) detailed analysis of Wesley's interest in "primitive Christianity" indicates the various sources through which Wesley came to have contact with early Christian sources, including the influence of his father and the Non-Juror tradition he encountered in the Oxford tutor John Clayton.[30] Through Clayton's influence (and library), Wesley's early Methodism came to emphasize weekly Communion, stationary fasts

---

26. Baker, *John Wesley.*

27. Bundy, "Christian Virtue."

28. Ibid., 149–50.

29. Carter, "High Church Roots," 70; cf. Duffy, "Primitive Christianity Revived."

30. "A catalog of Clayton's library survives and it lists nearly every book that influenced Wesley during this period, providing strong evidence that Clayton swayed Wesley's reading in a high church/non-juring direction." Hammond, "High Church Anglican Influences," 194. Wesley's practices in Georgia, too, reflect this "high church, non-juring" influence, including rebaptism of dissenters, trine (or triple) immersion, wine mixed with water in Communion, etc. (175–76).

(Wednesday and Friday fasts), and early church devotional practices.[31]
Finally, Richard Heitzenrater's essay on "John Wesley's Reading of and
References to the Early Church Fathers" (2002) raises the most significant questions about the mediating sources for Wesley's knowledge of
early Christian thought.[32] Heitzenrater, consulting Frank Baker's biblio-
graphic reading list, introduces some startling data into the discussion.
He claims that many of Wesley's references to the early church are merely
aphoristic or passing references. In fact, Heitzenrater claims that references to the early church fathers in Baker's bibliography are decidedly
sparse in the letters, published journals, private diaries, and other works.
Although three works contain especially noteworthy engagement with
early church theologians—*Letter to the Reverend Dr. Conyers Middleton*
(1749), *Roman Catechism, with a Reply Thereto* (1756), and *Farther
Appeal to Men of Reason and Religion* (1745)—they are polemical works
that reflect and counter his interlocutors' use of early Christian authorities. Given Wesley's "voracious" reading habits, Heitzenrater concludes:

> The paucity of Wesley's direct reading, the generality of his refer-
> ences, the 'Western' weighting of those references, and the apho-
> ristic nature of his quotations leave one wondering about the
> level of his reliance upon and knowledge of the primary sources,
> especially of the Eastern Church. . . . It is my suspicion that many
> of the early church ideas and practices passed through several
> filters before reaching Wesley from a number of sources.[33]

Thus, a strong body of scholarship exists that cherishes most Wesley's
established Anglican context and challenges any notion of extended
reflection on early Christian literature beyond his early years at Oxford
and Georgia. In this view, Wesley was not capturing early sources for
a new vision of the Church of England, but continuing a line of argu-
mentation that had already been applied in the prior century by English
theologians in the Restoration.

---

31. Notably, at the Consultation on Orthodox and Wesleyan Spirituality (2000)
Ted Campbell placed greatest emphasis on Wesley as "heir of a particular tradition of
Anglican patristic study that had developed in the late 1500s and the 1600s in response
to Puritans," i.e., Caroline Anglicanism ("Scripture and Tradition," 162).

32. Heitzenrater, "John Wesley's Reading."

33. Ibid., 30–31.

II.

While Wesley's interest in the early church certainly reflects the English High Church recovery of patristic scholarship, Wesley's appeal to early Christian thought and practice also signals his participation in a wider Enlightenment fascination with history. From this angle, Wesley's pursuit of early Christian thought and practice is instructive, but not unique. Wesley's attention to the early church is very much a product of his age. Any attempt to assess the appeal of antiquity in Wesley (or early Methodism, for that matter) should be made with respect to Wesley's conception of history and the task of the modern historian. Though certainly not a conventional historian, Wesley shaped and reformulated the writings of his predecessors through careful writing, translating, and editing in order to develop a *useful* account of Christian history.[34] In effect, John Wesley was a practically minded historian—a historian of Christian spirituality—who saw Methodism as simultaneously a revival effort within the Church of England and a mode of Christian practice that conserved genuine Christianity.[35]

Wesley's reflections on historical method can most clearly be found in the prefaces to two historical works (both abridgments in four volumes): (1) *A Concise History of England, from the Earliest Times, to the Death of George II* (1776), which appeared in Wesley's name and principally combined histories by Goldsmith, Rapin, and Smollett, "only with various corrections and additions"[36]; and (2) *A Concise Ecclesiastical History, from the Birth of Christ, to the Beginning*

34. John Whitehead's *Life of Wesley* went so far as to argue that Wesley lacked the requisite intellectual qualities of the historian, claiming that "[i]n historical compositions Mr. Wesley did not excel. His habit of generalising, and reducing to a few heads, every subject of which he treated, and the too great confidence he had in the authority of his own assertions, when he himself was convinced, in some degree indisposed him to enter into that detail of evidence from facts, so highly necessary to establish a general principle in history and biography. His works, therefore, of this kind have not the same merit as his other compositions." Quoted in Green, *Works of John and Charles Wesley*, 185.

35. Two recent publications indicate that scholarly recognition of Wesley's historical interests is growing: Seaborn, "Wesley's Views"; MacMillan, "John Wesley and Enlightened Historians."

36. Wesley, *Concise History of England*, 1:vii. I wish to thank the librarians of the Bridwell Library of Southern Methodist University for providing access to the first editions of Wesley's *Works*. Readers may also consult Wesley's "List of Works Revised and Abridged from Various Authors," in *Works* (1831), 7:510–91.

of the present Century (1781), which Wesley published under the name of his primary source: Johann Lorenz Mosheim, chancellor of the University of Gottingen.[37] The prefaces to these works provide a systematic statement of Wesley's historical methodology, explain his reasons for abridging these works, and offer an account of how history ought to be written. The prefaces also confirm that Wesley's own hand plays a formidable role in his labor to edit the works of others, including works from antiquity. Although he did not formally write these histories, he participated in far more than simply cutting out large chunks of the text. Wesley actively shaped these histories, sentence-by-sentence, in order to re-form the whole according to his own conception of God's work in history. The texts, in this sense, have very much become Wesley's own. In fact, I find it rather intriguing that of the sixty-five items bound in the fifteen-volume "Wesley's Tracts" (1746), "twenty-five of them (nearly 40%) were extracts by other authors, such as Jonathan Edwards, August Hermann Francke, Thomas Halyburton, Thomas à Kempis, Richard Baxter . . ."[38] Wesley's prefatory works reflect prominent Enlightenment interests that he encountered in his independent reading and polemical controversies alike.

Three essential principles define Wesley's historical method: impartiality, judiciousness, and spirituality. Wesley believes that *impartiality* is essential for the historian. He worries that historians too frequently lack impartiality and tend to privilege not only political interests, but also denominational concerns. Too often, Wesley claims, authors take up the cause of a single party while relating the events of a period: "Even in relating the uninteresting transactions which occurred many hundred years ago, most authors vehemently espouse the cause, either of one party or the other: as naturally, as, in reading Homer, some are earnest for the Trojans: others equally earnest for the Grecians."[39] Wesley's insistence on impartiality reflects trends in Enlightenment historiography, which moved towards writing histories that were universal in scope in order to avoid the party spirit that dogged earlier historians. Universality also included the elevation of antiquity in an effort to demonstrate his-

---

37. For the history itself, Wesley relied on both Mosheim's original Latin history as well as the English translation by Archibald Maclaine (Mosheim, *Concise Ecclesiastical History*).

38. Heitzenrater, "John Wesley's *A Christian Library*."

39. Wesley, *Concise History of England*, 1:iv–v.

torical progress and to offer words of instruction. MacMillan notes that "[i]n Gibbon's *History of the Decline and Fall of the Roman Empire*, for example, the first three centuries were given as much space as the last nine, and frequent comparisons were made between past and present events."[40] Wesley's interest in early Christianity, then, reflects the impartiality prized among Enlightenment historians.

Wesley believed that the ideal work of history ought to be written by *judicious* authors, as well. Good history must be well-written and entertaining, ought to overcome the temptation to show off one's learning ("a laboured panegyric upon my own understanding"), and should provide readers with precisely the information that is needed.[41] By producing inexpensive books that say precisely what is necessary, Wesley was able to justify his role as an abridger of the works of others.[42] In ecclesiastical histories, however, Wesley deplored the obsession with early church heresies: "Among these we may rank nine parts in ten of what relates to the Heresies, that were propagated in the several Ages of the Church, and in the several Provinces of the Empire." Historians tend to include every detail, but Wesley thought that such efforts showed "too much honour" to the "mere whims and absurdities of senseless or self-conceited men."[43] A historian's strenuous effort to bring all the heresies together frequently yields little more than a large "heap" of "the rubbish of seventeen hundred years."[44] The judicious historian avoids verbosity, while remaining cautious not to pass over seminal occasions that may give useful instruction to the reader.[45]

40. Macmillan, "John Wesley and the Enlightened Historians," 127.

41. Wesley, *Concise History of England*, 1:vii.

42. Mosheim's Latin work was valuable enough, but cost six shillings. The translation, for all the good it did by making the original accessible to the English reader, increased the price by five times. Wesley, *Concise Ecclesiastical History*, 1:iv.

43. Wesley, *Concise Ecclesiastical History*, 1:v. Wesley's recommended practice exemplifies the essence of Whitehead's criticism.

44. The author of a long-winded history risks losing the audience completely: "I ended the abridgment of Mr. de Renty's life. O that such a life should be related by such a historian! Who by inserting all, if not more than all the weak things that holy man ever said or did, by his commendation of almost every action or word which either deserved or needed it not, and by his injudicious manner of relating many others which were indeed highly commendable, has cast the shade of superstition and follow over one of the brightest patters of heavenly wisdom." Wesley, January 6, 1738, in *Works* (1984), 18:208.

45. The biographer of St. Catherine of Genoa, Wesley claims, has wrongly "aggrandized her into a mere idiot"; he further notes, in typical anti-Catholic rhetoric, that "we

Reliable historians, finally, must maintain *spiritual purpose and awareness* in their writings. Although partiality damages both secular and sacred histories, the gracious and providential activity of God in all things cannot be ignored. For Wesley, the historian unaware of God's active role in history is the one who fails to capture the fullness of truth. Wesley's discussion of the various histories of England, for example, turns sharply on the role of the divine in worldly affairs. Wesley wonders how it can be that all the major histories of England are "calculated only for Atheists, for there is nothing about God in them."[46] His meaning is clear: it is not so much an unawareness of the role of Christianity in the events discussed, as a complete lack of consideration of the providential hand of the divine within these events. God "governs the world" and his "kingdom ruleth over all"—not only in heaven but even here on earth:

> he alone *changeth the times and the seasons, removeth kings and setteth up kings*, and disposes all things by his almighty power, according to the counsels of his own will . . . from the whole tenor of their discourse, one would suppose, that God was quite out of the question: that the King of heaven had no more to do in the revolutions of *England*, than the emperor of *Japan*: and that his power over *Great-Britain*, was as effectually extinguished, as that of the *Danes* and *Saxons*.[47]

Wesley criticized the "atheistic" turn in contemporary historical works. For example, Wesley disapproves of William Robertson's *History of America*, in part, because Robertson completely eliminates the place of the Creator from his account and replaces God with mere chance: "Was it not enough never to mention the Providence of God where there was the fairest occasion? without saying expressly, 'the *fortune* of Cortez' or chance did thus or thus? So far as *fortune* or *chance* governs the world, God has no place in it."[48] Wesley remains cognizant that speaking of divine providence in history is "out of fashion," but questions whether "cultural prudence" enhances the progress of genuine Christianity: a "particular providence" must guide the affairs of history, since "any but a particular providence is no providence at all." When historians neglect

---

seldom find a saint of God's making sainted by the Bishop of Rome." Wesley, December 3, 1761, in *Works* (1984), 21:345.

46. Wesley, *Concise History of England*, 1:v–vi.

47. Ibid., 1:vi.

48. Wesley, July 6, 1781, in *Works* (1984), 23:214.

the providential work of God in the events of history, they not only misrepresent those events, but also fail to understand their audience and further the gap between historians and the reading public (for instance, Wesley notes that "the majority even of Britons, to this day, retain some sort of respect for the Bible").[49] While Enlightenment historians such as Hume and Gibbon avoided reference to divine intervention in the name of constancy, Wesley believed that history confirmed the work of God known by divine revelation.[50]

The problem of miracles exemplifies the intersection between Wesley's understanding of history and his attraction to the early church. Enlightenment historians increasingly ignored claims to miracles in antiquity, as Wesley himself acknowledges, due to the prevalence of "lying wonders" that "were so common in the heathen world."[51] Wesley's "Letter to Conyers Middleton" indicates the difficulty that Wesley and his contemporaries faced when deciding whether or not to trust early Christian accounts of miraculous events. Conyers Middleton's *A Free Inquiry into the Miraculous Powers, which Are Supposed to Have Subsisted in the Christian Church, from the Earliest Ages through Several Successive Centuries* (1749) argued that early Christian miracles associated with the Apostles following the death, resurrection, and ascension of Christ gradually declined until the gospel was left to make its own way by "the natural force of those divine graces, with which it was so richly stored, *faith, hope, and charity.*"[52] Middleton's treatise proceeds through a case-by-case study of the early church, allegedly demonstrating that early church leaders made spurious claims to the miraculous out of an inordinate love of power. Early Christian thought and practice, according to Middleton, reflects nothing more than superstition and deception, especially in their repeated pretensions to "*the gift of raising the dead; of speaking with tongues; of understanding the holy Scriptures.*"[53] Wesley's response is forceful and lengthy. He tackles each point of Middleton's argument in order to refute the pernicious nature of his reading of the ancient sources. But Wesley's argument is not merely about the role of

---

49. Ibid.

50. Cf. MacMillan, "John Wesley and Enlightened Historians," 125.

51. He continues, "they naturally supposed all the Christian miracles to be of the same sort." Wesley, April 2, 1788, in *Works* (1984), 24:74.

52. Middleton, *Free Inquiry*, xxix.

53. Ibid., xxxiii.

the miraculous, for Wesley's "Letter" is equally a reflection of his under-standing of God's active work in history and the ability of historians to identify that work.[54] The case of miracles in the early church brought central Enlightenment questions to the fore, as Campbell explains:

> The closing of the canon of scripture and the end of the "apostolic age" became, in Middleton's view, the final dividing line beyond which one could not step. Hume already had stepped beyond it, and Gibbon would treat it with disdain. Middleton thus repre-sents not the outcome of the Enlightenment, but a middle stage that illuminates the personal, intellectual struggles which the Enlightenment had provoked.[55]

Wesley, by contrast, slows the alleged waning of divine intervention to the time of Constantine's conversion, when "the decline of faith and morals among the Christians of Constantine's age led to a near cessa-tion of the miraculous powers."[56] His point is clear: miracles ceased only when and where the love of God had grown cold. Wesley and Middleton thereby represent

> two emerging forms of response to the tendency toward a uni-form interpretation of history in the post-Reformation period. One was the response of the Enlightenment, with its tendency to distrust particular tenets of revealed religion. The other was the response of the "religion of the heart," with its tendency to find divine interventions throughout the range of human history.[57]

In light of Wesley's involvement in such a fundamental controversy over history and the early church, it is no surprise that he implored histori-ans to maintain the place of the divine within their historical accounts: "Wholly to divest one's self of prejudice and partiality, is indeed a dif-

54. Wesley, "A Letter to the Reverend Doctor Conyers Middleton Occasioned by his late 'Free Inquiry,'" in *Works* (1872), 10:1–79.

55. Campbell, "John Wesley and Conyers Middleton," 43.

56. Ibid., 47; cf. Wesley's sermon "Of Former Times" (sermon 102; 1787), in which he highlights the role Constantine played in the corruption of the early church: "I have been long convinced from the whole tenor of ancient history that this very event—Constantine's calling himself a Christian, and pouring in that flood of wealth and power on the Christian church, the clergy in particular—was productive of more evil to the church than all the ten persecutions put together. From the time that power, riches, and honour of all kinds were heaped upon the Christians, vice of all kinds came in like a flood, both on the clergy and laity." §16, in *Works* (1984), 3:450.

57. Campbell, "John Wesley and Conyers Middleton," 49.

ficult thing. And I have found it equally difficult, to see God in all the affairs of men: among the multiplicity of visible causes, still to see Him that is invisible, the One Great Cause, sitting on the circle of the heavens, and ruling all things in heaven and earth."[58]

The same principle applies to histories of the church as well. The historian should recognize not simply the ostensible function of religion in the church but much more the true and interior state of the church. It is not enough for Mosheim to consider the internal state of the church according to its "state of learning, the form of government, the doctrine, the rites and ceremonies."[59] Wesley encourages historians to perceive the spiritual state of the church while cautioning against a naïve view of history that ignores the genuine defects and fallibility of the central characters of the church. Christian history is replete with troubled characters: it is "absolutely needful to apprise the pious Reader," Wesley maintains, "that he be not offended." Readers ought not expect a "History of Saints, of men that walked worthy of their high Calling." Certainly, some in every age were "burning and shining lights," but even they appeared in "a dark place" and a world "full of darkness and cruel habitations."[60] Only by such an impartial tone could the faithful historian avoid intermingling the seeds of error with truth.

Wesley's practical divinity resulted in the development of a deeply practical history—a history of Christian teaching and practice. In Wesley's *Christian Library*, a collection of fifty volumes that Wesley published to educate Methodist preachers and laity about the history of Christian belief and practice, Wesley includes "extracts from, and abridgements of, the choicest pieces of practical divinity which have been published in the English tongue."[61] The *Christian Library* was, by Wesley's own "rational" assessment, the most "complete Body of Practical Divinity" in the world.[62] Consistent with the Enlightenment interest in universality, Wesley gave a chronological ordering to the text—beginning with the

58. Wesley, *Concise History of England*, 1:viii.

59. Ibid., 1:v. Mosheim's "Introduction" provides a complete account of the differences between the external and internal history of the church—these categories provide the framework for the first three books (vols. 1–3), after which the Reformation and subsequent events appear under the categories of "general" (Christianity as a whole) and "particular" (sectarian/denominational) history.

60. Ibid., 1:vii–viii.

61. Quoted in Heitzenrater, *Wesley and the Methodists*, 178.

62. Wesley, *Christian Library*, 1:i.

Apostolic Fathers—so that "the serious reader may be the more clearly satisfied, that the genuine Religion of Jesus Christ has been one and the same from the beginning" and so that another might be able to continue his labors and "the more easily go on where I leave off."[63] Through the voice of his primary source, William Wake's *The Genuine Epistles of the Apostolical Fathers* (1693), Wesley recommends the life and teachings of the early church in particular: "We cannot therefore doubt, but what they deliver to us is the pure Doctrine of the Gospel: what Christ and his Apostles taught, and what these holy men had themselves receiv'd from their own mouths."[64] The first volume includes excerpts from Clement of Rome, Ignatius, Polycarp, and (pseudo-)Macarius. Surprisingly, some key figures are left off, however, such as Augustine and Ephrem Syrus.[65] Later volumes of the *Christian Library* turn to the acts of the martyrs, which extend the story of Christianity into later ages by providing examples of faithful lives, as well as accounts of the practical wisdom of divines in various places. Wesley includes a diverse body of Christians in the *Library*, too, including foreign leaders (such as Melanchthon and Calvin), members of the Church of England (such as Richard Hooker and John Donne), and, more than any other, Puritan divines (such as Whitaker and Thomas Wilson). Key mediating sources are also included in the *Christian Library*, such as Horneck's *Happy Ascetic* (vol. 29) and William's Cave's *Primitive Christianity* (vol. 31). Throughout, Wesley tailors the theological content of his texts. For example, in abridging Fox's *Acts and Monuments of the Christian Martyrs*, Wesley states that he has "purposely omitted, not only all secular history, but likewise those accounts, writings, and examinations of the martyrs, which contained nothing particularly affecting or instructive."[66] He frequently expunges erroneous teachings and, in extracting the works of Puritans, excises what he regards as blemishes of doctrine, since "they generally give a

---

63. Ibid., 1:v–vi; cf. Heitzenrater, "John Wesley's *A Christian Library*," 133–46.

64. Wesley, *Christian Library*, 1:i [17].

65. The meaning of these gaps demands further exploration, as Heitzenrater explains: "some obvious writers (some of them Wesley's favorites) are missing from the collection: Augustine, Ephrem Syrus, Thomas Hooker, Francis Atterbury, John Bull, Patrick Delany, August Hermann Francke, Robert Nelson, and John Norris. This is partly, though not completely, explained by his use of chronological order—he never got to the eighteenth century." Heitzenrater, "John Wesley's *A Christian Library*," 136.

66. Wesley, *Christian Library*, in *Works* (1831), 7:529.

low and imperfect view of sanctification or holiness."[67] Even Macarius, whom Wesley esteemed so highly, emphasizes the goal of Christian perfection without mentioning the central Eastern teaching of *theosis*.[68] In all, Wesley included fifty-two different lives in his *Library* and the complete set included works by seventy-one different authors from different periods in the history of the Christian churches.[69]

The *Christian Library* thereby forces students of Wesley's interest in the early church to grapple with a key question raised by Richard Heitzenrater's article on "John Wesley's Reading of and References to the Early Church Fathers" (2002). If John Wesley's thought is so deeply indebted to the authority of the early church, what does one do with his equally strong interest in the later ages of the church? Returning to the opening quote, one might ask: why does Wesley insist that Methodists are "downright *Bible Christians*" who interpret the Bible by the "primitive Church and our own"?[70] The answer, I believe, lies in Wesley's claim that Methodism was simultaneously a movement of reform even as it stood in continuity with Christian thought and practice from the apostolic age to the present.

One pivotal confirmation of my assertion is the final section of Wesley's edition of Mosheim's *Concise Ecclesiastical History*. Wesley wished to bring the history to a proper conclusion by clarifying the recent history of revival in England. He therefore decided to include his own account of the history of Methodism to counteract his detractor's accusations of enthusiasm: "As no other person can be so well acquainted with *Methodists*, so called, as I am, I judge it my duty to leave behind me, for the information of all candid men, as clear an account of it as I can. This will contain the chief circumstances that occurred, for upwards of fifty years, related in the most plain and artless manner,

---

67. Ibid., 7:530. A full account of Wesley's method of abridgment is beyond the limits of this article, but Monk's study shows how he not only used deletions, transitions, clarifications, and substitutions, but also provided what appear to be theologically-driven changes throughout: these items "raise tantalizing questions." Monk, *John Wesley*, 42, and ch. 3 generally.

68. Cf. Christensen, "Theosis and Sanctification," 85–87; Campbell, *John Wesley and Christian Antiquity*, 45.

69. See "Appendix 2: Exemplary Christian Lives in *A Christian Library*," in Monk, *John Wesley*, 255–56; and Heitzenrater, "John Wesley's *A Christian Library*," 136.

70. Wesley, *Short History of Methodism*, in *Works* (1984), 368.

before Him whose I am, and whom I serve."[71] Several points are worth highlighting about the inclusion of Wesley's history of Methodism in the *Concise Ecclesiastical History*. First, the inclusion of "A Short History of the People Called Methodists" confirms the notion that Wesley was doing more than merely republishing historical writings. By attaching his own work to Mosheim's—merging prefatory instructions and materials he had refashioned from Mosheim with a firsthand account of a contemporary movement—Wesley extended the received narrative of Christian history and controlled the story of Methodism. As the "Introductory Comment" to his account in the bicentennial edition explains, Wesley's abridgment already spanned four volumes, extending over 1200 pages. Yet the further material on the Methodists lengthened the whole by over one hundred pages, or eleven percent of the entire *History*.[72] Despite his own prefatory remarks on the importance of impartiality among historians, Wesley's history of Methodism is unabashedly apologetic. He wrote the piece in response to Maclaine's inclusion of a table that listed Wesley and Whitefield as heretics—a fact that he notes at both the commencement and the conclusion to the history, where he remarks:

> This is *the way* (*called Heresy* by Dr. M'Lean and others,) *according to which we worship the God of our fathers.* And we have known some thousands who walked therein, till their spirits returned to God. Some thousands likewise we now know who are walking in the same path of love, and studying to have a conscience void of offence towards God and towards man.[73]

Wesley is not simply letting the facts speak for themselves, as he might have implored the author of another historical narrative, rather Wesley establishes the movement as a part of the spiritual development of the nation and Christendom since the time of the earliest Christians. Moreover, as the conclusion to the whole four-volume history, Wesley places his own story and that of the Methodists in a line of succession— a history of those who have been faithful to God despite the external circumstances of the times. Even as the earlier volumes described the interior spiritual condition of the earliest churches, Wesley optimisti-

71. Wesley, *Concise Ecclesiastical History*, 4:169; cf. Wesley, "The Methodist Societies," in *Works* (1984), 9:425–503.

72. Wesley, "The Methodist Societies," in *Works* (1984), 9:425.

73. Wesley, *Concise Ecclesiastical History*, 4:280–81; cf. Wesley, "The Methodist Societies," in *Works* (1984), 9:503.

cally weaves his own story with that of the earliest believers: "they expect, that men should *say all manner of evil against them, for* their Master's *sake.* But they have counted the cost, and are willing to be *as the filth and offscouring of the world.* Yea, they have many times shewn, that they *counted not their lives dear unto themselves, so they might finish their course with joy, and testify the gospel of the grace of God.*"[74] Wesley thereby develops a continuous historical record of God's providential and progressive work in the world.

Wesley's understanding of history encouraged him to write, compile, abridge, and republish a wide range of writings (including his own journals) for the benefit of the Christian community. He participated in the Enlightenment debate over how history ought to be written and he shared with his contemporaries the belief that history ought to document an impartial record of truth. As I have explained, his histories are neither simple chronologies of events nor the pursuit of broad doctrinal developments. Wesley's historical work straddles premodern and modern conceptions of how history should be written. On one hand, Wesley perceives the work of providence in all history, believes that discerning historians will not neglect the role of the divine in political and social events alike, and maintains that God's design marks all history. Yet, on the other hand, Wesley also insists that valid historical writing seeks objectivity and impartiality. For Wesley, these two aims were not in conflict. Wesley models a distinctive historiography that promotes a particular form of spirituality drawn from the early church to his own day; a model of history as practical religion or, as he termed it, "practical divinity."

III.

In light of the three scholarly patterns identified in the first section of this paper and the fuller context of Wesley's participation in eighteenth-century historiography, some clearer judgments can be made about Wesley's understanding of the early church and its continued relevance today. Clearly, Wesley's various works indicate his knowledge of and reading in a wide range of early Christian writers, including Augustine, Chrysostom, Cyprian, Clement of Alexandria, Ephraem Syrus, Justin

74. Wesley, *Concise Ecclesiastical History*, 4:281; cf. Wesley, "The Methodist Societies," in *Works* (1984), 9:503.

Martyr, Origen, and Tertullian. Western theological voices are also strong, particularly when one considers that Wesley was chiefly interested in the ante-Nicene period of early church development, when genuine Christianity remained, in Wesley's view, uncorrupted by the Constantinian turn in the faith. Wesley's private diaries, for example, confirm his close study of Augustine during his time at Oxford (Augustine *Confessions* and *Meditations* were part of the standard curriculum at Oxford).[75] However, the *absence* of Augustine's works from the early Christian period of the *Christian Library* is surprising. Eastern theological resources, too, certainly evoke a number of themes that parallel or at least informed Wesley's thought, including some therapeutic aspects of the work of grace and notions of sanctification and perfection that overlap with pseudo-Macarian literature.

Still, above all, I have argued that Wesley's devotion to early Christian thought and practice derives from a longstanding interest in "primitive" Christianity as part of a larger, eclectic defense of the Methodist movement in England. Wesley's use of High Church patristic scholarship by Horneck, Cave, Reeves, and Marshall indicates that even as Wesley appealed to early Christian practices towards the renewal of the Church of England, he also hoped to show that Methodism was theologically consistent with the witness of the earliest Christians. Wesley's theological and historical debts are eclectic and his work as a historian of spirituality indicates that his true aim was to replicate neither Eastern nor Western sources. Rather, Wesley's aim was to renew the Church of England while defending Methodism as a conservation of preexisting forms of spirituality. In the process, Wesley trained Methodists through a carefully crafted history of faith; an account of Christian spirituality formed by his own hand through the mediating sources of the historic Christian communion.

Wesley's eclectic interest in the genuine gospel, concern for universality, and recognition of the work of the Spirit of God in every age of the church continues to challenge Christians in the twenty-first century. I thereby conclude with five implications of a "Wesleyan" understanding of the place of early church thought and practice in Christianity today.

(1) John Wesley's appeal to early Christianity informs a Christian commitment to *the authority of Scripture*. Wesley's recognition of the value

---

75. Heitzenrater, "John Wesley's Reading," 26.

of the rich traditions of the church—ancient *and* modern—reminds Christians that a high estimation of the faith and practices of antiquity need not diminish the authority of the Bible. Albert Outler's now-famous Wesleyan Quadrilateral has been widely received in Wesleyan and even non-Wesleyan circles, yet Wesley clearly never admitted any authority—church traditions, reason, or experience—equal to that of the Bible.[76] Church traditions, insofar as they reflect the biblical witness, provide examples of genuine Christian life and thought in continuity with the original apostolic witness. Wesley's interest in the early church provides Christians with a valuable example of the need for biblical commitment informed by the wider witness of the church. Wesley's biblical and historical work reflects his desire to avoid partiality, the "rock whereon so many split," so that he might steer a *via media* between the extremes of bigotry that ruled other historical studies: "And I am in hopes this will appear to all who are divested of prejudice, and who are lovers of naked truth."[77] The early church provides useful resources that clarify the richness of the authoritative biblical witness.

(2) Wesley's appeal to Christian antiquity also reminds Christians that the riches of the early church include not only thoughtful reflection on God, but also *faithful spiritual practices*. Wesley's earliest encounters with antiquity reminded him of the importance of faithful works of service, fellowship in communal life, and personal holiness. Early Methodists were criticized for their sacramentarian tendencies, but Oxford students around John and Charles were equally devoted to works of service among the poor and elderly and even committed to regular work among prisoners.[78] He valued the gathering of small groups of believers (Wesley's use of classes and bands distinguished early Methodist societies) because that was the practice of the earliest Christians. Wesley saw in the "primitive" Christian witness an example of lived holiness that was as much if not more important than their theological speculation. The homilies of Macarius, which Wesley highly valued, clearly distinguish between two ways of living—that of the world and that of the Christians—"[a]nd the

76. For one helpful guide to Wesleyan perspectives on the Quadrilateral, see Gunter et al., *Wesley and the Quadrilateral*.

77. Wesley, *Concise History of England*, 1:viii.

78. On early Methodist devotion, see Richard Heitzenrater, *Wesley and the Methodists*, 39ff.

difference between them is very wide."[79] Wesley's strong social concern is part of a broad Christian commitment to the holy life and the work of the Spirit in Christian sanctification.

(3) Wesley's practice of abridging and editing his sources serves as a *cautionary reminder*, too, that not all early Christian practices and teachings are equally useful. Because Scripture is always the test of church traditions, the authority of historical witnesses will undoubtedly vary. Wesley was careful to remind others that the story of Christianity is one of imperfection (a lesson he surely knew from his own experience!), the saints of old were quite fallible, and the story is not for the fainthearted. But Wesley's commitment to God's providential work allowed him to cherish the historic faith even through the troubles that accompanied every age since the Apostles. In his sermon "Of Former Times" (1787), Wesley advised his readers that antiquity was hardly the golden age that some imagine. Long before the time of Constantine, "abominations" existed in the churches of Corinth, Carthage, and beyond.[80] For Wesley, the recent appearance of deism ("the fruit of the general infidelity") reminds Christians that even a "dreadful evil" can serve as a "great and universal good" in the hands of the beneficent creator.[81] So, while Christians can join Wesley in cherishing the early church, they should also avoid naïve optimism about the purity of the church in either former times or our own.

(4) The writings of the early church encouraged Wesley to recover an awareness of *the work of the Spirit of God* long after the days of the Apostles. Wesley attributed Christian witness, expressed in miraculous and charismatic signs, to God's activity among those who followed Christ in the early church. The decline of spiritual gifts in the post-Nicene era came not because Christians no longer needed them, but rather because Christian love had "waxed cold."[82] Likewise, against Conyers Middleton's claim that the silence of the apostolic writers "must dispose us to conclude that [the gifts] were then withdrawn," Wesley insists that careful historical research demonstrates that the gifts of the Spirit (including

79. "The Homilies of Macarius," in Wesley, *Christian Library*, Discourse 4.

80. Wesley, "Of Former Times" (sermon 102), §§15–19, in *Works* (1984), 3:450–51.

81. Ibid., §20, 3:452.

82. Wesley, "The More Excellent Way" (sermon 89), §§1–2, in *Works* (1984), 3:264.

healings and tongues) continued to be active in the early church: "O Sir, mention this no more. I intreat you, never name their silence again. They speak loud enough to shame you as long as you live."[83] Wesley was neither a charismatic nor a pre-Pentecostal. However, Christians today struggle with matters of the Spirit and spiritual gifts even as Wesley and Jonathan Edwards each addressed the spiritual "enthusiasm" associated with eighteenth-century revivalism. Wesley's willingness to reevaluate received notions about the work of the Spirit in the early church left a strong legacy that, in time, impacted the American holiness movement and the later Pentecostal movement that continues to shape the face of world Christianity in our own century.[84] Christians today, with Wesley, can probe the practices and beliefs of the early church (as well as later ages that Wesley too-quickly dismissed, namely the Middle Ages) for further insight into the work of the Spirit in contemporary practice.

(5) Finally, Wesley's recovery of writings from the early church and beyond are a reminder of his deep commitment to the importance of "holy conferencing." As I have argued in this essay, Wesley's vision was one of theological eclecticism that draws from a wealth of historical resources. In practice, while he could be something of an autocrat, Wesley adopted the custom of gathering his preachers in "conference" from 1744 onwards, allowing him to learn from their advisement and gain connectional relationship.[85] His consultation of the range of lives and histories of thought in the *Christian Library*, too, exemplifies his commitment to universal knowledge and judicious judgments. Christians, similarly, can learn from the kind of broad holy conferencing that Wesley practiced and even move beyond it in at least two forms. Ecumenical dialogue between Wesleyans and Orthodox theologians has led to fruitful conversations that clarify areas of common spirituality as well as significant differences in faith and practice.[86] Too frequently, the labels "evangelical" and "modern," among others, signify "intentional discontinuity" with the historical faith.[87] Moreover, even as Christians should pursue fruitful

83. Wesley, "Letter to Conyers Middleton," in *Works* (1872), 10:23.

84. Consider the conclusion of Hempton, *Methodism*, 208–9.

85. On the conferences, see Rupert E. Davies, "Introduction," in *Works* (1984), 9:20–23.

86. Cf. Bundy, "Christian Virtue," 155.

87. Ted Campbell's critique of American Methodism equally applies to other American Christians. Campbell, "Scripture and Tradition," 167.

ecumenical dialogue, global conversations are a necessary antidote to religious jingoism in our day.[88] Today, "downright *Bible Christians*" can learn from Wesley's pursuit of truth that the lessons learned from the early church, no less than our own *global* communion, are essential to the character of the Christian.

88. Sources such as the Barrett, *World Christian Encyclopedia* provide powerful evidence of the utterly global character of Christian faith in the twenty-first century.

Why Read Wesley Reading the Fathers?
A Response to Jeffrey W. Barbeau

D. Stephen Long

Marquette University

WHY SHOULD WE STUDY the church fathers? Why should we study Wesley studying the church fathers? Professor Barbeau's essay provides some excellent answers to these questions, both by summarizing the most significant answers from the Wesleyan tradition and by presenting his own concluding five implications of a "Wesleyan understanding of the place of early church thought and practice in Christianity today." In this brief response I would like to review and assess those answers, adding a few of my own. Let me suggest that we can cull from Barbeau's essay (at least) five reasons for why we might not only read the church fathers but read Wesley reading them. First is antiquarianism. It is good to study and preserve old things. Second is to reclaim a golden age from its corruption by those of us in the present who preserve that golden age. Third is to demonstrate the superiority of the present over the past, so the past will not be repeated. Fourth is to correct the present by a retrieval of the past. Finally, and perhaps most importantly, is because we share with the fathers a quest for truth as it comes to us through faith, hope, and charity. Let me quickly examine each of these in turn.

Antiquarian Interest

Perhaps this is the least important and explicit of all Barbeau's answers, but I would nonetheless not underestimate its significance. On the cusp of the modern era, where the "new and improved" became our fate rendering everything that came before putatively obsolete, Wesley sought to preserve the wisdom of the past. Unlike the church that he inaugurated, he did not go chasing after trends in a superficial attempt to be relevant and deem that "practical." Instead he sought to preserve ancient wisdom through accessible volumes called the *Christian Library*. Wesley prefaced each of his fifty volumes with these words: "Extracts from and Abridgements of the Choicest Pieces of Practical Divinity Which Have Been Published in the English Tongue."[1] Publishing and therefore preservation mattered. Texts needed to be preserved and this required a proper antiquarian interest. What other evangelical scholar undertook such an important task?

Mere antiquarian interest has some importance. Preserving old things during a time committed primarily to the present is a good in itself. But Wesley was not a "mere antiquarian." This would be an insufficient reason to study the fathers or any other era of the Christian tradition. Wesley preserved and studied their work because they provided both theoretical and practical wisdom for living the Christian life. Barbeau notes this in his second implication: "Wesley's appeal to Christian antiquity also reminds Christians that the riches of the early church include not only thoughtful reflection on God, but also faithful spiritual practices." The very structure of the *Christian Library* confirms this. By "practical divinity" Wesley meant nothing along the lines of the so-called "practical disciplines" dominating theological education today. He meant a profound historical and theological encounter with Christian truth, which could be understood by ordinary, everyday Christians. He explains his purpose in his introduction to the *Christian Library*: "I have endeavoured to extract such a collection of English Divinity as (I believe) is All True, All agreeable to the Oracles of God, as is all Practical unmixt with Controversy of any kind, and all intelligible to plain men: such as is not superficial, but going down to the depth and describing the height of Christianity."[2] Wesley begins the *Library* with the stories and theology of Ignatius, Polycarp, Macarius, and the sixteenth-century Lutheran John Arndt. He thought Arndt's "nervous account of True Christianity" was "worthy of the Earliest Ages." In other words, "antiquity" defines less a

---

1. Wesley, *Christian Library*, 1:i. See also Long, *Living the Discipline*, 25–27.
2. Wesley, *Christian Library*, 1:iv–v.

time than a theological sensibility. Arndt could be included alongside Ignatius.

After presenting their work, Wesley explains what this sensibility entails. He wrote:

> I believed nothing could be more acceptable to the serious reader than to see this Christianity reduced to Practice. I was therefore easily determined to subjoin to these, The Acts and Monuments of the Christian Martyrs. Here we see that pure and amiable Religion, evidently set forth before our Eyes; Assaulted indeed by all the powers of Earth and Hell, but more than Conquerors over all. May we all learn from these Worthies, To be not almost only, but altogether Christians! To reckon all Things but Dung and Dross for the Excellency of the Experimental Knowledge of Jesus Christ. And not to count our Lives dear unto our Selves, so we may finish our course with joy.[3]

Here is "antique" Christianity. It is an "experimental knowledge of Jesus." What Wesley means by "experience" is not some internal, existential intuition that then functions as one of the four authorities for Christianity, as it unfortunately became in the infamous Wesleyan Quadrilateral. "Experimental knowledge of Jesus Christ" comes by imitating the lives of the martyrs. This is an important answer to the question, why study Wesley studying the Fathers?

The "Golden Age"

We think something went wrong after a golden age, and we are recovering that golden age. As Barbeau notes, one reason Wesley turned to this antique sensibility was because he wanted to justify the Wesleyan movement.[4] For him, the Wesleyan movement was neither schismatic nor heretical; it was a retrieval.

This use of the fathers has a long history in Christian tradition in both Catholicism and Protestantism. For the latter the retrieval is usually Scripture. It is used against "tradition" in order to claim a purer and

---

3. Ibid., 2:216.

4. As Barbeau writes, "Still, above all, I have argued that Wesley's devotion to early Christian thought and practice derives from a longstanding interest in "primitive" Christianity as part of a larger, eclectic defense of the Methodist movement in England." Wesley "hoped to show that Methodism was theologically consistent with the witness of the earliest Christians."

more original Christianity against the corruption of Catholic tradition. One sees this both in certain forms of evangelical Protestantism and in liberal Protestantism with its incessant quests for the historical Jesus that are then used to critique traditional Christianity. But Wesleyan evangelicalism rejects this. It reads Scripture in the context of tradition, especially through the lives of holy witnesses primarily found in antiquity.

Wesley reiterated he was a "man of one book" even while he was a consummate reader of many. I think we should not dismiss this as mere pious rhetoric. He did not think we had to set Scripture over and against tradition as somehow two distinct sources. As the *Christian Library* notes, the Christian life is to be "performed." In that sense it is an experiential knowledge. One of the best performances was that of the early Christian tradition. It provides us an embodied historical presentation of Scripture and thus should be looked to in order to understand the Bible. Scripture and tradition are not two sources. They are one. We read the fathers because they show us Scripture.

This reading of Scripture and tradition, especially the patristic tradition, finds an analogy in the Catholic "ressourcement" of the twentieth century. Once again the fathers were read to help us read Scripture well. This bore great fruit as can be seen in the Vatican II document "Dei Verbum," written by Henri de Lubac, a key figure in the "ressourcement." "Dei Verbum" states:

> Hence there exists a close connection and communication between sacred tradition and Sacred Scripture. For both of them, flowing from the same divine wellspring, in a certain way merge into a unity and tend toward the same end. For Sacred Scripture is the word of God inasmuch as it is consigned to writing under the inspiration of the divine Spirit while sacred tradition takes the word of God entrusted by Christ the Lord and the Holy Spirit to the Apostles, and hands it on to their successors, in its full purity, so that led by the light of the Spirit of truth, they may in proclaiming it preserve this word of God faithfully. (1.9)

Wesley would agree that we find in "sacred tradition" and "Sacred Scripture" a single source. Given this I would concur with Barbeau's "first implication": "John Wesley's appeal to early Christianity informs an evangelical commitment to the authority of Scripture." Like "Dei Verbum," Wesley saw sacred tradition "informing" Sacred Scripture. It shaped it, showed us how to read it. He would certainly quibble that the single source constituted by Scripture and tradition is entrusted primarily to the Catholic magisterium. For him the source is found in its faithful embodiment, in the holiness of those who bore witness. Doctrine and ethics unite.

To Demonstrate the Superiority of the Present over the Past So It Will Not Be Repeated

Another reason we study the past, as the famous saying goes, is so that we will not repeat it. Wesley was no mere antiquarian; nor does he exude any romantic sentiment that the past was preferable to other ages of Christianity. As Barbeau notes, Richard Heitzenrater constantly reminds us of this. The attempt since Outler to read Wesley as somehow repristinating early Eastern Orthodoxy makes little sense. First, the church fathers should not be read through the eleventh-century schism; "East" and "West" did not have the oppositions some contemporary Wesleyan theologians read back into them. Second, Wesley was as comfortable extolling Christian tradition in the Reformation and the Middle Ages as in antiquity. He read and advocated the works of John Norris and Ralph Cudworth, as well as Aquinas, Scotus, Malebranche, and Clarke. In his "Address to the Clergy," Wesley questions the clergy's competence in metaphysics by asking:

> Do I understand metaphysics; if not the depths of the Schoolmen, the subtleties of Scotus or Aquinas, yet the first rudiments, the general principles of that useful science? Have I conquered so much of it as to clear my apprehension and range my ideas under proper heads; so much as enable me to read with ease and pleasure, as well as profit, Dr. Henry More's works, Malebranche's "Search after Truth," and Dr. Clarke's "Demonstration of the Being and Attributes of God?" Do I understand natural philosophy?[5]

5. Wesley, *Christian Library*, 10:492. For Wesley "natural philosophy" treats of two topics: God and creatures or invisible and visible beings. Natural philosophy originated with Aristotle and was preserved by "Arabian" philosophers. However, for Wesley, natural philosophy transgresses when it seeks knowledge of God and invisible being.

After discussing the usefulness of natural philosophy to explain visible, creaturely being, Wesley wrote in his essay "Of the Gradual Improvement of Natural Philosophy": "What remains of natural philosophy is, the doctrine concerning God and spirits. But in the tracing of this we can neither depend upon reason nor experiment. Whatsoever men know or can know concerning them, must be drawn from the oracles of God. Here, therefore, we are to look for no new improvements; but to stand in the good old paths; to content ourselves with what God has been pleased to reveal; with 'the faith once delivered to the saints'" (*Works* [1995] 13:447).

This would not be a position advocated by those contemporary Eastern theologians who find scholastic rationalism the source of Western failure. Someone who thought everything went wrong in the scholastic era (Luther would seem to join forces with such Eastern theologians here) or who failed to see the good in his own contemporaries would not have raised this question. Wesley did not deny true gains in knowledge. As Barbeau notes, he was willing to engage in the historiography of his age. I would affirm his third implication: "Wesley's practice of abridging and editing his sources serves as a cautionary reminder, too, that not all early Christian practices and teachings are equally useful." But nor did Wesley use the present against the past as though the latter was only something negative to be overcome—a "dark age" that had now been dispensed with because of our "Enlightenment." Despite what many contemporary Wesleyan interpreters suggest, he was not the first modern theologian, worried primarily with today and willing to jettison anything not relevant to modern shifts that replaced metaphysics with epistemology and method.[6]

Something Is Wrong with the Present that Could Be Corrected through a Retrieval of the Past

A fourth reason to turn to the fathers is the direct opposite of the reason just stated, but similar to the second. We look to them because they help us correct inherited errors infecting the present era. We have many variations on this theme.

There is the Anabaptist sentiment—one Wesley shared—that Constantine's conversion corrupted Christianity. Wesley wrote:

> Persecution never did, never could give any lasting wound to genuine Christianity. But the greatest it ever received, the grand blow which was struck at the very root of that humble gentle patient love, which is the fulfilling of the Christian law, the whole essence of true religion, was struck in the fourth century by Constantine the Great, when he called himself a Christian and poured in a flood of riches, honours and power upon the Christians, more especially upon the clergy.[7]

6. For a critique of the many works that espouse Wesley's importance as what it allows us to do "today," see chapter 1 of my *John Wesley's Moral Theology*.

7. "The Mystery of Iniquity," in *Works* (1984), 2:463.

Once Christianity is showered with "riches, honours and power," then true Christianity becomes more difficult to recognize.[8] The fathers who were not so infected help us see it.

For many in the Wesleyan tradition corruption lay in the Western tradition itself. Outler fostered this notion by claiming Wesley turned not only to the fathers but also to the East. Randy Maddox, one of the foremost Wesleyan experts, has developed this argument. He states that Wesley "not only became aware of many of these Greek authors through his study, he seems to have imbibed a marked preference for them over the Latin writers!" This prompts Barbeau to state, "Maddox firmly relocates Wesley's theology in the traditions of Eastern thought."

Only with fear and trepidation would I disagree with Maddox in interpreting Wesley. So I won't. It is not his interpretation of Wesley that I find troubling, but the differentiation between East and West. As many church historians and theologians have noted, this differentiation arose from the popularization of what has become known as "de Regnon's paradigm." It purportedly showed the distinct differences between the Western and Eastern theologians. Systematic theologians took up this paradigm and ran with it, finding the supposed Eastern "social" Trinitarianism preferable to the Western "psychological" one. Rahner, Moltmann, Zizioulas, Lossky, and others perpetuated this divide, a divide that has been significantly challenged by Michel Barnes, Sara Coakley, Lewis Ayres, David Hart, and others. Too often we read Wesley reading the fathers with something like de Regnon's paradigm in place. The result is, as Heitzenrater rightly reminds us, we fail to see how eclectic he is, and how willing to affirm Latin as well as Greek sources. Wesley did not canonize East versus West, antiquity versus scholasticism, Bible against tradition. No single golden age existed. The Spirit was always at work and we could discern its agency. Here I make common cause with Barbeau's fourth implication: "The writings of the early church encouraged Wesley to recover an awareness of the work of the Spirit of God long after the days of the Apostles."

Of course, another reason we Protestants turn to the fathers is because the Reformation has been in a crisis for quite some time now. *Sola scriptura* did not constitute an adequate church authority. It did not help

---

8. In that same sermon then, Wesley wrote that after the conversion of Constantine, "The few Christians that are upon the earth are only to be found where you never look for them." Ibid., 2:465.

us negotiate the divisions caused by the North American slavocracy, as Mark Noll has noted. It does not help us negotiate our conflicts over sexuality at present. Turning to the fathers will certainly not resolve these issues, but the need to have some accountability for our individualistic and therefore idiosyncratic reading of Scripture is necessary. Barbeau poses an important question: "Wesley's well-known appeal to Scripture still resonates with evangelicals today. But what about his devotion to the historical writings of the church?" Could that expansion of the "canon" create the needed unity of thought and practice God desires for his church?

Truth and Charity

Finally, and perhaps most importantly, we turn to the fathers because we share a common quest with them, a quest to live lives of truth and charity that bear witness to our faith and therefore offer hope. It is the content of what we find in reading their works that matters most; something which I have neglected in this essay up to this point, and something I fear that gets neglected too often when we answer the question, why read the fathers? We do not so much study the fathers to study them, but to study what they themselves studied. This means that we must not choose one of the five reasons I have too summarily outlined here. They all matter, but they must matter by first and foremost being attentive to the content of what the fathers wrote. And for that we must read them. We need a "Christian Library." Even more importantly, we need the reason for such an endeavor—"holy conferencing." Barbeau's fifth implication points the way forward for why we should read Wesley reading the fathers. It will help us see, as Wesley himself said, "Christianity is essentially a social religion" that requires a common quest for holiness.

3

The Use and Abuse of the Christian Past

Mercersburg, the Ancient Church, and American Evangelicalism

DARRYL G. HART

Johns Hopkins University

JOHN WILLIAMSON NEVIN AND Philip Schaff would apparently have much to teach contemporary evangelicals who look to the ancient church for Christian roots deeper and older than Billy Graham and Carl Henry. Nevin and Schaff briefly engaged in tag-team wrestling with the rest of American Protestantism from the provincial setting of Mercersburg, a small village in south central Pennsylvania, off the beaten paths of either the Philadelphia-Princeton-New York-Boston postal roads or the trails that would become a corridor between Philadelphia and Harrisburg. Perhaps even more indicative of Nevin and Schaff's isolation was their ecclesiastical identity as theologians and ministers in the German Reformed Church, a communion even less familiar to Anglo-American Protestants, whether Congregationalist, Presbyterian, Methodist, Episcopalian, or Baptist, than German Lutherans or Dutch Reformed. Even so, when Nevin and Schaff grew frustrated with the ecclesial and liturgical possibilities of American Protestantism during the two decades before the Civil War, they turned for help to parts of the ancient church.

The unusual mélange of German Reformed confusion, Nevin's interest in Hegelian philosophy, and Schaff's recent migration to the United States and interest in church history all combined in uneven amounts and at fitful intervals during the last phases of the Second Great Awakening to form what became known as the Mercersburg Theology. It ran strong from roughly 1842 to 1853 and then ran out of gas. Nevin himself experienced spiritual and psychological fatigue that almost left him in the Roman Catholic Church. Schaff eventually accepted an offer in 1870 to teach church history for New School Presbyterians, a group of conflicted Calvinists who were calibrated more to the engines of modernity than anchored to authority of antiquity. All along the Mercersburg Theology was the bull's-eye for opponents of liturgical Protestantism within the German Reformed Church from both the East in Philadelphia and the West in Ohio. Arguably the greatest legacy of Mercersburg within the German Reformed church was a new hymnal and liturgy that almost divided the communion in the decades after the Civil War. For the American church more generally, Schaff's historical scholarship resulted not only in an eight-volume history of the church that devoted several volumes to the early church but also the incomparable collections of the ante- and post-Nicene church fathers.

That brief overview of the buzz Nevin and Schaff created and the burn out that followed may function as a word of caution to contemporary evangelicals in search of a usable ancient past to correct born-again Protestant deficiencies. The Mercersburg men learned firsthand that appropriating the ancients for modern America created as many problems as it solved. Perhaps even more cautionary for contemporary evangelicals is the reason that motivated Schaff's, and especially Nevin's turn to early Christianity. The Mercersburg Theology stemmed from the conviction that the Protestantism emanating from the revivals of Charles Grandison Finney and the reforms of New England's Congregationalists and New School Presbyterians was an eviscerated form of Christianity that lacked significant continuity with the church, whether Protestant, Roman Catholic, or Orthodox, before the nineteenth century. In which case, Nevin and Schaff turned to antiquity not to bolster evangelicalism but to abandon it, almost entirely.

What follows is a relatively brief survey of the way that Nevin and Schaff, in the heyday of the Mercersburg Theology, appealed to the ancient church. As much as their turn to early Christianity shaped what critics and supporters associated with the Mercersburg Theology, it was a short-lived project that never fully developed. Nevin and Schaff would eventually leave the seminary that had initially sustained their endeavor, and the only vestige of their historically and ecumenically informed theology was their participation on a denominational committee to revise the church's liturgy. The controversy that erupted from this committee's work demonstrated the real difficulties of combining diverse streams and periods of Christian witness and ministry. Even so, the experience of Nevin and Schaff, while not necessarily encouraging for contemporary Protestants who want to appropriate the ancient church, is still illuminating and instructive.[1]

New Measures, Old Church

If location is everything in real estate, context rules in history and the specific context for Mercersburg's turn to the early church was the revivalism of Finney and the Second Great Awakening.[2] In 1843 and 1844, Nevin wrote *The Anxious Bench* and a revised edition with a fuller conclusion, a work that took issue with the methods, theology, and devotion of revival. Nevin himself had experienced the enthusiasms of the Second Great Awakening, first with a feeble personal conversion while an undergraduate at Union College in Schenectady, New York, and then as a seminary professor while leading worship at a local German Reformed congregation where a Presbyterian evangelist with the stamp of Finney on him tried to enlist Nevin for the altar call. The latter experience prompted Nevin to write a relatively lengthy critique not only of the Arminian theology of the nineteenth-century awakenings but also of its undergirding system. In particular, Nevin decided that revivalism possessed a seriously impoverished understanding of the nature of the Christian ministry. As such, Nevin contrasted the system of the bench with that of the catechism, with the bench standing for the individual's

1. For overviews of the Mercersburg Theology, see Nichols, *Romanticism in American Theology*; and Gunnemann, *Shaping of the United Church of Christ*. For orientation to the theological landscape of nineteenth-century American Protestantism, see Hatch, *Democratization of American Christianity*; Noll, *America's God*; Mullin, *Episcopal Vision/American Reality*; Kuklick, *Churchmen and Philosophers*; and Gerrish, *Tradition and the Modern World*.

2. Much of what follows in this paper is condensed from Hart, *John Williamson Nevin*.

lone decision to walk the aisle, and the catechism signifying a churchly form of devotion that stressed church membership and growing in faith through word and sacrament.

In the conclusion to *The Anxious Bench*, Nevin outlined the difference between the system of religion implied in the new measures and the rival system signified by the catechism. By the catechism he did not mean simply the method of instructing children in the faith by question and answers, such as the German Reformed Church's own Heidelberg Catechism. The catechism did, though, point to a system of religion by which its adherents grew up into or inherited the faith, not unlike that of passing on the faith through the memorization of received Christian wisdom. For Nevin the catechism symbolized the regular ministry of the church, "sermons full of unction and light," systematic instruction, an earnestness for holiness, pastoral visitation, catechesis, church discipline, and "patient perseverance in the details of ministerial work." These were the God-appointed means of growing the church and her members. And this was the system that was antithetical to the new measures. Nevin wrote:

> The spirit of the Anxious Bench is at war with the spirit of the Catechism. Where it comes decidedly to prevail, catechetical instruction, and the religious training of the young generally, are not likely to be maintained with much effect; and it will not be strange, if they should be openly slighted even, and thrust out of the way as an encumbrance to the Gospel, rather than a help.[3]

In contrast to the way that many evangelical Protestants who promoted Finney's revivals viewed such a churchly scheme—as human artifice as opposed to the immediate and dramatic work of the Spirit in conversion—Nevin reversed the terms of debate. In fact, his point, reinforced by the Mercersburg Theology, was that the ministry of the church was the divine work of salvation.

Of particular importance to Nevin even as early as 1844 was an organic conception of the church as the body of Christ. Instead of viewing sin as merely a function of bad habits that an individual could overcome with a momentary decision for Christ and dedication to live a holy life, Nevin believed, as a good Augustinian, that sin went deep. As such, to overcome the organic union between all people and Adam, the father

3. Nevin, *Anxious Bench*, 55–56.

of sin, persons needed to be united to Christ, become part of his body, the church, and draw upon his life-giving Spirit in order to persevere in the Christian faith. Salvation, according to the catechetical scheme, consisted of a new life emanating from this union with Christ who is "the organic root of the Church."[4] Nevin's ideas here certainly showed continuity with the federal theology he had learned at Princeton Seminary, but through reading in German sources thanks to his situation among the German Reformed, he was also adding pieces of philosophical idealism for reinforcement.

By conceiving of Christianity in organic or corporate, as opposed to individualistic, categories, Nevin was at this early stage, even before Schaff had migrated to America, specifying a significant feature of the Mercersburg Theology, what James Hastings Nichols called, "the first enunciation of what was to become the Mercersburg doctrine of the church."[5] In effect, the organic character of Christianity and the idea of union with Christ as articulated in *The Anxious Bench* would become the opening through which Nevin would explore the early church in search of support for his lonely position.

Swiss Reinforcements

With Schaff's 1844 arrival in Mercersburg, the notion of a unified theology connected to the German Reformed seminary made sense. It was no longer the idiosyncratic construction of an ethnically confused professor who had grown up Scotch-Irish and now labored in German fields of hops. A native of Switzerland, Schaff was clearly the junior professor to Nevin, born in 1819 some sixteen years after his American colleague.[6]

Despite his youth—Schaff was twenty-five upon his arrival in the United States—he came with a wealth of knowledge. He had studied first at Tübingen, the center of biblical criticism, for half his university education and studied with Isaac Dorner, who attempted to appropriate the theology of Schleiermacher and the philosophy of Hegel for pious ends. From there Schaff transferred to the pietist center of Halle and its university where Friedrich A. G. Tholuck made the greatest impression.

4. Nevin, *Anxious Bench*, 2nd ed. (1844), reprinted in Yrigoyen and Bricker, *Catholic and Reformed*, 105–7.

5. Nichols, *Romanticism in American Theology*, 59.

6. On Schaff, see Shriver, *Philip Schaff*; and Graham, *Cosmos in the Chaos*.

(Tholuck may have given Schaff a foretaste of American Protestantism since a number American theologians had traveled to Germany and taken courses with him, among them Charles Hodge from Princeton, Edward Robinson, Henry B. Smith, and George L. Prentiss from Union in New York, and Edwards A. Park from Andover.) The theological influences on Schaff were not confined to the universities where he matriculated, however. Informally, Schaff had read Johann A. Neander, whose ideas about organic development in church history were important for Schaff's own scholarship. These intellectual influences contributed to Schaff's high-church ecclesiology, a position that dovetailed with Nevin's emerging convictions. In his inaugural address at Mercersburg, delivered on October 25, 1844, entitled "The Principle of Protestantism," Schaff developed a notion of historical development that he would refine in his writing and editing on church history. The argument that the Protestant Reformation had evolved from Roman Catholicism generated much opposition within the German Reformed church against Mercersburg because of the implication that the kind of anti-Catholicism surfacing in the United States during the Nativist rising of the 1840s and 50s was an overreaction to the differences between Roman Catholics and Protestants. When Schaff claimed that "*The Reformation is the legitimate offspring, the greatest act of the Catholic Church*," he seemed to be denying an important category for low-church, revivalist-committed Protestants in America.[7]

Yet, by 1844 and the consolidation of the so-called Mercersburg position, Schaff and Nevin were not yet interested in the early church. Schaff was clear in affirming the material and formal principles of the Reformation in his 1844 inaugural. But he also took exception to Protestantism's chief defects of rationalism and sectarianism. His solution was for American Protestants especially to wean themselves from Anglo-American philosophy and discover the virtues of German idealism. Nevin, who wrote the introduction to the printed version of Schaff's lecture, sided with Schaff's point about historical continuity. For Nevin, the Reformation was not a repristination of second-century Christianity but grew organically out of the medieval Roman Catholic world. At the start of the Mercersburg Theology, then, the main point was to recover a high estimate of the church along the lines that Rome propounded, without either capitulating to Roman Catholic ecclesiology or descend-

7. Schaff, *Principle of Protestantism*, 49. Emphasis original.

ing into Protestant individualism. Both men believed that Puritanism was guilty of Protestantism's chief errors.

For the remainder of the decade in which Mercersburg would thrive as a distinct theological position, Nevin performed the bulk of heavy lifting from the early church. The reason for turning to early Christianity was to pursue the question of the church's status as a divine institution—in other words, to test the waters of high church Christianity. Was the idea of the church as a mediator of supernatural grace present in Christianity from the start? Or had Roman Catholicism foisted it on western Christianity, with the Protestant Reformation recovering the ancient church's purer teaching? This, by the way, was the position of Mercersburg's critics as early as Schaff's inaugural address, "The Principle of Protestantism." In the context of Nevin's mounting frustration a form of Protestantism in the United States overrun by revivalists and do-gooders, he explored the earliest forms of Christianity.

Nevin's quest for the historical church had begun as early as 1846 with his work on the Lord's Supper in *The Mystical Presence*. One section of that book prefigured his later studies by comparing Puritan understandings of Christ's presence in the Lord's Supper with those of specific church fathers. He followed with a series of articles in the *Mercersburg Review* on the Apostles' Creed. In a manner similar to his argument about the sacrament, Nevin explored the historical origins of the creed, the later attestation by Roman Catholics and Protestants alike to its authoritative standing and its meaning. The series also provided him with another opportunity to work out the organic nature of Christianity and the church, with Christ incarnate being the life-giving source of the church, and the creed functioning as the embodiment of that vitality. The Apostles' Creed, Nevin wrote, "represents not a system of thought, but a system of life. . . . It is the free spontaneous externalization of the christian [*sic*] consciousness, the substance of living christianity [*sic*] as a whole, in its primary form of faith." As such the early church was not the "artificer that hammered" the creed into shape, "part by part, and one article after another." Instead, the church was "the organ, through whose life as an actual fact it brought itself to pass."[8] One practical implication that Nevin drew from the significance of the creed was that it functioned as the lens through which the Bible needed to be understood—not the other way around. This was a way of contrasting the Bible-only wing

8. Nevin, "Apostles' Creed," 219.

of American Protestantism with historic Christianity. By favoring the hermeneutic of private judgment, born-again Protestants were cutting themselves off from the historic pattern of faith, which read the Bible from within the context of the church ands its creed.

Nevin concluded his first series on the early church with an essay, "Puritanism and the Creed," that put the others in perspective. His aim was to show that modern Protestantism was a novel, deformed variety of Christianity that had departed from the ways of historic Protestantism because it was dislocated from saints who had gone before. Nevin thus implied that the divide between modern and historic Christianity was greater than that between Protestants and Roman Catholics. He wrote:

> Here are two *minds*, two theological habits, the old catholic consciousness and the modern Puritan consciousness, "having no kindred spirit," each of which claims to be, not at once the Bible, (neither the Creed nor the New England Primer is *that*,) but still the only true and safe preparation for coming to the right sense of the Bible. . . . *I* build upon the Scriptures, it exclaims; the Creed is a human production, and teaches false doctrine; follow *me*. Truly, a very great and solemn demand! Let it be heard with all becoming seriousness and respect. Still, we tremble at the thought of such a deep rupture with the old Christian consciousness, and venture to ask: By what authority doest *thou* this thing, and who *gave* thee *such* authority?

Nevin did not want to be misunderstood. He conceded that Puritanism's Bible-only faith had many merits. But so did Roman Catholicism. And as of 1849 Nevin was prepared to believe that both the one extreme (the Bible plus private judgment) and the other (church and outward authority) could be harmonized. Still, the contemporary descendants of New England Puritanism had a duty to search for coherence. Without it the Puritan faith was "at war with reason and right."[9]

Two years later, when Nevin returned to the topic of early Christianity, he seemed to have abandoned hopes of harmonizing modern Protestantism and the early church. By 1851 the stakes had been raised from whether America's low-church Protestantism was out of step with the faith of Calvin and Ursinus to whether Protestantism in its essence possessed a suspicion of the church as a mediator of grace. A contributing factor was the wave of anti-Catholicism among American Protestants

9. Nevin, "Puritanism and the Creed," 601, 603.

that associated Rome with everything un-American—papal tyranny vs. individual freedom, religious superstition vs. enlightened inquiry, ecclesiastical hierarchy vs. popular sovereignty, the list of contrasts could go on. This anti-Catholic prejudice was in many respects one of the chief catalysts for Nevin's theological development. Initially, Nevin responded to Protestant inspired nativist anti-Catholicism by arguing that evangelicalism in the United States veered significantly from the Reformation. By the 1850s he took up the challenge of defending Rome itself. He did so by looking at the earliest Christian expressions. The point was to see whether the anti-Catholic prejudice of his Protestant peers was plausible. Was it truly the case that the faith of American Protestantism, which stressed the Bible only and the rights of private judgment was a repristination of the ancient church?

In a three-part series from 1851, Nevin weighed in against any number of recent expressions of Protestant anti-Catholicism. His chief point was to challenge precisely the "Puritan" theory of church history, a term with broad application not simply to New England Congregationalists but including also Baptists, Presbyterians, German Reformed, and low-church Episcopalians. The basic idea was that Christianity began unadulterated as a religion solely of the Bible and individual interpretation. Worship resembled that of New England or Scotland. No papacy, priesthood, liturgy, or superstitious ceremonies encumbered genuine Christianity. This pure form of the Christian religion lasted only until the third century when allegedly "the prelatical system with its whole sea of corruptions and abominations" began to prevail.[10] This system was supposedly responsible for turning the church into a synagogue of Satan, thus requiring the Reformation to set right the early church's pure and simple devotion.

In one of his most compelling critiques of this form of Protestant smugness, Nevin raised the question of whether the Puritan theory actually made any sense of the wonder of the incarnation, the earthly ministry of Christ, and the witness of his apostles. "The whole course" of the early church's history, he wrote, "seemed to show clearly, that the powers of a higher world were at work in the glorious movement, and that it embodied in itself the will and counsel of heaven itself for the full accomplishment of the end towards which it rested." In fact, many Christian apologists cited the success of the early church as "one of the

---

10. Nevin, "Modern Civilization," 208.

external proofs of its divine origin, a real supernatural seal of its truth."
But after such an amazing and divinely blessed beginning, the work of
Christ and the apostles virtually came to naught. "Hardly before the last
of the apostles had gone to heaven, before signs of apostasy began to
show themselves in the bosom of the infant church . . ." So far did the
church depart from the truth of the gospel in Puritan accounts that its
fall was not only partial and transient but universal "in its collective and
corporate character, with an apostasy that was to reach through twelve
hundred years." This mean that "Satan in the end fairly prevailed over
Christ."[11] The implausibility of this conclusion, Nevin believed, was
enough to show the error of the Puritan reading of church history.

Aside from the intellectual difficulties attending this interpretation
of the early church, Nevin argued explicitly that Puritanism differed
from the early church in six significant ways. The first concerned the
church, whether it was a human institution designed basically to teach or
whether it was a divine institution that actually mediated grace by virtue
of membership in it. The rest of the differences stemmed directly from
this: second, the ministry (pastors as "religious counselors and teachers"
vs. being part of a "divinely established hierarchy"); third, the sacraments
(gestures of the faithful vs. disclosures of divine grace); fourth, the rule
of faith (the Bible interpreted privately vs. Scripture interpreted corporately by the church); fifth, the order of doctrine (theological novelty vs.
the Apostles' Creed); and sixth, faith in miracles (supernaturalism vs.
rationalism).[12] This last point was the newest in Nevin's litany of charges
against Puritanism and by it he was referring to the early church's belief in signs and wonders that accompanied the spread of Christianity,
as opposed to charge of superstition that many American Protestants
hurled against Roman Catholics. These contrasts led inevitably to the
conclusion that "No scheme of Protestantism . . . can be vindicated, on
the ground of its being a repristination simply of what Christianity was
immediately after the age of the Apostles." Nevin added, "To take away
from the church its divine historical existence," to place a large set of
brackets around the period from the fifth to the sixteenth centuries, "is
to turn it into a wretched Gnostic abstraction. To conceive of it as the
mere foot-ball of Satan from the beginning, is to suppose that Christ was

11. Nevin, "Early Christianity," 211–12.

12. Ibid., 232–53.

either totally unmindful of his own word that the gates of hell should not prevail against it, or else unable to make good his word."[13]

In Nevin's second historical series on the ancient church, he looked specifically at the church father Cyprian, the third-century bishop of Carthage. This study turned into a four-part series that mainly added depth to the point already made, namely, that modern Protestantism was far removed from the earliest Christian forms of faith. In the first Nevin sketched Cyprian's life. In the second he looked at the persecution the church suffered and the controversies that ensued over how to address believers who had forsaken their faith in the face of such opposition. Nevin could not help observing that in the context of persecution membership in the church became an issue of life and death, and its ministry a source of hope for Christians under siege. "Cyprian lays so much stress on the solemnity of penance and absolution in the case of the lapsed, as the necessary condition of their being restored to her communion and peace," Nevin wrote, because of the bishop's understanding of the church as "the real organ and medium of salvation."[14] Still, the historical circumstances that prompted Cyprian to require penance from the lapsed and to make absolution a formal rite of public restitution was not Nevin's main point. Cyprian's larger significance was to represent a high view of the church pervading the entire span of the early church. In this regard, Cyprian's faith was a forerunner of Augustine. "No one had ever a deeper sense of [the church's] glorious significance," Nevin wrote. "It lay at the foundation of his spiritual life. It formed the very hinge of his conversion."[15]

Yet, even as Nevin wrote he also read in the religious press about ongoing attacks upon Roman Catholicism for holding a view of the church like that of the church fathers. He singled out an article in the *New York Observer* that opined that the "introduction of *a sacramental religion*" into Christianity was "a complete perversion of the gospel" because it removed the necessity of "an intelligent reception of the truth" and rested the "whole affair" in the hands of a priest. The writer for the *Observer* even ridiculed "some learned men in the Protestant churches [who] are seeking to exhume from the catacombs of a past age, and

13. Ibid., 309.
14. Nevin, "Cyprian (Second)," 382.
15. Nevin, "Cyprian (Third)," 443.

impose upon the wonder-loving credulity of the nineteenth century."[16]
Nevin appeared to take less offense from the *Observer* than interpreting
the editorial as a sign of his own vindication. Here was an understanding
of Protestantism "which boldly repudiates as an apostasy and mystery of
iniquity the whole sense of what Christianity was taken to be in the beginning, back at least to the very age next following that of the Apostles."
Nevin elaborated his gripe with American low-church Protestantism:

> For it is not with this or that questionable point only, that the
> issue of the N. Y. Observer is concerned. It goes at once to the
> very foundations of the ancient faith. The idea of a sacramental
> religion, we are told, overturns the Gospel. A ministry exercising
> in any true sense Divine powers, is taken to be such a concep-
> tion as opens the way at once for the full reign of the Antichrist.
> Why? Only of course because the *Church*, the proper home of
> such a ministry and sacraments of such supernatural force, is not
> believed to be the grand and awfully solemn mystery which it
> was held to be in the beginning. All comes to this at last.[17]

By the end of the series in the fall of 1852, Nevin was clearly growing weary of the tension between modern Protestantism and historic
Christianity, whereas in his previous historical inquiries he had held
out hope for finding a high view of the church in the Reformers. Such
a bracketing of American Protestantism and the Reformation allowed
Nevin wiggle room to remain a Protestant. But by the end of the series
on Cyprian his tone had changed markedly. He concluded that not even
sixteenth- and seventeenth-century Protestantism could measure up to
the ancient church. "Early Christianity," he concluded, "was in its con-
stitutional elements, not Protestantism, but Catholicism."[18] Nevin recognized that he was heading to a position where the only way to find the
sacramental and churchly conception of the church that he valued was
to join the Roman Catholic Church. Many of his colleagues and family
members believed Nevin was preparing to cross the Tiber.

Still, Nevin had significant reservations about Roman Catholicism.
If forced to choose between Puritanism and Rome, he could clearly
sound like a convert in the making. But during these same critical
years between 1849, when the *Mercersburg Review* started, and 1853,

16. Ibid., 447–48.

17. Ibid., 449.

18. Nevin, "Cyprian (Fourth)," 561.

when he retired from all things Mercersburg, Nevin published a steady stream of reflections on Roman Catholicism. These pieces revealed that his Protestant faith went even deeper than his anguish over the state of American Protestantism. By the end of these reflections, however, thanks to personal and professional exhaustion, Nevin resigned from his duties at Mercersburg. It would turn out to be simply a leave of absence. Nevin returned to teaching and administration at Franklin & Marshall College, Mercersburg Seminary's sister institution (and neighbor once the seminary relocated to Lancaster, Pennsylvania). But he never recovered his initial productivity when the Mercersburg Theology was a definable entity. He remained in the German Reformed Church and took some responsibility for revising the church's liturgy. Still, beyond work on the liturgy and some teaching and administration at Franklin & Marshall, Nevin's contribution to the Mercersburg Theology had basically dried up by 1853.

During this period of creativity and historical investigation by Nevin, Schaff was more or less a bystander. That may seem a harsh verdict. In fact, because Nevin and Schaff both taught at Mercersburg and their efforts to leaven an American ethnic church with yeast from contemporary expressions from Germany, historians have treated these colleagues as if their ideas were interchangeable. Although they both affirmed a high view of the church that made them seemingly friendly to Roman Catholicism, each man came to his views and executed them in different ways. The most obvious divergence was that each worked in different theological disciplines, Nevin in theology and Schaff in history, though this is hardly a firm distinction since the former's theology relied heavily on historical consciousness and the latter's historical awareness sprang from certain theological convictions. Even so, Schaff's major contribution to the Mercersburg Theology came upon his arrival in the United States with his inaugural lecture, "The Principle of Protestantism."

Beyond that book his published contributions were meager. What is more, Schaff's own interest in the ancient church and the source materials and narratives he produced came well after his time with Nevin at Mercersburg (and Lancaster later). Once Schaff left the German Reformed Church to affiliate with the Presbyterians at Union Seminary in New York City, he would emerge as one of the most productive historical theologians in the history of the United States, with authoritative series on the Nicene and post-Nicene fathers, chairing the committee responsible for the Revised Standard Version, and writing a seven-volume history of the Christian church. As James H. Nichols put it, "No other American theological scholar of the century rivaled this production."[19]

But as prolific as Schaff was after becoming a Presbyterian, Nevin bore the brunt of duties in constructing the Mercersburg Theology. Once Nevin left the seminary and limited his later career to Franklin and Marshall College, Schaff was no match to pick up the slack. It was Nevin who articulated the centrality of the incarnation in Mercersburg's thought. He was also responsible for a sacramental theology that had important repercussion for the nature of the Christian ministry. What is more, Nevin attempted to give coherence to these strands of theological development and defended them polemically, whereas Schaff was content to fill in here and there. Of most importance for this conference, it was Nevin who turned to the early church to carry on his battle with low-church Protestants in the United States and cultivate a churchly understanding of Protestantism. Had they not worked together at Mercersburg they would each have been examples of German idealism's influence on a few odd figures in nineteenth-century American Protestantism. Without a common employer, their writings would not have added up to a coherent or distinct school of American theology.

The one exception was the contribution that each man made to the German Reformed Church's revised liturgy of 1866. Despite reluctance by both Mercersburg professors to serve on the denominational committee, their work was the one monument to their decade of collaboration at the seminary. As it turned out, Schaff took the lead in producing the liturgy and steering it through the committee and Nevin provided the ammunition when the liturgy needed defense. Schaff was the chairman of the committee along with ten ministers and four elders. Nevin was one of the ministerial members despite his resignation from the seminary and ambivalence about Protestantism.

The Mercersburg orientation of the committee was clear from its statement of liturgical principles. The intention was to look not solely to the sixteenth century for guidance but also, and with greater rigor, to the early church. It read: "The liturgical worship of the Primitive Church, as far as it can be ascertained from the Holy Scriptures, the oldest ecclesiastical writings, and the liturgies of the Greek and Latin

19. Nichols, *Romanticism in American Theology*, 9.

Churches of the third and fourth centuries, ought to be made, as much as possible, the general *basis* for the proposed Liturgy."[20] This did not mean that the Reformation was necessarily defective, because, as the committee also explained, the "merit of the Reformation" was not to produce new liturgies but to hand down older ones translated into the vernacular, "purifying them from certain additions," "reducing them to greater simplicity," and "subordinating them to the preaching of the Gospel." The committee sought to provide the church with forms for all parts of congregational life, from the Sunday service, baptism, the Lord's Supper, and marriage, to family worship and a lectionary. This product would in effect be a prayer book—a historical novelty for a communion that had never had one.

The anomaly of the situation finally became apparent even to some of the members of the committee who had initially supported Nevin and Schaff. In particular, John H. A. Bomberger, pastor of a German Reformed congregation in Easton and a long-time sympathizer of Schaff and Nevin, wound up turning on Mercersburg. Although Bomberger would emerge in the history of the denomination as little more than a low-church pastor, the Easton minister was in fact one of Nevin's chief defenders. At roughly the same time that Berg left the German Reformed Church to minister among the Dutch Reformed, Bomberger wrote two articles defending Nevin's teaching on the Lord's Supper, the incarnation, and church history from those who accused him of harboring Roman Catholic sentiments. Bomberger had admitted that he was not in complete agreement with all of Nevin's views. But he also believed that Nevin's critics had not proven their case and that they carelessly threw around the charge of "papist."[21] Bomberger was also not an advocate of free worship. Since 1849 he had been working for the recovery of the Palatinate Liturgy because he believed the church's custom of worshiping without forms was creating liturgical chaos. These affinities between Bomberger and Nevin were largely responsible for the committee's harmonious labors from 1852 to 1858. After 1860 those affinities were hardly discernible and these two became the chief antagonists in the German Reformed Church's version of civil war. This worship war even produced a new college for the German Reformed Church. Because Franklin &

20. Quoted in Maxwell, "Liturgical Lessons of Mercersburg," 126.

21. J. H. A. Bomberger, "The Provisional Liturgy," *Weekly Messenger*, November 11, 1857, quoted in Maxwell, "Liturgical Lessons," 252.

Marshall was tainted by Nevin's theology, Bomberger founded Ursinus College in Collegeville, Pennsylvania, as a competitor. If the controversy can be simplified, it boiled down to whether the new book of worship would function as a prayer book with set liturgies and readings for all services—what Bomberger would have called "sacramental" worship— or whether it would be a resource with a variety of prayers and forms that each pastor and congregation could adapt for local purposes.

The German Reformed worship wars lasted longer than the United States' Civil War, but close to the end of the national conflict Nevin produced the most important work of his last part of his career, *Vindication of the Revised Liturgy* (1867), a shortish pamphlet designed specifically to answer Bomberger.[22] In the first section, devoted to the history of the committee's work and to the place of liturgy in the German Reformed Church, Nevin carried a full-scale assault on Bomberger in some of the most vituperative writing of his career. In the second half of the *Vindication* Nevin turned from personal polemics and church politics to the theology behind the revised liturgy. All of the major themes of his earlier writings were evident. Nevin outlined his defense around three themes: the christocentric character of the liturgy's (read: Mercersburg) theology, its dependence upon the Apostles' Creed, and its objective and historical nature. But these sections were secondary to the topics of Christ's mystical presence, the spirit of the anti-Christ, and the church as a medium of salvation, each of which followed from Nevin's conception of the incarnation. For instance, Nevin wrote that the gospel of the Apostles' Creed was entirely christological, that is, it "concentrates itself in Christ, throws itself, in full, upon the Incarnation, and sees in the objective movement of this Mystery of Godliness . . . the whole process of grace and salvation." In contrast, the gospel of Puritanism was subjective, "causing metaphysical abstractions to stand for the proper objects of faith . . ."[23] The opposition to the revised liturgy denied that the office of Christian ministry flowed from Christ's ascension, that ordination was an "investiture with a supernatural commission," and that sacraments were actually "seals of grace present."

Nevin also appealed to sixteenth-century views to justify his own churchly orientation. So when it came to objections that in the service

22. Nevin, *Vindication of the Revised Liturgy* (Philadelphia: Rodgers, 1867) reprinted in Yrigoyen and Bricker, *Catholic and Reformed*.

23. Nevin, "Theology of the New Liturgy," 49.

of ordination with the laying on of hands comes "the gift and grace of the Holy Ghost," Nevin countered that the reformers had insisted that ordination was the "sacramental seal of their heavenly commission," and a "symbolical assurance . . . that their consecration to the service of Christ is accepted, and that the Holy Ghost will most certainly be with them . . ."[24] To the objection that the declaration of pardon after corporate confession of sin was a form of sacerdotalism, Nevin replied that the forms clearly stated that the minister's authority to absolve sin came strictly from that delegated by Christ. And because of that delegated authority, the minister's official declaration had in its own sphere "a real force."[25] To the charge that the revised liturgy taught baptismal regeneration, Nevin responded that the forms did not state that baptism saved the unbaptized child but instead put him or her in the "way of salvation," thus making the sacrament a means that God designed to "carry with it the benefit it represents." Finally, to criticism that the liturgy implied transubstantiation in its forms for the Lord's Supper, Nevin contended that only a Puritan outlook could read it that way; in point of fact the old Calvinistic understanding of the Lord's Supper did actually conceive of the sacrament as a "medium of a real mystical communion with [Christ's] glorified life."[26]

After 1867 German Reformed worship debates went ahead with little input from Nevin. Bomberger responded to Nevin's *Vindication* with his own pamphlets and by 1869 the church had two different proposals for a new liturgy, one indebted to the Mercersburg Theology, the other in reaction against it. The church's General Synod wrestled with these two proposals throughout the 1870s and finally appointed a Peace Commission to overcome the antagonism that the liturgy wars had created. This committee would work for almost another decade before finally adopting a *Directory for Worship* in 1887 more in line with Bomberger's proposal than Nevin's. Although the final *Directory* did not fundamentally compromise Mercersburg's positions, it functioned more as a directory than a book of common prayer, thus giving congregations the freedom to choose the forms they would use, if any. In effect, the German Reformed Church may have been high church on paper but in practice the communion was divided between congregations more

24. Ibid., 52, 54.
25. Ibid., 57.
26. Ibid., 61, 63.

comfortable with the Mercersburg liturgy and those who preferred the low-church character that prevailed in the denomination before the advent of Nevin and Schaff. By then Schaff was leading ecumenical efforts among Presbyterians and Nevin was dead.

Organicism and the Novelty of Historicism

One of the effective points that Bomberger made against Nevin during the debates about worship was the novelty of the Mercersburg proposals. As creative, historically aware, and thoughtful as the Mercersburg Theology may have been, Schaff and especially Nevin were guilty of introducing forms and ideas that were foreign to German Reformed congregations. Indeed, the German Reformed Church, like colonial American Lutherans before the consolidating efforts of Henry Muhlenberg, was a quirky coalition of congregations united more by ethnicity and language than by a shared understanding of Reformed Protestantism. The creation in 1825 of a seminary at Mercersburg was one of the first attempts by the denomination to establish a measure of coherence among its pastors and congregations, many of which had been shaped by the low-church Protestant piety that prevailed within the American Protestant mainstream trickling down from the Puritans and expanding under the influence of revivalism. To try to give the German Reformed Church greater unity by turning to the ancient church, while laudable in theory, was clearly too much too soon. More importantly, it violated the very notion of organic historical development that Nevin and Schaff promoted. At one level, Nevin's liturgy was as novel as Finney's "new measures" because it veered so widely from the experience of German Reformed pastors and church members in the United States and even from sixteenth-century Heidelberg.

This may be the most valuable lesson for contemporary evangelicals who are prone to look upon proposals for an "ancient-future" faith as a welcome development. Aside from normative questions about the actual teachings and practices of the early church, or the prior question of establishing criteria by which to evaluate the oldest expressions of Christianity, the idea of taking an expression of the Christian religion forged in very different times and cultures from those prevailing now is fraught with inherent problems. Is it possible to take pieces of the early church and use them in a contemporary setting without appropriating the entire package of ancient Christianity? Obvious differences involve the nature of the church, the episcopate, church authority, and sacramental theology. Can low-church, highly decentralized congregations appropriate teachings and practices of the early church for individualistic Christians accustomed to subjective and emotional expressions of the faith? And what about the born-again experience that seems to trump all creedal, liturgical, and ecclesiastical norms? Any fair-minded account of the differences between the early and contemporary churches would put them at almost opposite ends of the ecclesial and liturgical spectrums. In fact, Nevin may have had an easier time than today's evangelicals because at least he worked within a denomination, in contrast to most of the contemporary evangelical world, which thrives in a setting of independent churches and parachurch organizations. If it was difficult for the German Reformed Church to embrace the Mercersburg proposals, how much more difficult will it be for those in the Southern Baptist Convention, the Assemblies of God, or the Orthodox Presbyterian Church? Perhaps the best way for evangelicals to return to the ancient church is to follow the example of Peter Gilchrest and other evangelicals and join one of the Eastern Orthodox communions. But that would seem to require abandoning the very characteristics and impulses that have constitute evangelicalism. Either way, the example of the Mercersburg Theology's attempt to recover the ancient church is clearly not a success story but a sober lesson about Christian differences.

Mercersburg Doctrine as a Double-Edged Sword

A Response to Darryl G. Hart

Douglas A. Sweeney

Trinity Evangelical Divinity School

As usual, Darryl Hart has written a paper that is meaty and provocative. An expert on the life and work of John Williamson Nevin, Hart surveys the ways in which Nevin and his colleague, Philip Schaff, appealed to early church fathers in their "tag-team wrestling [match] with the rest of American Protestantism," advancing a theology far more catholic than anything on offer in the evangelical mainstream. Through their writings on the nature of the church and church history, the Apostles' Creed, Cyprian, the church fathers generally, and liturgical concerns, they sought to show that Protestantism at its best was also catholic. It evolved organically from the teaching of Jesus and the apostles, the early church fathers, and medieval catholic soil—and failed to flourish when uprooted from the rest of the Christian church.

Hart tells the story of their efforts as a cautionary tale, aimed at those working today to find "a usable past for evangelical Protestants." He warns that Nevin and Schaff "knew first hand that appropriating the ancients for modern American Protestantism created more problems than it solved." Indeed, their own reforms failed, for modern American evangelicals had languished far too long in arid, rationalistic climes to be replanted overnight in the fertile ground of Christ. Hart suggests, furthermore, that the "reason" Schaff and Nevin turned to the fathers to begin with was to demonstrate this point, to account for their own struggle or, in Hart's words, "to show that the evangelicalism emanating from the revivals of [Charles Finney] and the reforms of New England's

Congregationalists was an eviscerated form of Christianity that lacked any significant continuity with the church." Nevin and Schaff, claims Hart, "turned to antiquity not to bolster evangelicalism but to abandon it, almost entirely."

This caution comports well with Hart's more famous efforts to deconstruct modern evangelicalism, replacing it with older forms of confessional Protestantism. He interprets Nevin and Schaff as noble forebears in this effort, people who recognized the dangers inherent in modern evangelicalism and wielded ancient tools to nip these problems in the bud and, failing that, to gain some distance from the movement. If you are like me, however, you turned to this chapter hoping to hear what Darryl thinks of the promise of appropriating ancient Christianity, not so much by Finneyites or *maverick* evangelicals—the foils of Nevin and Schaff—as by people who embrace Nevin's "system of the catechism"— *classical* evangelicals rooted in Augsburg, Heidelberg, and even Hart's Westminster—participants in ecumenical evangelical ministries who also do their best to hold fast to the confessions and traditions of their churches. So my comments on his paper are written mainly as an effort to draw more from Dr. Hart about the use of ancient sources by the people whom he takes to be the right kinds of Protestants.

I have a quibble and three questions that I hope will serve this purpose. First, the quibble: Nevin and Schaff (especially Nevin) criticized Charles Hodge and the Princeton theologians nearly as much as they censured anyone but the Finneyites. In *The Mystical Presence* (where this was implicit) and in numerous other publications penned from Mercersburg (where it became much more explicit), they claimed that modern Protestants, especially in America, and even at Princeton Seminary, had fallen away from the faith of the Reformation. They had modernized, rationalized, flattened out, and disenchanted classical Protestantism, leaving its catholic substance behind. Darryl's paper might suggest to uninitiated listeners that Nevin opposed only the kind of pietistic, revivalistic evangelicalism that Darryl himself deconstructs. Truth be told, however, Nevin also opposed his alma mater—nineteenth-century Princeton—and its modern Reformed version of confessionalism. He said that Old School Presbyterians should root themselves more deeply in the history of the church and the more catholic view of the church upheld in the early Reformation. It was not just, for Nevin, then, that the "system of the bench" was too sectarian, schismatic, rationalistic, and subjective (though he did believe these things). Even the "system of the catechism," as used by modern Protestants like Hodge and his compatriots, was largely disconnected from the ancient, incarnational view of the church and its union with Christ that had long made it a source of spiritual life and special grace.

This leads to my first question: Why did Nevin and Schaff have trouble retaining confessional Protestant views during the times when they explored the early history of the church? As Hart has noted, Nevin's itinerary led him near to Rome. Later in the century, after Schaff had gone to serve the liberal New School Presbyterians at Union Seminary, his work on the early church and ancient creeds of Christendom was accompanied by an actual move away from confessional Protestantism. By the time that he published his book on *Creed Revision in the Presbyterian Churches* (1890), he was convinced that Presbyterians should shuck their Calvinism. "Let us be honest," he said, "and confess that old Calvinism is fast dying out. It has done a great work, and has done it well, but cannot satisfy the demands of the present age. We live in the nineteenth, and not the seventeenth century. Every age must produce its own theology and has its own mission to fulfil. . . . We must look to the future, when God will raise another theological genius, like Augustin[e] or Calvin, who will substitute something better, broader, and deeper than the narrow and intolerant system which bears their honored names." Schaff's organic, evolutionary, catholic view of history—much like that of Nevin—would not sustain his earlier type of confessional Calvinism. Why was this the case? Did the Mercersburg men sense that mainstream American Calvinist thinking about the past—and continuity with the past—had grown parochial, predictable, self-serving? Did their ancient-future faith give them perspective on the present that embarrassed them about the net results of such thinking? Did their dalliance with Romanticism and modern German idealism make them too progressive in their understanding of history to commit themselves firmly to formulations from the past?

My second question pertains to whether Nevin and Schaff were right, or the degree to which they were right. Hart concludes that they should not have rushed their modern reformation, that their turn to the ancient church, "while laudable in theory, was clearly too much too soon." Their liturgical reforms were much too novel and abrupt. They were not grown organically from German Reformed soil. But were

Nevin and Schaff correct about the need for evangelicals to steep themselves in tradition and revise their view of the church, the incarnation, and the sacraments? Perhaps if they had succeeded in their efforts at reform fewer historically minded Christians would have left evangelicalism—and fewer would leave today. I wonder if Hart wishes they had succeeded.

Now to my third and final question: Were Nevin and Schaff too critical of modern Protestantism? Hart has written compellingly in defense of some of their foils, people like Princeton Presbyterians (and my own confessional Lutherans) who attempted to be catholic but not to be Roman Catholic, to retain the Protestant principle, the confessions of their churches, *and* a strong and deep connection to the universal church. Didn't Nevin and Schaff champion the need to maintain both the "Protestant principle" as well as "catholic substance"? Shouldn't they have noticed that, even during the heyday of the Second Great Awakening, there were other evangelicals trying to balance these things as well?

I think that Hart is right to suggest that our modern, free, selective, custom-built appropriation of the faith of ancient Christians is inimical to the actual teaching of many of them. It is sad that evangelicals often look to the tradition only because its smells and bells render our services more chic and intensify our spiritual subjectivism. Still, it seems to me that our pragmatism, independence, and long-standing tendency to reinvent religion for ourselves make it easier—not harder—to retrieve and reincorporate the ancient Christian faith—or at least the parts we like—into our Christian faith and practice. So it's crucial that we discern, in communion with the saints, whether the ancient church was right about the things that we retrieve. Evangelicals will continue to seek an ancient-future faith whether or not they get our help. I would like to suggest that we help them. And I wonder what we should learn from Nevin and Schaff as we do so. Were they onto something that might well instruct evangelicals and bolster evangelicalism? Or do they simply teach us that we have to make a choice between the latest forms of modern evangelical religion and the whole enchilada of traditional Catholicism (whether in Roman or Eastern flavors)? Can we have it both ways? Can we find a healthy balance of tradition, Protestant doctrine, and evangelical relevance? Can Nevin and Schaff help us to be "evangelical catholics"?

4

The Chicago Call and Responses

ELESHA COFFMAN

Waynesburg University

I FOUND THIS PAPER DIFFICULT to approach. You see, I never met Bob Webber. I was just a baby when he, Donald Bloesch, Thomas Howard, Peter Gillquist, and others organized a conference to call evangelicals to deeper engagement with historic Christianity. Many evangelical scholars have been studying, and living, that engagement longer than I've been alive. What could I possibly say that those eminent thinkers did not already know?

Lacking any other options, I thought I would try to use this "newcomer" status to my advantage. I decided to approach the subject of *The Chicago Call* as a historian, asking a historian's questions and drawing mainly from archival and print sources. My goal was to sketch the past thirty-odd years from a fresh angle. That sketch begins with a look at who joined *The Chicago Call* (as well as who didn't) and where their efforts originated. Next I'll attempt to situate the Call in historical context—a difficult task, given the multiple streams of American religion converging and diverging in the 1970s, as well as the cross currents embodied in the Call itself. In combination, this who, where, and when help explain why the Call has occasioned such diffuse and, to some, disappointing responses. It is possible to view this document as a call *without* response, or, as Michael Gallo once wrote in *Touchstone* magazine, "a small puff of smoke on the theological horizon," the suggestion of a fire beneath the surface of evangelicalism that never quite burst into flame.[1] I think, though, that *The Chicago Call* both recapitulated some of the inherent challenges in engaging church history and truly moved that engagement forward for evangelicals. As a young Christian historian, I have benefited from that effort, despite having been unaware of *The Chicago Call* before embarking on this research.

And now, a brief note to others who might share my former unawareness: Robert Webber, who died in 2007, was a theologian who sought to renew American evangelicalism, especially through serious attention to the early church and to Christian worship. In 1977, he spearheaded a gathering of more than forty people who produced "The Chicago Call: An Appeal to Evangelicals." The Call was printed in *Christianity Today* and then published, along with explanatory essays, as *The Orthodox Evangelicals* in 1978. The appeal included eight sections: a call to historic roots and continuity, a call to biblical fidelity, a call to creedal identity, a call to holistic salvation, a call to sacramental integrity, a call to spirituality, a call to church authority, and a call to church unity. In keeping with my approach as a historian, I'll especially focus on the first section, the call to historic roots.

Who

In contemporary historical studies, these three categories abide: race, class, and gender (and the greatest of these depends on your dissertation adviser). These have been key categories for historical investigation since about the 1960s. They moved to the fore as historians became more aware of oppressed and underrepresented minorities, the power dynamics encoded in social structures, and the importance of "social location" for scholars, the people they study, and the students they teach.[2]

When examining the signatories of *The Chicago Call*, there is not a lot to report on the diversity front. Those who gathered at Cenacle Retreat Center in Warrenville in 1977 were practically all white men, and while they might have varied somewhat in social class, their professions—the overwhelming majority worked in Christian higher education, publishing, or full-time ministry—were not the type likely to yield

1. Gallo, "*Chicago Call* Ten Years Later."
2. For a quick overview, see Alford, "Why Do Historians Write."

fabulous wealth. To be sure, the group was not without theological and denominational diversity. In his 1978 book *Common Roots*, Webber distinguished no fewer than fourteen evangelical subcultures, and, as members of any of those subcultures could surely tell you, the distinctions are not inconsequential. Nonetheless, if one imagines the original group intoning the Call's refrains, "We confess," "We deplore," "We affirm," the voices blend seamlessly.

I am by no means the first person to comment on this unanimity. A search for documents in the Billy Graham Center archives turned up a note from Sharon Gallagher, editor of the Christian World Liberation Front magazine *Right On* (later *Radix*), in response to Webber's press release about the upcoming Chicago Call conference. Gallagher had scrawled across the top of Webber's cover letter:

(1)   Do you have any understanding of Pete Gillquist's new theology?

(2)   <u>No</u> women on planning board or attending—<u>Gross</u>!

(3)   The format seems reactionary.

(4)   Do the Wheaton elite who mostly comprise the board really have anything to offer the entire American Church?

P.S. A friend suggests "The Wheaton Wheeze" as a working title.

The file included another note from Gallagher, which read, "Please excuse the P.S. on my note to you. It was really uncalled for. I am serious, though, about the questions raised."[3] In other words, she reconsidered the "Wheaton Wheeze," but she didn't take back her complaints about male dominance and elitism. (Four women did end up signing the document: Isabel Erickson of Tyndale House Publishers, Lois Ottaway of Wheaton College news service, and authors Kathryn Lindskoog and Luci Shaw. None of the women contributed an essay to *The Orthodox Evangelicals* or appeared in Michael Gallo's "*Chicago Call* Ten Years Later" follow-up.) Benedict Viviano, the only Roman Catholic participant at the conference, similarly characterized the Call as "an elite appeal to an elite."[4]

It is a serious question how far the initial impact of the Call can be widened beyond the forty-two signatories. Kenneth Woodward, reporting on the meeting in the May 23, 1977, issue of *Newsweek*, stated:

3. Chicago Call collection, BGC archives.

4. Gallo, "*Chicago Call* Ten Years Later."

The Chicago Call reflects a growing effort among educated Evangelicals to find deeper roots. Some feel cramped by Evangelicalism's low regard for reason and high tolerance of boisterous Biblicalism. Others want more disciplined forms of worship than the long sermons and emotional hymns typical of many Evangelical services.[5]

While limiting his comments to *educated* evangelicals, a label that certainly fit the group that issued the Call, Woodward suggested that evangelical discontent was growing and already broad enough to encompass multiple strains. As evidence, he cited reports of a spate of conversions to Anglo-Catholicism and the Episcopal Church at evangelical schools like Gordon and Wheaton. That evidence was equivocal, though: conversions did signal some kind of trend, but in sufficient numbers, the conversions would eventually *decrease* evangelical restlessness, as a result of the restless ones leaving the fold.

Christianity Today's coverage of the Call suggested an even more ambivalent initial reception. In a news item, Donald Tinder called the conference "an ad hoc group of 46 comparatively unknown Christians . . . more or less identified with evangelical institutions or views," who were concerned with "areas of alleged reductionism." In an editorial in the next issue, editor Harold Lindsell more warmly suggested, "One does not have to agree with each of [the Call's] confessions and affirmations (or with whatever one cares to read between the lines) in order to endorse heartily, as we do, the giving of 'careful theological consideration' to these matters." Of course, the editorial also stated that the Call "will not cause much to happen that would not have happened anyway." Regarding the dismissiveness of Tinder (who nonetheless signed the Call) and the tepid praise of Lindsell, my respondent, David Neff, stated in his introduction to the 2009 reissue of *Common Roots*, "Arguably most evangelicals in 1977 would have seen things more as [Tinder] did than as Webber and Lindsell did." I'm not even sure I'd put Webber and Lindsell on the same side of that binary, for reasons I'll get to in a bit.

Where

Gallagher's "Wheaton Wheeze" gibe raised the subject of geography. *The Chicago Call* was, in actuality, a heavily suburban effort. Not everyone

5. Woodward and Maier, "Roots for Evangelicals," 76.

involved was a Wheatie. Signatories also represented Bethel, up in St. Paul, Minnesota; Fuller, out in California; Gordon-Conwell, in Boston; and Dubuque Seminary, in Iowa; along with a few other places. Mostly, though, their institutions were all places even a Wheaton College student without a car could easily access: the college itself, Tyndale House, Good News Publishers, College Church. With a little help from public transit, I could get to Elmhurst, North Park Seminary, and Trinity International University, too.

I don't want to press this point too hard, and I don't want to be reductionistic, but viewing this geography as a historian and, even more so, from my other academic discipline—religious studies—I have to say that Wheaton is exactly the place you'd expect to find a youthful religious rebellion turning toward history and the high church. Religious historian Daniel Sack has painted a memorable portrait of "whitebread Protestants" who, becoming satiated with casseroles and Jell-O salad, might well go seeking more interesting, authentic fare. They're not likely to seek it just anywhere, though. Sociologists of religion have repeatedly demonstrated that higher education tends to propel people toward "higher" churches, as, for example, in the 1958 formulation of E. Digby Baltzell:

> The average American is born the son of a Baptist or Methodist farmer, after obtaining an education he becomes a businessman in a large city where he joins a suburban, Presbyterian church; finally, upon achieving the acme of economic success, he joins a fashionable Episcopal church in order to satisfy his wife's social ambitions.[6]

One need not cast the members of *The Chicago Call* group as crass social climbers in order to observe that, while their statement was in many ways countercultural, they did not entirely swim against the sociological tide. Many of them were already well-educated, suburban Presbyterians (and members of other churches in the Reformed wing of evangelicalism) in 1977. Ecclesially speaking, they had nowhere to go but up.[7]

6. Baltzell, *Philadelphia Gentlemen*, 225.
7. Sack, *Whitebread Protestants*; Baltzell, *Philadelphia Gentlemen*.

When

The timing of *The Chicago Call*, however, complicated the narrative considerably. I can place the Call on multiple timelines, each suggesting different conversation partners, impulses, audiences, and outcomes. Back when I was editor of *Christian History* magazine, we printed a timeline in every issue, and we always tried to place the issue's subject in multiple, layered contexts in hopes of highlighting parallels and resonances that might not otherwise be evident. I'll try to do that now, labeling the three bands of my timeline Cultural, Ecumenical, and Evangelical.

The 1970s—it was the best of times, it was the worst of times, it was definitely the disco- and polyester-est of times. The 70s were a transitional decade between the idealism and upheaval of the 1960s and the resurgent conservatism of the 1980s, a span often described as suffering from "malaise." The disheartening endgame of Vietnam and the betrayal of Watergate had undermined confidence in institutional authorities. There were nuclear fears, an oil crisis, rampant inflation, and the Cold War, and all President Carter could suggest to the American people was to put on a sweater? (I'm glad I was too young to remember all of this.)

Not much in *The Chicago Call* seemed to refer to this cultural context. The document began, "In every age the Holy Spirit calls the church to examine its faithfulness to God's revelation in Scripture." But, given the other historical referents in the document, that "age" could really be any time after the nineteenth century. Two passages in the section "A Call to Holistic Salvation" more specifically highlighted post-World War II concerns:

> Wherever the church has been faithful to its calling, it has proclaimed personal salvation; it has been a channel of God's healing to those in physical and emotional need; it has sought justice for the oppressed and disinherited; and it has been a good steward of the natural world.
> As evangelicals we acknowledge our frequent failure to reflect this holistic view of salvation. We therefore call the church to participate fully in God's saving activity through work and prayer, and to strive for justice and liberation for the oppressed, looking forward to the culmination of salvation in the new heaven and new earth to come.

If I were teaching this as a primary source document in my American religious history class, I would call students' attention to the phrases "oppressed and disinherited" and "justice and liberation," as well as the mention of stewardship of the natural world. Those concerns weren't new in 1977, or even in the 1960s, but the document used language of a particular era. The writers were clearly aware of civil rights, postcolonialism, liberation theology, and *Silent Spring*.

A historian could also spot indications of cultural context in the document's "Call to Church Authority." Granted, that section was explicitly ecclesial, not political, but its laments about "legalistic, domineering leaders on the one hand and indifference to church discipline on the other," and its exhortation to "all Christian organizations to conduct their activities with genuine accountability to the whole church" bespoke a search for confidence amid a widespread crisis of authority. Among other things, *The Chicago Call* was an epistemological cry: How do we know what's true? Who and what can we trust? Earlier in his career, Webber had examined these questions through the lens of existentialism. By 1977, he had turned to the early church instead.

I'm calling the second band of my timeline Ecumenical both because it encompasses events from a variety of Christian traditions and because it involves self-consciously ecumenical movements of the twentieth century.

In the latter category, the two standouts would have to be the World Council of Churches and the Second Vatican Council not that participants in the Chicago Call conference were great fans of either. Evangelicals never cottoned to the World Council, formed in 1948 in alliance with the Federal Council of Churches in America, an organization solidly on the modernist side of the fundamentalist-modernist divide. Nonetheless, the World Council raised the visibility of Eastern Orthodoxy in the West and offered one example of a bridge between Orthodoxy and Protestantism. Also, against its founders' ecumenical ideals, the Federal (now National) and World councils exposed and deepened the clefts between conservative and liberal Christians across confessions. By calling their book on The Chicago Call *The Orthodox Evangelicals*, I don't think Webber, Bloesch, and the other essayists were explicitly making common cause with conservatives in the East, but I don't think that interpretation runs counter to their intentions. Such an outreach wouldn't have been unique in the history of Protestantism, either. Martin Luther tried rhetorically to enlist the "Greek Church" on his side of theological wrangling, and Philipp Melanchthon worked personally with a deacon sent by the Patriarch of Constantinople. (The sixteenth-century exchange determined that Lutherans actually had more in common with Rome than with Constantinople, but not nearly enough simply to patch things up.)

Vatican II definitely constituted a more immediate backdrop for *The Chicago Call*. Meeting in four sessions, under two popes, between 1962 and 1965, Vatican II marked a collapse of barriers between Roman Catholicism and other branches of Christianity as dramatic in its way as the fall of the Berlin Wall in 1989. As documented by Robert Wuthnow and other sociologists of religion, it too made possible collaboration among like-minded Christians across branches of the church.

The word "catholic," capitalized and lower-case, appeared in several places in *The Orthodox Evangelicals*. In his chapter giving a behind-the-scenes look at the planning of the conference, Webber reprinted large sections of a letter from Jim Hedstrom that, in Webber's retelling, "advocate[d] caution against mere external changes that would adopt the trappings of catholicity" and instead "set us on a course that determined to bring together the Catholic, reformed, and evangelical perspectives."[8] Historian Richard Lovelace, in his chapter on the "Call to Historic Roots and Continuity" section, mustered one cheer for Vatican II, prior to which, he wrote, "Catholic observers regarded their Protestant brethren somewhat in the way ocean-dwelling fish might look at their tiny cousins condemned to live in fishbowls." Continuing the metaphor, he mused:

> Evangelicals worry that Catholic ecumenism is the threat of an ocean to swallow a pond, and they do not even feel easy about digging trenches between themselves and other ponds. Denominationally, however, there are no oceans, only lakes, and the life in these is joined in an ecosystem that cannot flourish while they are separate.

To facilitate this hydro engineering, Lovelace appealed to a timeless principle of small-c "catholicity" rather than to any particulars of the preceding decade.[9]

In the first of two responses to the Call printed at the back of *The Orthodox Evangelicals*, critic David F. Wells of Trinity Evangelical Divinity School skipped over Vatican II and instead reminded readers of the Fourth Lateran Council, held in 1215, and its declaration that

8. Webber, *Orthodox Evangelicals*, 26–27.

9. Ibid., 49, 62.

there is no salvation outside the Roman Church. Wells decried "the grey and shadowy presence of a Catholic outlook" pervading The Chicago Call, and he didn't like the "drift toward the Eastern churches," either.[10] The final word in the book, though, tellingly belonged to Benedict T. Viviano, a Dominican professor of New Testament who consulted on and signed the Call. Viviano saw important points of agreement between the Call and Vatican II on subjects including the authority of Scripture and the importance of biblical preaching. He feared a very different grey and shadowy menace—the "culture-endorsing humanism" of Bultmann, Tillich, "and worse" that he perceived as a threat to the renewal begun by "the Council, . . . nothing less and nothing other than a return to the gospel." In a vibrant example of Wuthnow's postdenominational restructuring of religion, Viviano signed The Chicago Call to express his "solidarity" with Christians whose antipathy toward Hans Küng ran as deep as his own.[11]

Viviano mentioned one other item that belongs on the Ecumenical timeline: the Hartford Appeal of 1975. Viviano saw in that declaration, as in The Chicago Call and in Vatican II, a reassertion of christological faith against the culture-embracing tide. The Hartford Appeal boasted a small, but high-profile roster of signatories, representing institutions like Yale, the University of Chicago, Notre Dame, and Union Theological Seminary. Actually, I find the breadth of the group remarkable: William Sloane Coffin Jr., Avery Dulles, George Lindbeck, Ralph McInerny, Richard Mouw, Alexander Schmemann, Lewis Smedes, Robert Wilken, Stanley Hauerwas; Lutheran, Methodist, Episcopal, Reformed, Roman Catholic, Orthodox. Despite this variety, Baptist minister Robert G. Middleton, writing in The Christian Century, dismissed both the Hartford Appeal and the similarly timed, but very differently aimed, Boston Affirmations as "coterie theology . . . based on the assumption that the viewpoints and practices of the groups drafting the statements are characteristic of the churches in general." (I laughed out loud when I read that—in The Christian Century, a magazine founded on that very assumption. But that's a line of argument for another day.) I couldn't find any overlap between the Hartford Appeal and Chicago Call groups, or any textual evidence that the Chicago Call conference actively referred to Hartford, but the finding aid for the Chicago Call collection here in

10. Ibid., 217, 215, 219.

11. Ibid., 231–33. Robert Wuthnow, Restructuring of American Religion.

the BGC archives did state that the Call "was to be loosely modeled after 'The Chicago Declaration,' 'The Hartford Appeal,' and 'The Boston Affirmation.'"[12]

Reference to "The Chicago Declaration" segues to the third layer of my timeline, the context in which Webber and his cohort operated most directly and self-consciously: Evangelicalism. From the veritable flurry of Christian declarations in the 1970s, *Christianity Today* placed the Chicago Call alongside the 1973 Chicago Declaration, the statement on evangelical social concern that launched Evangelicals for Social Action and the "Evangelical left" more generally, and the 1974 Lausanne Covenant, a confession of faith and call to action formulated at Billy Graham's International Congress on World Evangelization.[13] Webber apparently concurred with this contextualization.[14] And, of course, the Call was subtitled "An Appeal to Evangelicals," the broader "Appeal to Christians" having been rejected after hours of debate in committee.[15] In reporter-speak, the cultural and ecumenical timelines provided "deep background," while second-generation American evangelicalism was the story.

Attempting to recount a recent history of American evangelicalism in this room seems positively silly, as most of you have lived it and many of you have built fine careers writing about it. Instead, I'll use the words of Richard Lovelace, who contributed the essay on the "Call to Historic Roots and Continuity" to *The Orthodox Evangelicals*. This will indicate where drafters of the Call thought they stood in history, and then I'll embellish with the benefit of hindsight. Lovelace wrote:

> The resurgence of the evangelical movement in American Christianity, widely noted by the press during the presidential campaign in the bicentennial year [1976, *Time* magazine's "Year of the Evangelical," the year mainstream journalists scrambled to figure out what Jimmy Carter meant by "born again"], appears to be a reality and not simply a media event. Certainly the last decade has involved a fairly large numerical multiplication of evangelical Christians in this country.
>
> But there is still a question in the minds of many observers about how much more is involved beyond mere growth in num-

12. Middleton, "Bosford Declaration"; "Chicago Call Collection."

13. See *Christianity Today*, June 17, 1977, 27.

14. Webber, *Orthodox Evangelicals*, 32.

15. Ibid., 31.

bers. . . . New converts and newly awakened parishioners are enthusiastic and effusive, but not many show the effects of the deep
conviction of sin and awareness of the glory of God characteristic
of past "great awakenings." . . .

All of this can be readily explained as the result of immaturity
in the awakening movement. Evangelicalism has been growing
rapidly since it began to reform its tradition in the 1940s, and
it has reached an adolescent stage in which some of its latent
powers are still undeveloped. The shaping and transformation of
thought, society, and culture may still lie in the future.[16]

Lovelace's description calls to my mind the image of a puppy that hasn't
grown into its feet yet. Lots of energy, lots of muscle, but no self-awareness, and certainly nothing you'd call polish or class. A serious tendency
to blunder into things, despite innocent intentions. And so, while the
Chicago Call was an answer to the epistemological question, "How do
I know what's true?" it was even more emphatically an exhortation to
evangelicals to grow up, get serious, train your (ecclesial) body, and get
a handle on where you stand in time and space. Figure out who you are
and what you've been put on this planet to do.

Unfortunately, from my perspective at least, American evangelicalism as a whole sort of skipped that maturity bit and moved
straight into transforming thought, society, and culture—and not in
particularly nuanced ways. The 1970s would not be known for deep
evangelical reflection, but for Harold Lindsell's divisive *Battle for the
Bible*, Jerry Falwell's even more divisive Moral Majority, the rise of
televangelism, and the eschatological thriller *The Late, Great Planet
Earth*, published in 1970 and made into a movie in 1979. (I don't think
I've ever seen that movie, but I too vividly remember the 1972 classic
A Thief in the Night from high school youth group.) Like unruly adolescents, evangelicals earned a reputation for bullying, shocking, and
scaring the bejabbers out of people.

Responses

I know I'm caricaturing the 1970s here. I know there was a lot more going on in evangelicalism then, some of it very mature and godly and important. Where I'm heading with this is a hypothesis on *why* the Chicago
Call didn't elicit a more robust response from its intended audience. Put

16. Ibid., 44–45.

briefly, I see the Call pointing one way—toward the past, toward tradition, toward contemplation—at a moment when the strongest currents in evangelicalism were flowing the other way—toward an apocalyptic future; toward change in the presentation, though not the content, of the gospel; toward action, action, and more action. You just can't stop adolescents in their tracks by unpacking for them the riches of history. I teach intro history surveys to college freshmen. I know of what I speak.

The authors had even more strikes against them than the seriousness and countercultural aspect of their chosen task. First, as I said before, the authors of the Call were elites—white, male, educated elites—and if I've learned anything from my research into the early twentieth century Protestant mainline, it's that elites don't have nearly the influence in American Protestantism that they and everyone else assume they do. This is populist country, for good and ill. "Coterie theology" *can* make a difference, but primarily for an inner circle. The Chicago Call changed some people's church affiliations—their entire lives. Most people never heard it.

Second, the authors of the Call operated from a base that was essentially suburban and parachurch (publishing houses, non-denominational schools, and denominational schools connected to the least hierarchical branches of their churches), meaning their impulses would not find ready institutional homes. In fact, Webber and company weren't seeking to institutionalize the Call, at least not at first. "Apparently," Michael Gallo reported in *Touchstone*, "the initiators of the Chicago Call conference had no intention of forming any sort of follow-up organization or networking to reach the rank and file of Evangelicalism."[17] Their goal, like that of all restorationist movements, was to burrow beneath the tangle of ecclesial branches and tap into "common roots," unifying Christians rather than staking a new plant to compete for the sun. (The archetypal restorationists were the nineteenth-century Christians, or Disciples of Christ, who declared "No creed but the Bible" and adamantly resisted being labeled a new denomination.) A few fledgling institutions did peek up in this milieu, like Peter Gillquist's New Covenant Apostolic Order, Ray Nethery's Grace Haven in Ohio, and Beth B'rith Christian Mission in Chicago. Most remained obscure. Gillquist's group, the one with the most momentum, became the Evangelical Orthodox Church on its way to absorption within Antiochian Orthodoxy. Webber's passion for wor-

17. Gallo, "*Chicago Call* Ten Years Later."

ship found brick-and-mortar embodiment at the Calvin Institute for Christian Worship and, in the 1990s, at the Robert E. Webber Institute for Worship Studies in Florida, but you could argue that the institute we're inaugurating here is the first institutional response to The Chicago Call's overall agenda.

The lack of a clear, institutional lineage frustrates the historian, because it means she doesn't know which names to Google and which archivists to badger, but it doesn't mean that The Chicago Call had no legacy. In *The Orthodox Evangelicals*, Webber listed three results he hoped to see:

> First, I hope the Call will help to restore a sense of historical awareness among evangelical Christians. . . .
>
> Secondly, I hope the Call will help restore the content of Christianity to evangelicals. . . .
>
> Thirdly, I hope the Call will eventuate in a sense of community among evangelicals.

Webber also listed three spheres in which progress toward these goals would need to occur: "the schools—particularly our seminaries, Christian liberal arts colleges, and Bible colleges," "evangelical publishing houses," and local churches.[18]

I don't feel like I really have the tools to assess how far evangelicals have come in building a sense of community, or to comment on developments at the local-church level. The Religious Right engendered a sense of *solidarity* within its ranks, but I don't know if I'd exactly call that community. A newer movement in evangelical churches trades a focus on the evangelical *bloc* for attention to neighborhood *blocks*, creating geographic communities that don't necessarily contribute to the wider kind of community I think Webber was talking about. I'll leave this subject for other scholars.

There has definitely been progress in the publishing arena toward helping evangelicals connect with the content of their faith. I can cite Thomas Oden's Ancient Christian Commentary on Scripture series, published by InterVarsity, Evangelical Ressourcement and Webber's Ancient-Future series at Baker, plus lots of scattered titles. In the realm of periodicals, the Chicago-area evangelicals who moved through

18. Webber, *Orthodox Evangelicals*, 35–38.

Beth B'rith Christian Mission to Christ Covenant Church to All Saints Orthodox Church launched *Touchstone: A Journal of Mere Christianity* to proclaim the "Great Tradition" among like-minded Protestants, Catholics, and Orthodox. I don't know if *Christian History* magazine and its original parent, the Christian History Institute, founded in 1982, responded to The Chicago Call in any conscious way, but they also aimed to bring church history to evangelicals through film, church bulletin inserts, a print quarterly, and later a website. Evangelical publishers never stopped producing the superficial "pop-evangelicalism" that irked Webber, but they took up the challenge to provide heartier material as well.[19]

In the third sphere in which The Chicago Call aimed to stimulate action, evangelical colleges and seminaries, I really don't see a lot of movement toward serious and sustained engagement with church history. This institute would, of course, be an exception (though it took thirty years), and I think evangelical schools have made efforts to build their faculties, curricula, and resources in both theology and worship studies, two other key emphases of the Call. Church history, though, not so much.

Evangelicals are not alone in this struggle. In his revealing 2003 presidential address to the American Society of Church History, Brooks Holifield recounted the arduous process by which church history gained acceptance in higher education:

> [I]t took a long time for the history of Christianity to secure a place in American classrooms. For that matter, it took a long time for any history to secure a place in American classrooms. As late as 1884 (a time distant from us by only four generations of scholars), when more than four hundred institutions offered higher learning in the United States, no more than fifteen professors and five assistant professors exclusively taught history in the colleges and universities.[20]

In the early 1800s, schools like Princeton Seminary and Harvard Divinity School allowed professors with expertise in other areas (systematic theology, ethics, rhetoric) to offer lectures in church history as time permitted. Andover had an endowed chair in history, but when its occupant, James Murdock, attempted to teach history there, other

19. Ibid., 36.

20. Holifield, "On Teaching the History of Christianity."

faculty members complained, the board tried to force him out, Murdock threatened to appeal to the Supreme Judicial Court of Massachusetts, the students petitioned on his behalf, and Murdock ultimately lost his job. Nor was this only a Protestant problem. When the Catholic University of America was founded in 1887, the school wanted to offer a course on the early church, but the only person who could teach it was still in Berlin studying the subject.

Why all the pushback? Some Christian educators considered history irrelevant, or at least far, far less important than biblical studies and practical divinity. Others, though, judged history to be downright dangerous. Quoting Holifield again, on the Andover brouhaha:

> [T]he next faculty meeting fell into chaos, with otherwise staid faculty members shouting at each other and storming out of the room. The theologian Leonard Woods told the trustees that the study of history should be "altogether subordinate," and Ebenezer Porter worried openly about its effect on doctrinal solidity. If students had an early exposure to the "multifarious forms of religious beliefs in past ages," they would either waver in their creed or blindly submit to human authority. Leonard Woods agreed: too much history would draw them aside from a biblical standard of truth.[21]

I hear echoes of the same concerns in *The Orthodox Evangelicals* and in responses to The Chicago Call, both tacit and explicit. Essayists in *The Orthodox Evangelicals* bent over backwards to assure their readers (all 5,500 of them, the book's print run) that they were not straying from Protestantism's *sola scriptura* commitments. Nonetheless, one participant at the Chicago Call conference opted not to sign the final statement, wary that the Call leaned too far toward Roman Catholicism and Eastern Orthodoxy (both churches characterized by, among other things, high regard for human authority) and that the Call was "soft on Scripture." Similarly, in a letter to *Christianity Today*, one reader reacted against the Call's assertion that Scripture must be interpreted "with respect for the historic understanding of the church." The letter-writer warned, "Such folly will only serve the cause of scriptural disobedience . . . and will sow the seeds of a new battle for the Bible some decades

---

21. Ibid., 239, citing Thompson, "Church History Comes to Andover," 214.

hence."[22] In a grudge match between the timeless verities of the Bible and the contingencies of history, the Bible had to win.

In the spirit of this longstanding rivalry, perhaps it is only to be expected that The Chicago Call would stop short of a total embrace of church history, and that the response to the Call within the evangelical world would be even more restrained. (Randy Sly, writing for Catholic Online in 2008, called the evangelical reception of The Chicago Call "less than half-hearted.")[23] Regarding the reticence toward history in the Call itself, I'm mainly thinking of Webber. Richard Lovelace's essay on the "Call to Historic Roots" surveyed the whole of church history, but Webber was primarily interested in just the first five centuries of the common era, and most especially just the first two. As he wrote in the preface to *Common Roots*,

> My argument is that the era of the Early Church (AD 100–500), and particularly the second century, contains insights that evangelicals need to recover. Obviously the early church is not perfect. Like other periods of history, the early church needs to be judged by the apostolic norm. But the best insights of the early church, those they struggled to maintain, were in fact those convictions they regarded as apostolic. Thus, to recover this era of the church is to restore the earliest expressions of Christian theology and church practice that grew out of apostolic teaching.[24]

In addition to the Restorationist overtones I mentioned earlier, there is a primitivist impulse here, a longing for the golden past that, as documented by Theodore Dwight Bozemen in *To Live Ancient Lives*, animated the English Puritans. This impulse is distinct from historylessness, the disregard for the past that is endemic to America, but it is also distinct from *historical consciousness*, the belief that "all ideas, values, institutions, and behavior patterns known to human beings are produced by human beings, and therefore bear the imprint of the historical setting in which they emerge."[25] To state the point metaphorically, Webber wanted to tap into the roots of Christianity without first boring through the gnarls and burls and wormholes and growth rings of the tree. He,

22. Webber, *Orthodox Evangelicals*, 33–35.

23. Sly, "Special Report," online: http://www.catholic.org/national/national_story.php?id=27157.

24. Webber, *Common Roots*, 32.

25. Wacker, *Augustus H. Strong*, 10.

and the Chicago Call in general, did not start with the historian's mantra, "change over time." He sought the timeless, not the contextual; the normative, not the contingent. As evidence, in the "Call to an Ancient Evangelical Future" that Webber headed up not long before his death, the first article addressed not historic roots and continuity but the primacy of the biblical narrative. This latter call, along with much of Webber's published work, also spurned modernity, of which historical consciousness is an intellectual cornerstone.

And yet, and yet, history *is* dangerous, as the Andover board suspected nearly two centuries ago. It consistently answers more than what we ask of it. I can't draw any lines of causality, but I do know that in the thirty-odd years since The Chicago Call there has been a flourishing of evangelical history, as scholars like George Marsden, Mark Noll, Joel Carpenter, Grant Wacker, and Nathan Hatch—not all of them card-carrying evangelicals, but all near kin—have become stars in their field and helped to engineer a shift by which religion has recently become the number-one subfield in American history. I am one of the beneficiaries of their pioneering work. I didn't set out to be a historian—I was an English lit major here at Wheaton—but the more I learned about the subject through my work on *Christian History* magazine, the more I realized that the past told me things about grace, the church, and the human condition that I absolutely needed to know, even if I hadn't gone looking for them. My hope is that this institute will also yield abundantly, fulfilling, and exceeding the call sounded a few miles from here back in 1977.

The Chicago Call:
Catholicity through History

A Response to Elesha Coffman

DAVID NEFF

Christianity Today

I WANT TO THANK ELESHA Coffman for applying her excellent historian's eye to the Chicago Call. There are, of course, other eyes through
which to view it.

Unlike Elesha, I have been aware of the Chicago Call for close to
thirty years. I moved to Chicago's Western suburbs just four years after
the Call was issued. In my first month at my new job at InterVarsity
Press, a friend invited me to go to church with him. That church was
St. Barnabas Episcopal in Glen Ellyn, Illinois, and my family and I were
treated to a rich liturgical experience and many enthusiastic handshakes.

After we got home, I headed to my filing cabinet. Many of the
names I had heard in after-church introductions seemed familiar. I took
from a file drawer an article I had clipped from the March 1978 issue of
Eternity magazine. It was written by Wheaton College historian Mark
Noll and was titled, "Evangelicals on the Canterbury Trail." Scanning the
article, I saw that indeed, many of the people I had met that day were
named in Mark's article. Among them was Robert Webber, architect of
the Chicago Call.

The Call's message was still very much in the air then. And as someone who was dissatisfied with his sectarian upbringing, I was looking for
elbowroom. I knew I could find that in the Episcopal Church, and a little
over a year later my wife and I were confirmed in that denomination.
The night before the confirmation I went out for drinks with several
new friends, including a Gordon College English professor who had

125

signed the Call. (If memory serves, his favored beer of the evening was Moosehead.) The next day, Tom Howard attended our confirmation and said to my wife and me, "Welcome to this branch of the catholic church."

Tom's comment sticks in our memory because just three years later, he bolted for another branch of the church catholic—the one with headquarters in Rome. But the significance of his comment highlights an important aspect of the Call. It is about *catholicity*, or, if you will, *evangelical ecumenicity.*

It is easy to read the Call as if it were primarily a call to re-engage the church's early history. The first of its eight points is "A Call to Historic Roots and Continuity." Before the May 1977 gathering at the Warrenville Cenacle where the Call was drafted, Webber had completed the manuscript for his book *Common Roots. Christianity Today* was to publish the Chicago Call[1] before Zondervan put *Common Roots* into bookstores, but it was the writing of *Common Roots* that laid the foundation for Webber's work on the Call. That book has a similar starting point, with the first chapter entitled "A Call to Historic Christianity."

In that first chapter, Webber asserts that the revitalization and maturation of evangelical Christianity will not take place without "a purging of our modernity and a return to Christianity in its historic form."[2] The chapter goes on to make multiple references to the "historic substance" of Christianity.

Thus, these parallel discussions in the Chicago Call and *Common Roots* are framed with words like *history* and *roots, historic* and *historical.* But is *history* the focus of the summons Webber issued?

I would argue that for Robert Webber and his colleagues in the Chicago Call, the goal was not historical recovery but spiritual health, and that they believed the spiritual health of the evangelical movement would not be possible without a renewed understanding of its place in the church catholic.

Thus, while the Chicago Call begins its ascent with "A Call to Historic Roots and Continuity," it reaches its peak with its final point: "A Call to Church Unity." Between those two appeals come calls for "Church Authority," "Sacramental Integrity," and "Creedal Identity."

1. "The Chicago Call: An Appeal to Evangelicals," *Christianity Today,* vol. 21, no. 18 [June 17, 1977], pp. 28–29.

2. Webber, *Common Roots*, 14.

Half of the Call's main points, then, deal with the need to recover the churchly character of evangelicalism, and with it a sense of catholicity.

This is a very difficult task for those with an evangelical sense of identity. The Reformational roots of evangelicalism were clearly about the renewal of the whole church. The church's internal struggles over the Reformers' challenges and subsequent martyrdoms and wars hardened the two sides into enemy camps. But this hardening into enemy camps undermined the purpose of reform. Such hardening has been repeated many times in our history. The fundamentalist-modernist controversy is the instance that continues to haunt us. Like it or not, we who move in the orbits of Billy Graham, Wheaton College, *Christianity Today*, and the National Association of Evangelicals live in the penumbra of fundamentalism.

The Evangelical Movement of the mid twentieth century struggled to break free of that fundamentalism. Graham's generous orthodoxy helped us along that path. But fundamentalist fears of catholicity persisted.

So as late as 1977, when *Christianity Today* editor Harold Lindsell editorialized about the Chicago Call, he touched on both themes: historicity and catholicity. He labeled the Call "a warning against ignoring or scorning the past." But then he explained the particular danger for Christians who ignore the past: "For the Christian," he wrote, "ignoring the past is . . . an implicit denial of a cardinal truth: there is *one body* of Christ; all believers, whether now alive on earth or not, are members of that body. Gifted teachers, writers, exegetes, and theologians are God's gifts to the body for subsequent ages as well as their own."[3]

So Lindsell highlighted the Chicago Call's inner movement from history to catholicity by underscoring the way in which ignoring the past denies the unity of Christ's body.

Dr. Coffman's paper has focused on the relation of the Chicago Call to history, and I have tried to shift our understanding of that document to ecumenicity and catholicity. That is to say, from the word *Roots* in the title of Bob's book to the word *Common*, to a stress on what all Christians share.

I do not wish, however, to deny the ironies Dr. Coffman's historian's eye has detected.

---

3. Lindsell, "Religious Roots."

If she detects a restorationist and primitivist note in the Chicago Call rather than a true historical consciousness, she is right. During the writing of *Common Roots* and the drafting of the Chicago Call, the Webbers and their friends were not attending a properly churchly church that one would associate with phrases like "creedal identity," "sacramental fidelity," and "church authority." No, it was the 70s, and they were in a house church.

I was recently talking with another signatory of the Call who was part of that house church.[4] He reminisced with a kind of embarrassed nostalgia about their desire to live without the institutional limits of traditional churches. Letting the children experience "church" with a balloon in their hands and a puppy in their laps was what it was all about, he said. Even though Bob Webber dated his conversion to liturgical worship to a 1972 Easter Vigil at St. Michael's Catholic parish in Wheaton, in this period the Webbers were not on a high-church pilgrimage. They were living out the primitivist impulse.

The 60s and 70s were times of cultural and ecclesial ferment. And so have been the "naughts"—or whatever you label the immediate past decade. Bob Webber saw it coming at the end of the 90s when he wrote his first book in the Ancient Future series, *Ancient-Future Faith*. This was published at roughly the same time as Brian McLaren's first book, *Reinventing Your Church*. Both men saw the challenge of the postmodern context. McLaren has progressively departed from the historic faith in his attempts to shape "a new kind of Christian" and "a new kind of Christianity." But because Webber grounded his vision in the common roots of the whole church (that is, the *ancient* in ancient-future), he was able to keep a firm hold on orthodoxy as he issued his call for evangelical reform and renewal. At least two kinds of postmodern renewal have been under way. I give high credit to those behind the Chicago Call for pointing many to the ancient-future path, a path that drinks deeply from classic faith while forging a way into the future.

4. Personal conversation, March 14, 2010.

PART TWO

Evangelicals and the Early Church:

Recovery • Reform • Renewal

5

Why Study Early Christian History and Literature

EVERETT FERGUSON

Abilene Christian University

I AM GLAD TO SHARE with you in the celebration of the beginning of
The Wheaton Center for Early Christian Studies. Since I have made
the study of early church history the primary focus of my professional
work, I rejoice to see more persons taking an interest in this field of
study and the establishment of institutions to promote that study.

In announcing my topic as "Why Study Early Christian History
and Literature," I may be giving, in paraphrase of Cardinal John Henry
Newman, an *apologia pro vita mea*. Those already convinced of the importance of this study may take the title to mean, "why one *should* study
early church history." Others not yet convinced can take it to mean, "why
some people *do* study early church history."

The New Testament is, of course, our earliest Christian literature.
As inspired apostolic and prophetic writings, the canon of Scripture is
the standard for the faith and practice of the church. So I preface my lecture with the affirmation—which I expect I share with most of you—that
the Bible is our authority in religious matters. Neither the second century, the fourth century, the sixteenth century, the nineteenth century,
nor the twenty-first century is our authority. Although the Bible is the
church's authority, it, as any written text, must be interpreted.

131

The earliest non-canonical Christian literature overlaps in time the latest New Testament writings, but this literature is not our authority. Hence, I begin with a disclaimer: I have no desire to substitute church tradition for Scripture as the standard for Christian faith and life. I do not want even to supplement Scripture with early non-canonical Christian writings. My position rather is that early church history may help us interpret the Bible and understand what it says in a better way. To use a courtroom analogy, early Christian writings outside the New Testament are not the judge, nor are they the jury, in deciding Christian teaching. They function rather as witnesses in the case. And my plea is that they are witnesses who need to be heard in the court of interpretation. As with any human witness they may be in error, and we may have to correct them by the apostolic word. Yet, if they can help us interpret the Bible correctly and can strengthen our faith, or in Robert Wilken's words deepen our faith, they have a value for us.

I begin with some "ivory tower" reasons for studying early Christian history and literature.

First, some people enjoy being "antiquarians." For instance, the students said of George Williams, my major professor at Harvard, that he did not lecture on church history, he reminisced. He commuted daily to the fourth century, or whatever century he was lecturing about at the time. There is something to be said for pure scholarship, devoting one's time to basic historical research, just as there is for pure or basic science.

Related to this, second, is the challenge of learning and discovering. Sir Edmund Hilary, when asked why he wanted to climb Mt. Everest, is quoted as saying, "Because it is there." I submit that this is a justifiable reason for following many academic pursuits. Here is a body of material: its very existence is a challenge to the inquisitive mind.

Now, let us concentrate on what I may call the "faith" reasons, reasons that grow out of faith. These may be more practical considerations for you.

First, early church history provides confirmation and elucidation of the New Testament. I do not mean the approach that interprets the first century in the light of the fourth century, or the sixteenth century for that matter. There is always the danger of reading later practices and doctrines back into the early period.

I often employ what I call the historical argument in support of a given Christian practice. There are two aspects to it. One part of the argument is that those closest in time were in a better position to testify to apostolic examples than later witnesses. That should be obvious, even if this consideration is often ignored. A second aspect may require more explanation. This aspect pertains to a historical continuum. If something existed in the first-century church, there should be some trace of it later. Conversely, if something is not found in the early centuries, it may be questioned whether it was in the New Testament, or one must provide a very good explanation for it being totally lost so soon. In the same way, what existed later (even if false) must be derivable from the New Testament. Some have an ahistorical approach to the interpretation of the New Testament. Some have an understanding of New Testament teaching that could not have led to the early church's understanding. Even if the early church's understanding is wrong, one must be able to explain how the New Testament teaching could have resulted in this outcome. I am reminded of an anecdote from rural east Texas where I was born. A stranger trying to find a certain place inquired of a local person for directions. The local thought for a moment, scratched his head, and finally said, "You can't get there from here." That is my reaction to some interpretations of the Bible I hear. You can't get to the historical Christian development from what is presented.

The opposite error is to think that in the first century one already has the fourth-century practice. Historical continuity does not mean historical sameness.

Let me give an example of historical confirmation. 1 Corinthians 14:16 refers to others saying "Amen" to a person's thanksgiving. Our church history sources, such as Justin Martyr's account of a worship assembly (*1 Apology* 67), attest to a congregational unison "Amen" at the conclusion of prayer. Jerome commented that the congregational "Amen" was loud enough to be heard far outside the walls of the basilica (*Comm. Galatians* 1.2). These later writers make clear that Paul was not speaking hypothetically but was referring to actual congregational practice.

As an example of elucidation I refer to the early church's understanding of the water in John 3:5, "born of water and the Spirit." Here I step on some toes. The uniform testimony of the orthodox Christian writers is that this verse refers to baptism. In fact, John 3:5 is the most quoted baptismal text in the second century. Only a few Gnostics in the early period disputed the importance of baptism. Modern believers who would dehydrate the new birth need to ponder who their theological ancestors are in the ancient church.

You may respond that the early writers were not always right. A stream may become contaminated quite near its source, but it is much more likely to be pure near its origins. And, as I have indicated, we have to have a very good explanation of how and why *everyone* got something wrong from the beginning.

A second "faith" reason for studying early church history is that it shows the path of change from the New Testament.

What stands out to me is the development in the organization of the church. The later New Testament documents (Acts, Titus, 1 Peter) and the earliest non-canonical documents (*Didache, 1 Clement*) show a plurality of elders, also called bishops and pastors, in each church. Quite early there is the emergence of a single bishop at the head of the presbytery of each church, first attested in the letters of Ignatius of Antioch.

Many changes, such as this one, were almost imperceptible at first, and only in historical perspective can the significance of certain things be seen. An exception was the dramatic change from a persecuted to a victorious church in the fourth century, but even in that regard many aspects of the changed situation were slow in taking hold.

In the process of change, practices preceded dogma. We who do theology may be reluctant to acknowledge this, but most persons are doers first and thinkers later. A good example from early church history is the relation of infant baptism to the doctrine of original sin. Many, but not all, who practice infant baptism today do so because of belief in original sin. But the historical relation is the reverse. Augustine's argument with the Pelagians demonstrates this. Everyone at the time agreed that baptism is for the forgiveness of sins, and the Pelagians accepted infant baptism as the custom of the church. Augustine argued from the practice of infant baptism that since infants had no sins of their own, their baptism indicated their inheritance of the guilt, not just the consequences, of Adam's sin. After Augustine prevailed over the Pelagians, original sin became the principal doctrinal support for infant baptism, whereas originally the practice of infant baptism was the argument for the doctrine of original sin.

Christians in the early centuries made mistakes. People in the New Testament did too, as we know from the problems addressed in the New Testament letters. Those in error were corrected by the apostolic word.

We may have to correct the early church too by the apostolic word. Nonetheless, the writings of the second to fourth centuries help us understand better that apostolic word in its context.

A third value derived from studying early church history is the example of noble lives.

Who is not inspired by Polycarp of Smyrna's noble confession in about the year 156? When called upon by the Roman governor to swear by the *genius* of the emperor and revile Christ before the pagan crowd gathered in the stadium, Polycarp boldly declared, "For eighty-six years I have served him, and he has done me no wrong. How can I blaspheme my King who saved me?" (*Martyrdom of Polycarp* 9.3).

Or, from the domestic sphere consider Nonna, the mother of Gregory of Nazianzus, who paid her the tribute of being the coworker of her bishop husband, his teacher in piety, an example in prayer and fasting, a thrifty manager of the family possessions, and a generous giver to God and the poor (*Oration* 18.7–9).

A fourth value of studying early church history, as of studying other periods of history and other cultures, is the contribution to distinguishing the eternal from the cultural.

If we see Christianity in only one cultural context, it is easy to confuse the two. Americans have been particularly susceptible to doing this. Even missionaries have often found this distinction difficult to recognize. The broader one's historical knowledge, the clearer the perception of the gospel.

A fifth "faith" reason for studying early church history is to learn how others solved or failed to solve similar problems to ours. Early Christians give us guidance in dealing with issues that are still with us.

One such problem is the relation of faith and philosophy. How do we make intellectual adjustments to our society? The early church faced this question in an acute form. The philosophical climate was no more favorable to Christianity then than it is now. Christian thinkers laid down the lines of approach that can guide us today. Justin Martyr enunciated the view, "Whatever things were rightly said among all men are property of us Christians" (*2 Apology* 13). In order to make the intellectual case for Christianity, we must produce better-informed Christians and more Christian scholars, and that is a goal of this Center for Early Christian Studies. The early church won in part because it produced better brains than its pagan rivals did. Early Christians not only out-lived and out-died their pagan contemporaries but they out-thought them as well.

A related issue is the relation of Christianity and culture. What is our strategy—if we are not in favor of conformity with the world, will we pursue a policy of engagement with the world or of withdrawal from the world? The cultural standards of pagans were far different from Christian standards. In the fourth century this disparity became evident in the church itself. Today the accepted standards in society at large and what Christians regard as acceptable are far apart and pulling farther apart. What is our solution? Christian education is a counter-attack, not a retreat. Some in the early church chose the path of withdrawal in monasticism. Paradoxically, the monks often succeeded best when they modified their own ideals and went back into the world to preach and teach or welcomed the world that came to them for advice. In so doing they sometimes transformed society.

A specific issue within the larger discussion of culture has to do with moral questions. Abortion, abandonment of children, homosexuality, and sexual promiscuity were prevalent in the early Christian centuries, and Christian writers often commented on these matters. Here Christian teaching maintained a consistent stance in support of life and of sexual purity.

Another problem faced in the early centuries that exercises Christians today is church-state relations. On this question the situation in the early centuries was different from that in the modern Western world. However, the affirmation that primary loyalty belongs to God is still central. Tertullian was one of the early voices for something we wish were more widely recognized today. He said, "It is not the nature of religion to compel religion. Religion ought to be adopted voluntarily and not by force" (*To Scapula* 2.2). Coercion can take the form of subtle pressure as well as more overt exercises of force.

As a sixth of my "faith" reasons for studying early Christian literature, I elaborate on the thought already suggested: its value for the interpretation of Scripture.

Robert Wilken developed this in his lecture here last fall. I want to take a different approach, that of a historian rather than a theologian. We should do the history before doing our theology. Wilken follows this sequence, but there are many who do their theology before doing the history. And a further caution: in doing the theology we should take the whole biblical witness and not just some selected texts, to which we make the rest conform.

My special concern is the New Testament. The accurate interpretation of the New Testament in its historical context includes the foreground as well as the background. Biblical scholars have learned the value of background studies. We need the historical foreground to complete the picture. For example, Greek lexica regularly cite early Christian writings to illustrate the meaning of words. In the same way we should extend the practice to other matters than word usage. The early Christian writings clarify matters of doctrine and life.

It helps to read the New Testament as part of a historical continuum. The early Christian writers lived in close enough proximity in time to the early disciples to be able to preserve and transmit authentic information. They spoke and wrote the same language as the New Testament writers. They shared to a large extent the cultural and social setting of the first century. They lived in nearly the same historical context and shared in the same tradition of faith. Therefore, they were in a good position to preserve the original sense of a passage of Scripture or the intention of the apostolic teaching and so to tell about Christian faith and practices. I know, for example, that I have often found in John Chrysostom's homilies insights that modern New Testament scholars think they have discovered about the meaning of a word or idiom.

Growing out of this point is a seventh "faith" reason for studying early Christian literature: that is the theological reflection on the biblical data. There were legitimate and illegitimate doctrinal developments out of the teachings of Jesus and the apostles. Thus we have the conflicts between the orthodox and the Gnostics in the second and third centuries. More work is still needed on theological clarification of many doctrines. Wheaton would seem to be a place for progress in this study to be advanced.

In doing this theological reflection on the apostolic message, there are some dangers to be avoided.

One danger is making tradition the practical authority. A person can be so impressed with early Christian literature, on discovering it, as to elevate it to a place equal to Scripture. Some churches accept on principle tradition as well as Scripture as normative. They are often as arbitrary in what they accept from tradition as others are about what they select out of Scripture to follow. To listen attentively to the early

Christian development as a testimony to the meaning of the Bible is not the same as making that development normative for present Christian practice.

Another danger is reading the later development back into the New Testament. There were many changes in Christian practice, some occurring quite early. The church's early history is to aid, not determine, the interpretation of the New Testament. If something is not in the New Testament, then early Christian literature cannot put it there, nor can it interpret something not there.

A third danger is overgeneralization—taking an isolated or individual view out of the historical evidence and considering it the general position. Of course, a single writer or source may preserve the correct understanding over against the majority position. To avoid the mistake of overgeneralization there must be a breadth of knowledge in the sources. It is more likely for an individual writer or the church in a certain region to go astray than for such a thing to happen to the church over a broader territory. Of course, given enough time this consideration loses its force, because ideas spread. It is important to determine if there is a uniform testimony of many witnesses so as to establish a definite tradition of teaching. The earlier and more extensively such a consensus can be established, the stronger and more persuasive it becomes as traceable to earliest Christian times or as resting on something other than an individual's innovation. Nonetheless, another caution is that a majority does not necessarily establish truth. Still one must beware of the danger of overgeneralization.

Well, I trust I have made a case for the importance of The Wheaton Center of Early Christian studies. I close with some personal reflections.

The study of early Christianity will bring an understanding and sympathy for others, their beliefs and actions. This study will give a frame of reference for self-understanding and seeing more clearly the options before us. We understand ourselves better when we see ourselves in relation to others. This will lead, I trust, to two qualities often difficult to keep in balance—firmness of conviction and broad-minded charity—a balance to be seen in Jesus but often not evident in his followers.

Someone, after reading my textbook *Church History: From Christ to Pre-Reformation*, wrote to me assuming I must be Catholic or Orthodox because I interpreted the history sympathetically. That is the task of the historian: to understand the people and periods under study. (And I add parenthetically that one should understand before assigning blame or praise.) My correspondent then expressed surprise to learn that I identify myself with Churches of Christ.

The first four centuries were the formative period for the history of Christianity, and nearly all branches of Christianity look back to this period as having special significance. Perhaps more than any period between the New Testament and today this is the period of history you should know. And I include the Reformation in making this sweeping statement, although I enjoy Reformation studies and liked teaching it.

Roman Catholics, Eastern Orthodox, and to some extent Anglicans claim the early period as their own. When I entered this field, some (both Catholics and those of my own fellowship) wondered what I was doing here, and I still get questions about it. My studies, however, led me to conclude that these early writings are more mine than theirs, if you want to put it in terms of possession.

A more appropriate question, however might be this: Will the church that produced hundreds of martyrs like Polycarp, Justin, and Blandina; that produced persons of spiritual insight like Antony, Ephrem, and John Cassian; that produced mothers and homemakers like Nonna, Macrina the Elder, and Paula; that produced bishops and ecclesiastical statesmen like Cyprian, Basil the Great, and Leo the Great; that produced theologians like Athanasius, Gregory of Nazianzus, and Cyril of Alexandria; that produced towering intellects like Origen, Gregory of Nyssa, and Augustine—will that church claim *us* as *its* heirs?

6

Evangelicals and the Public Use of Creeds

Scot McKnight

North Park University

O N MY DRIVE HOME from teaching an evening Bible class at Willow Creek recently, I spotted on my cell phone an e-mail from a former student of mine when I was teaching at Trinity Evangelical Divinity School. This former student has been flourishing as a professor for a number of years at an evangelical college [not Wheaton]. I e-mailed him my phone number, from a stoplight of course, and within a few minutes we were chatting. It was a conversation I have had numerous times with a dozen or so former students from Trinity. The gist of our conversation began upfront with his comment: "Scot, I'm about to finish RCIA [the Rite of Christian Initiation of Adults into the Catholic Church] and would like to talk to you about it." Though each conversation along this line has its particularities, each also has its commonalities, including my typical question, "What does your wife/spouse think?" this particular conversation had a special wrinkle: the professor has been told by the administration that he will have one academic year left on his contract after his Easter Vigil entrance into the Roman Catholic Church, after which time he will be looking for a new academic post. (Once again, this is not Wheaton and it was not certain that the move would be made.)

In an article I wrote some years back, called "From Wheaton to Rome," which is now in a book of mine called *Finding Faith, Losing*

Faith, I sifted anecdotal evidence of converts from evangelicalism to Catholicism, and discovered four observable crises that precipitate such a conversion: a need for certainty, a sense of history, a yearning for ecclesial unity, and a desire for empirical authority. There is no need here to sort through those points again, nor to evaluate whether conversion to the Roman Catholic Church actually provides resolutions to those issues. Instead we need to observe that these four crises wedge their way into the cracks between the four distinguishing features of evangelicalism as sketched in David Bebbington's quadrilateral,[1] and rupture one's evangelical faith into an unwanted mess for many. One can plausibly contend that evangelicalism's present shape, theology, and praxis precipitate such crises. Once again, there is no need to discuss Bebbington's four points so I mention them: biblicism, crucicentrism, conversionism, and activism. I don't find these terms all that clear, so I'll say them slightly differently. Evangelicals are those who believe in (1) the truthful adequacy and sufficiency of the Bible for revealing the gospel and what is to be believed, (2) the fundamental sacrificial and atoning death of Jesus for human sinfulness, (3) the necessity for each person to have a personal experience of conversion in order to be finally acceptable to God, and (4) the expectation of a life shaped by active participation in church and in evangelism and in social justice. Neither ecclesiology nor pneumatology emerge in Bebbington's sifting of evangelicalism, and the absence of both presents dramatically difficult problems for any evangelical who wants to take on the issue of evangelicals publicly reciting creeds, as I will do in this study.

Converts to Catholicism from evangelicalism join hands, probably between points one and two, to say that the first, biblicism, will not support the weight it has been asked to carry even if it has carried that weight, rather happily, for the better part of two centuries. Precisely in this crack the issue of creeds arises and makes one ask the question how biblicism alone can warrant the need and weightiness of theological articulations. Sure, the Bible can provide the grist and the grit, but which interpretations will become normative or authoritative, and even more, who will decide, can't be adjudicated simply, or at least for some it can't be adjudicated on the basis of biblicism. Something more is needed, and for evangelicals this has been more or less a robust, unofficial commitment to Bebbington's four marks. There are signs of changes.

1. See Bebbington, *Dominance of Evangelicalism*, 21–40.

Oddly enough, there are a variety of evangelicals today searching for a voice of authority, but in strikingly different ways, and I want to continue my meanderings into the problem by calling attention to a few examples. I once heard Albert Mohler, president of Southern Seminary, interviewed on TV about Mormons and he said they weren't Christians because they didn't believe the Nicene Creed. I grew up Baptist, and my parents were more or less Southern Baptists, and I never once heard anyone suggest Mormons weren't Christians because they denied some creed. They weren't Christians, so we believed, because they didn't believe the clear teaching of the Bible. What struck me was Mohler's appeal to the Nicene Creed. Frankly, I liked his surprising-to-me appeal, but that's for later. Alongside such appeals to some kind of *regula fidei* to guide our interpretation of the Bible and to mark off the faithful, we have an increasing number of evangelicals today framing new doctrinal alliances, like the Gospel Coalition and the Alliance for Confessing Evangelicals. Michael Horton, for instance, has said that the framing ideas—like Bebbington's quadrilateral—may be enough to form alliances for evangelicals, but they aren't enough to frame what a church believes and needs to conduct itself with faithfulness, which means for Michael the official Reformed confessions.

Let's add to these converts and confessions by evangelicals a rather new and bold adventure: the recovery of the theological interpretation of Scripture, which in some ways is challenging the adequacy of the biblicism criterion of Bebbington. There's all kinds of excitement about this movement even as many of us are trying to make sense just what they are doing, and I see it in Kevin Vanhoozer, Daniel Treier, J. Todd Billings, the Brazos theological commentary on the Bible from Baker, and the monumental InterVarsity Press projects led by Tom Oden and Gerald Bray, all with the word "ancient" headlining their efforts. This project is one that some would see as confusing or others would say is downright wrong but which is clearly being embraced by a growing number of evangelicals. Good grief, I sometimes say, some of this stuff is being published by InterVarsity Press, the home of John Stott, who may well have recited creeds in public worship but who can't be said to have let any theological interpretation overtly or consciously shape his Bible reading.[2]

---

2. Which is not to say that a theology didn't influence him; it did. But I can't say that I've seen much of Stott's work overtly constrained by creedal statements. Gerald Bray

Which is exactly where I'd like now to stop, and make this claim: *The trends I have mentioned are indicative of and attempts to address a fundamental problem in contemporary Western evangelicalism: the loss of an authoritative, official, ecclesiastically-constrained theological heritage, which is leading to, or perhaps derives from, the diminution of the gospel and of theology overall.* While it is not often said, there is today at least a fissure in the evangelical conviction of the complete adequacy of Scripture, and alongside that well-kept secret is an increasing willingness to tether one's faith to confessions. David Wells has spent the last two decades complaining about theological diminution, and he's right (sometimes).[3] American evangelicalism—and here I'm pointing to generic, populist, and widespread evangelical churches that believe the Bible, preach conversion, focus on the cross and more or less expect Christians to participate—is falling apart theologically. I am convinced that, with due respect to the Reformed evangelical tradition, which has more than enough theology to carry the day, there is little theological robustness at work in generic-brand evangelicalism. What matters is a seeker-sensitive approach to church services and the narrowing of theological concerns to that which we can all agree on, which basically gets down to that God loves us, Jesus died for us, the Bible is our book, and we need to get busy.

John Stott agrees with David Wells but from a slightly different angle, from Roger Steer's new biography, recording an interview with the fine editor at *Christianity Today*, Tim Stafford. When Stafford asked Stott how he evaluates the immense growth of evangelicalism in his lifetime, Stott said this: "Growth without depth . . . [the growth] has been largely numerical and statistical growth. And there has not been sufficient growth in discipleship that is comparable to the growth in numbers." And he locates the issue in the gospel, and in so doing opens himself to a problem we will point out later. I quote from Stott: "But we must look beyond evangelism to the transforming power of the gospel, both in individuals and in society." And he points both to the superficial concern with holiness and the need to expand the agendas of social concern to include such things as environment and the rights of women and chil-

helpfully pointed out to me in conversation that what I am saying pertains to Stott's more public ministry and writing but less to his ecclesial ministry.

3. Beginning with his *No Place for Truth or Whatever Happened to Evangelical Theology?* and finishing with *Above All Earthly Pow'rs: Christ in a Postmodern World*.

dren.[4] Two leading evangelicals of the twentieth century, and now into the twenty first, both observing similar weaknesses in evangelicalism.

I don't believe I have the answer to all of this, but I do believe the rapture of creeds from weekly church worship is part of the problem and probably a symptom of an anti-intellectual incorrigibility about populist evangelicalism, which will lead me to a later proposal. I want to offer a mild defense of the use of creeds in low-church evangelical churches, but I want to do so under the umbrella that theology and creed, on the one hand, and gospel, on the other, are not at odds with one another. (I will suggest that gospel and creed are to be connected.) There is an assumption at work in much of populist evangelicalism that the gospel is simple and theology arcane. Creed saddles theology, and therefore creed too is arcane. The next step for many in this camp is to appeal to evangelicalism's biblicism: "Let's just get back to the Bible, before there was any theology, before there were any creeds, back when it was all gospel and all good."

I disagree with that kind of biblicism, which might be called *scriptura nuda*, but I do want to propose that we get back to, or at least begin with, the Bible. What we find smack-dab in the middle of the New Testament are very early Christian creeds, and these creeds are profoundly theological, their theology is good, and they are also gospel articulations so that gospel and theology aren't a cosmic leap from one another. I am proceeding to the New Testament first because, to make a defense of creeds for evangelicals, one better find something about it in the New Testament.

New Testament and Creeds

New Testament experts and early Christian historians lock horns on which text in the New Testament is a creed or a confession and which is not. Anglican scholars find baptism and nascent liturgy and even lectionary patterns all over the place and they think they are "obvious," while non-liturgical evangelicals are baffled by the conversation and hadn't even thought of any of these connections. To suggest that 1 Peter is a baptismal liturgy appeals to the former and offends the latter. Church historians smile at the latter and agree with the former, unless they are old-school Baptists. But at least we can all land on this: no one seriously

---

4. See Steer, *Basic Christian*, 267–68.

disputes that texts like Philippians 2:6–11 and Romans 10:9–10 and 1 Peter 3:18–22 and 1 Timothy 3:16 and 2 Timothy 2:11–13 are liturgical or proto-creedal or confessional.[5]

Take, first of all, what is probably some kind of *baptismal confessional* set of lines, now found in Romans 10:9–10.

> because if you confess with your lips that Jesus is Lord and believe in your heart that God raised him from the dead, you will be saved. For one believes with the heart and so is justified, and one confesses with the mouth and so is saved.

A confession was evidently required (upon baptism?) to find acceptance, and that confession included confession that Jesus is the exalted Lord (and I can hear Tom Wright adding "not Caesar"), and that same confession involved believing that God had actually broken the bonds of mortality to death and raised Jesus up bodily. And if you don't confess those two things, you aren't saved. Then Paul adds that one believes in the heart and this leads to justification and one confesses with the lips and this leads to salvation. And I've never seen a gospel tract today that requires belief in Jesus' exalted Lordship and belief in his bodily resurrection, let alone even uses the word justification, and neither have I ever heard such words at a baptismal service.

What strikes me about the earliest Christian proto-creeds, second, is *their christological center*. Notice these statements, and as you listen you might compare them to the stuff we hear in Christian music today:

> [6] who, though he was in the form of God,
> did not regard equality with God
> as something to be exploited,
> [7] but emptied himself,
> taking the form of a slave,
> being born in human likeness.
> And being found in human form,
> [8] he humbled himself
> and became obedient to the point of death—
> even death on a cross.
> [9] Therefore God also highly exalted him
> and gave him the name
> that is above every name,
> [10] so that at the name of Jesus

---

5. See Neufeld, *Earliest Christian Confessions*. A recent use of such categories can be found in Hurtado, *Lord Jesus Christ*, 140–43.

> every knee should bend,
> in heaven and on earth and under the earth,
> [11] and every tongue should confess
> that Jesus Christ is Lord,
> to the glory of God the Father. (Phil 2:6–11)

And . . .

> [18] For Christ also suffered for sins once for all, the righteous for
> the unrighteous, in order to bring you to God.
> He was put to death in the flesh,
> but made alive in the spirit,
> [19] in which also he went and made a proclamation to the spirits
> in prison . . .
> [22] who has gone into heaven and is at the right hand of God,
> with angels, authorities, and powers made subject to him.
> (1 Peter 3:18–22)

And . . .

> Without any doubt, the mystery of our religion is great:
> He was revealed in flesh,
> vindicated in spirit,
> seen by angels,
> proclaimed among Gentiles,
> believed in throughout the world,
> taken up in glory. (1 Tim 3:16)

The earliest Christian creeds, then, are one-sidedly focused on Jesus Christ and his role as God's Savior as they also confess the resurrected and exalted Lord.

And now for a third point about these proto-creeds, and on this one I want to focus on *the gospel creed found in 1 Corinthians 15:3–5*, though some would also add 15:23–28 as part of this proto-creedal confession.

> [3] For I handed on to you as of first importance what I in turn had
> received:
> that Christ died for our sins in accordance with the scriptures,
> [4] and that he was buried,
> and that he was raised on the third day in accordance with the
> scriptures,
> [5] and that he appeared to Cephas, then to the twelve.

²³ But each in his own order: Christ the first fruits, then at his coming those who belong to Christ.

²⁴ Then comes the end, when he hands over the kingdom to God the Father, after he has destroyed every ruler and every authority and power.

²⁵ For he must reign until he has put all his enemies under his feet.

²⁶ The last enemy to be destroyed is death.

²⁷ For "God has put all things in subjection under his feet." But when it says, "All things are put in subjection," it is plain that this does not include the one who put all things in subjection under him.

²⁸ When all things are subjected to him, then the Son himself will also be subjected to the one who put all things in subjection under him, so that God may be all in all.

I have three observations, each of which will help us in our case for the value of creeds as a widespread weekly element in public worship in evangelical churches, especially low-church evangelical churches.

First, this early Christian creed or baptismal formula or confession swallows up the central saving events in Christ *by connecting it to Israel's Story.* The operative expression here is "in accordance with the scriptures," never mind if one cannot find the explicit text to which Paul points when he says that Jesus "was raised on the third day in accordance with the scriptures." Some suggest Hosea 6:2, though Gordon Fee seems to have the lion's share when he says it is probably an allusion to the sweep of Scripture, with texts like Psalm 16:8–11 and 110:1 involved somehow.[6] We can debate such issues and miss the point: the earliest creedal formulation of the gospel saw the saving events that God wrought in Jesus Christ, the Lord, as culminating the Story of Israel. Notably, then, the separable lines in 1 Corinthians 15 become, in effect, new chapters in Israel's story.

Which leads me to some unavoidable finger pointing. The moment our gospel confessions and creeds become simple lines in a saving process or theological articulations shooting off in one direction and then another, and either way lose their connection to Israel's story, our gospel gets disconnected from the only story our gospel has to tell. At Paul's rawest gospeling moment, when he was preaching on the Areopagus in Athens (Acts 17), he could not avoid telling the Gentile philosophers

---

6. Fee, *First Epistle to the Corinthians*, 726–28.

what he believed in the context of Israel's Creator God and Israel's Scriptures.

Second, 1 Corinthians 15:1–2 sets us up to believe that this proto-creed is actually *the gospel itself.* "Sure, sure," I can hear my evangelical friends say, "1 Corinthians 15 is the gospel." And the moment you ask them to share their faith with someone out the door goes 1 Corinthians 15 and in the door comes the four spiritual laws or the bridge illustration or Alpha, each of which has been used mightily by God and (sometimes) disastrously by Christians. These gospel articulations make me wonder if they are the reason there's so little theology left. Evangelism, or what I prefer to call "gospeling," if I'm reading Paul aright, is about telling the story of Jesus as (1) the saving story that (2) brings to a climax the story of Israel. Paul clearly implies that 1 Corinthians 15:3–5 is the content and order of the earliest Christian gospel.

Some more finger pointing could follow but I suspect it will be clear enough in my third point. Third, 1 Corinthians 15 alone provides a foundation upon which we are to understand three developments. The first one may in fact be behind this passage, the second one is clarified by it, and the third one explains the theological robustness at work in 1 Corinthians.

(1) There are seven gospeling events in the Book of Acts: 2:14–39; 3:12–26; 10:34–43; 11:5–18 and 13:16–41; 14:15–17; and 17:22–31. One could add other references, but these are the major gospeling events. What we call the gospel today more or less is not what was gospeled by Peter or by Paul; what they "gospeled" is often enough not gospeled by evangelicals today. Ergo, our gospel is not their gospel and their gospel is not our gospel. In brief, *the apostolic gospel consisted of narrating the saving events of Jesus' story as the climax of God's story with Israel, and it involved the demand to repent and to be baptized for the forgiveness of sins as the forms of entrance into that saving Story.* Both Peter's and Paul's sermons are fleshing-outs of the gospel tradition we find in 1 Corinthians 15. Maybe 1 Corinthians 15 is a summary of their sermons.

(2) I suggest that 1 Corinthians 15, which again is the gospel as the redemptive narrative about Jesus, explains something that only first-year college students ask, the answer to which is largely ignored by most of us. The question: Why did the earliest Christians, if not the authors themselves, call the first four books of the New Testament "Gospel"?

Which leads to a backhanded question: Do the four Gospels tell the gospel? And is their gospel the gospel we today preach as the gospel? That last question is the easiest one to answer: No, in fact, most people today don't preach a gospel that at all sounds like Matthew, Mark, Luke, or John. So the finger-pointing is deserved: *the reason the earliest Christians called Matthew, Mark, Luke, and John "the Gospel" is because they were in fact the gospel.* The gospel, in other words, is the narration of the story of Jesus as the climax of Israel's story. Which is exactly what 1 Corinthians tells us, and it is not at all new to say that 1 Corinthians 15 might be taken as an outline of each of the Gospels.

(3) My third point has to do with creeds: *the early Christian creeds, or at least the second article (Jesus Christ), are based on 1 Corinthians 15* and flesh out what they thought was inherent in that passage in order to maintain fidelity to and faithful witness to that primitive gospel tradition. To be sure, they become Trinitarian from the *Epistula Apostolorum* and from Justin Martyr (*First Apology* 61) and from Irenaeus on (*Demonstration of the Apostolic Teaching* 3; see also *Against Heresies* 1.49). Prior to Irenaeus we find both unmistakable adherence to and additions to 1 Corinthians 15. Thus, Ignatius, *To the Trallians* 9.1–2:

> from Jesus Christ, who is of the stock of David who is of Mary, who was truly born, ate and drank, was truly persecuted under Pontius Pilate, was truly crucified and died in the sight of the beings of heaven, of earth and the underworld, who was also truly raised from the dead . . .

One finds something similar in Tertullian's rule of faith (see *Veiling of Virgins* 1) and in Hippolytus of Rome's short treatise against the patripassionism of Noetus (*Against Noetus* 1), and even more in his baptismal formula (ca. 215; *Apostolic Tradition* 21.11–19).

While Nicaea is later, and while it adds plenty and subtracts "Israel's story" a bit too much for my liking, it doesn't take but a moment's notice to see that the Son clauses are rooted in 1 Corinthians 15.

> We believe in one Lord, Jesus Christ,
> the only Son of God,
> eternally begotten of the Father,
> God from God, Light from Light,
> true God from true God,
> begotten, not made,
> of one Being with the Father.

Through him all things were made.
For us and for our salvation
he came down from heaven:
by the power of the Holy Spirit
he became incarnate from the Virgin Mary,
and was made man.
For our sake he was crucified under Pontius Pilate;
he suffered death and was buried.
On the third day he rose again
in accordance with the Scriptures;
he ascended into heaven
and is seated at the right hand of the Father.
He will come again in glory to judge the living and the dead,
and his kingdom will have no end.

The same can be said of The Apostles' Creed:[7]

And in Jesus Christ his only Son our Lord; who was conceived by
the Holy Ghost, born of the Virgin Mary, suffered under Pontius
Pilate, *was crucified, dead, and buried; he descended into hell; the*
third day he rose again from the dead; he ascended into heaven,
and sitteth on the right hand of God the Father Almighty; from
thence he shall come to judge the quick and the dead.

Much more needs to be said, and I suspect many in this room could
say it with more finesse than could I, but this one thing needs to be
observed: *the Nicene Creed, or the regula fidei leading up to it, and the*
creeds that flowed out of Nicea, are not exercises in theological sophistry
or speculation but profoundly gospeling events. To recite the creed for
these early Christians was not to dabble in the theologically arcane but
to articulate and confess—aloud and often—the gospel itself. To deny
these creeds was to deny the gospel. Creed and gospel are not arcane
and simple, but creed fleshes out what gospel really meant and means.
This has been traced well by Ted Campbell in his book *The Gospel in*
Christian Traditions.

Theology has become intellectual sport for so many that the average evangelical Christian, and here again I remind you that I'm thinking more of populist evangelicals and not IVP readers, that the minute

7. Found at the end of the NT ms Codex E; in Ambrose; in Sermons 213, 215
by Augustine; in Sermons 57–62 by Peter Chrysologus, bishop of Ravenna (400–
450); and then completely in Rufinus of Aquileia's commentary on it (c. 404). From
Johnson, *Creed*, 31.

anything smacks of theology it gets shoved into the box of the speculative or divisive or unnecessary. Not so with those early Christians. I'm impressed with St. Irenaeus of Lyons's *On the Apostolic Preaching*, which in many ways might be taken as what Peter and Paul might have said had we been given their full sermons—yes, yes, of course, dropping out the anachronisms of the second century. Here we find a profound storied grasp of the Bible, but Irenaeus's grasp here isn't anything other than how he understood the *gospel itself*. And Cyril of Jerusalem, in his *Catechetical Lectures*, reveals just how serious this gospeling and baptism were in the warnings and moral exhortations he provides for those who are candidates for church membership. Creed for him was a summary of the Bible (*Catechetical Lectures* 5.12). You can't find them reducing gospel and getting people dunked or dipped or sprinkled *and only then giving them theology if they were the academic sort.*

Evangelicals won't confess creeds or use confessions unless they can be convinced they are biblical and unless they are connected to the gospel and conversion. I've tried to do just that in what I've said so far. I'd like now to move into two proposals.

Recovering Creeds

The earliest Christian creeds were articulations of what the gospel was and they were the preferred means of connecting the newly baptized and the mature believer to the gospel and to the church. As such, creeds were ways of providing *clarity, heritage, depth, width, and memory* to the church. The absence of creeds, not to mention the nearly total absence of reading Scripture aloud, as a lectionary (and not just as a launching pad for a sermon), deprives evangelicalism of that same clarity, heritage, depth, width, and memory. The theological superficiality of much of populist evangelicalism, I am contending, is symptomatic of the absence of creeds. I don't know which came first. Populist evangelicalism has almost no heritage, it lacks depth, it fears width, and its memory goes back all of a decade or two. It's clarity, then, is thin.

So I make two proposals before this audience today, hoping that some of this will gain traction with some. The first one is this: I propose that we who believe in the value of creeds become active in getting our churches, especially if we are part of a church tradition that does not recite the creed publicly, to begin a course of instruction for the elders, deacons, and teachers on the history of the creeds. And I don't mean read a book about them; I mean read them and study them together. In this proposal, then, I am also suggesting that one doesn't have to stop with Nicea or the Chalcedonian Definition. I would urge such churches to have a monthly rotation in public: begin with the Nicene-Constantinopolitan Creed or the Apostles' Creed, bring in some Reformation creedal form (and I was struck recently in reading the Genevan Confession by how profoundly different it is from the Apostles' Creed or Nicaea because of its soteriological orientation), and then add to that one's denominational or local church confessions.

The absence of theological robustness might be regained in some small measure simply by the routine recitation of the faith we have always believed and do believe. These creeds and confessions will raise questions, it will lead good evangelicals back to their Bibles, and perhaps raise the level of theological sophistication.

A second proposal, and it's a soapbox. Most of us write things no one but specialists can understand. Most of the people in our churches, and probably more than most, aren't reading the sorts of things we professors write these days. Some professors think we are writing popular theology because we don't overload our books with footnotes. Instead, we've only got about 100 footnotes in a 200-page book. That's not popular theology, and its total sales frequently enough are an ignored commentary.[8]

Some of us, perhaps most of us, believe in trickle-down theological education. We'll write theological tomes and learned journal articles and seminary students will read them—and some of them actually do, but don't kid yourselves—and then when they become pastors they'll pass on our profundities to lay people and, *voila*, in a decade or two the problems will be resolved. Just in case you haven't noticed, that's been the theory for the last four decades and you can see where it has led us. We need to embrace something more robust than a trickle-down theory of education.

The need here is so great that one is tempted to call a moratorium on evangelical theologians writing for the guild, or at least reducing their guild writing, and require each theologian, each biblical expert, and each church historian to write one book for the church—for ordi-

---

8. I'm not suggesting we cease publishing academic books for the guild.

nary lay people with enough snap to it to make it genuinely readable, pleasurable, and inspiring—before they can write academic pieces.

Perhaps an illustration will help. Dispensationalism rose to its pervasive heights because its principal theologians, Lewis Sperry Chafer, Charles Ryrie, Dwight Pentecost, and John Walvoord, wrote easy-to-digest theologies. I have often heard it said that their theologies were too simplistic. Perhaps so. You won't have much trouble getting me to agree with you against dispensationalism. But perhaps we should turn this around to say it another way: dispensationalism gained its power, at least in part, because of the rhetorical powers of its theologians. They could write theology in such clear ways that the ordinary Christian could grasp it and remember it and never forget the stuff! The reason ordinary pastors struggle getting dispensationalists to see things another way is because dispensational theologians were masters of rhetoric and theological writing.

How many theological books, other than those by C. S. Lewis, are being read across the evangelical church today? Perhaps we can ask this through an entirely different set of questions: What books are being read? Who is writing them? Who do you think is having the biggest influence? What are their rhetorical powers? Something I want to take to heart and I hope others will give me an ear: Don't complain about what the ordinary evangelical knows and believes until you are willing to speak to them, in their words, and in ways that compel belief and memory.

Somewhere along the line—I think it was in the wake of Carl F.H. Henry and George Ladd and the rise of neo-evangelicalism—we professors jumped the shark when it comes to communicating theology to the evangelical church. We regret the situation we are now in. We can do something about it. In our own day, perhaps the signal writer who is most influential is N. T. Wright. I have often said that one reason Tom's ideas catch on is because his prose is so pleasurable and "Caesar's is not."

A Response to Scot McKnight

Daniel J. Treier

Wheaton College

Scot McKnight is an excellent, holistic biblical-theological scholar, who is building bridges to people and communities with whom many of us interact poorly. I respect him for listening well to the churches, plus speaking boldly when he believes that is needed. I am in broad agreement with the major claims of his paper, so the following five thesis statements merely offer friendly amendments or suggested nuances.

Thesis 1: *If creeds are to have the pedagogical function we hope for, we must give careful attention to surrounding cultural shifts and countercultural practices.* The creeds come to us from a context in which disciplined, prayerful attention—to texts, and to God through text—had a different kind of cultural normalcy and force, even as literacy itself had a vastly different meaning and narrower reach. Without apocalyptically overemphasizing the uniqueness of our own time, I suspect that my contemporary addictions—to self-important and institutionally-imposed busyness, along with endless technologically-promoted distractions as coping mechanisms—do not promote such worshipful attentiveness. So it seems unlikely that creedal recitation of the sort that Scot proposes would make a major dent in evangelical learning of the faith unless that recitation happens within the context of, or helps to foster, a larger set of practices. Those practices would need to focus on biblical literacy along with countercultural habits of solitude, electronic fasting, communal engagement on terms not personally chosen, and so forth. As suggested within the volume on *Nicene Christianity* edited by Christopher Seitz, the creeds go in search of churchly communities that would practice the form of life within which they make sense. They are worth reciting apart from pedagogical accomplishments, but we must be realistic about the different goals involved in democratizing evangelical learning today as compared with the patristic generations.

Therefore, Thesis 2: *We need to clarify what evangelical "biblicism" means, both positively and negatively, but the underlying issues we must address concern ecclesiology.* David Bebbington speaks of biblicism, as Scot does at points, to underscore evangelicals' *de jure* respect for Scripture's authority. At times, though, Scot seems to use the term in a popular yet ideological sense, to speak more of *nuda scriptura* (*de facto*) than *sola scriptura*. By that standard there are theological traditions within evangelicalism that do not qualify as biblicist, as he notes. That may be part of the reason for ambiguous relationships between the term "evangelical" and groups of Lutheran and Reformed Christians (among others), for whom there are creeds and confessions with substantial authority under Scripture.

Yet to this increasingly murky picture we must add the plethora of "doctrinal statements" or "statements of faith" that guide evangelical parachurch institutions and even supposedly nondenominational or anticreedal churches. If evangelical biblicism really leads to neglect of creeds, then it must do so in a very particular way. It is plausible to argue that many nondenominational and anticreedal evangelicals reject focusing on the classic creeds precisely because they are ancient and ecumenical. It is further plausible to wonder if many confessional evangelicals, at the popular level anyway, function similarly: they may salute the Westminster Confession in a way they refuse for the Nicene Creed, simply because the former is associated strongly with the authority of Scripture and the latter with Eastern Orthodoxy and/or Catholicism. Perhaps these are the realities to which Scot points, and he may be right to detect some signs of change.

But, even so, it might be just as important to address the underlying presuppositions rather than speaking generically of biblicism. If we have creed-like statements functioning all over the place, yet they particularize scriptural understanding rather than unite Christians across time and space, then I think the root tendency feeding such fragmentation may involve narratives of ecclesiastical decline. All evangelicals legitimately hold such a narrative to some degree, if they embrace a Protestant identity. Many evangelicals, however, remain ignorant of the degree to which the magisterial Reformers valued the catholicity of the church and saw themselves moving beyond internal protest to external separation only when forced. These evangelicals remain ignorant of the Reformers' appeals to the early creeds and the true understanding of much that the ancient fathers said. Still other evangelicals trace decline much farther than aspects of the medieval church, however. They see decline almost as a perennial principle of ecclesiastical history—to the extent that doctrinal statements must be exceedingly particular for the sake of heresy prevention, and ecclesiastical division must be exceedingly regular for the sake of spiritual cure.

There is a pejorative sense of the word "biblicism" that captures some of these realities, but in my view it would be more precise to reflect on the ecclesiological issues at stake. Then we could not only confront noncreedalism, as Scot does, on the grounds that it is unbiblical—by far the most promising rhetorical strategy among evangelicals, or so I would hope! We could also confront the challenge of evangelical diversity, trying to assess to what extent we may realistically seek a pan-evangelical approach to creeds—either theologically or practically. To the extent that we may do so, perhaps contemporary realities of postdenominational American Christianity deserve reflection at least as much as outdated or knee-jerk notions of biblicism.

Now to Thesis 3, regarding just how we should associate the creeds with Scripture: *There is debate, from what I understand, in technical circles of patristic scholarship about the extent to which we should cast the rule of faith primarily in narrative terms.* Scot is right to indicate the narrative shape of the Nicene Creed, and to find parallels with 1 Corinthians 15:3–4 and the biblical Gospels. It is helpful for him to challenge us regarding the primacy of Israel's story and the tendency of the church fathers, except when they were confronting "gnosticism," to neglect this. It appears wise to root our appeals to theology more organically in the gospel and in the dramatic events of its creedal rearticulation. We do not want, for instance, theories of atonement to become rhetorically primary replacements for the creedal, ecumenical narration of the good news. Yet it is compatible with a certain focus on narrative to believe that occasional footnotes or digressions remain necessary for the story's telling—regarding the identity of the divine protagonist and the appropriate worshipful responses on the part of other participants. That is what Nicaea gives us: the law of prayer is the law of faith.

Further regarding the relation between Scripture and creed, Thesis 4: *"Theological interpretation of Scripture" refers to a varied movement or conversation, having more directly to do with scholarly fellowship than congregational life at this stage, and involving canon and culture not just creed.* People can read elsewhere what I think God might be orchestrating in the hubbub over theological interpretation; suffice it to say that certain biblical and theological scholars are finding fellowship over shared concerns—maybe in terms of questions to pursue more than answers to agree upon—among some fellow scholars rather than their churches or academic disciplines as such. For now, I'll simply say that John Stott clearly read Scripture and preached with canonical awareness, and he was a pioneer in challenging evangelicals to address culture biblically by "bridging two worlds"; so, irrespective of how frequently or focally he referenced the ecumenical creeds, Stott's reading of Scripture appears to be substantially theological. I also consider many biblical scholars' readings of and worries over theological interpretation to be overloaded on its patristic elements.

Finally, a word on Scot's pleas to follow Stott, Lewis, and Wright by writing for non-specialists. Thesis 5: *Yes, we need more "bridge" people between academy and church, but we also have to assess soberly who wants to walk across, and to where.* Trickle-down theological education has unfortunate political connotations for some of us, but also a grain of truth for all of us. Trends in contemporary evangelical churches are readily traceable to intellectual moves—or non-moves—made thirty to fifty years ago, whether or not the people who think and live out those trends have any awareness of them at all. Moreover, Lewis and Wright, at least, are the writers they are because of exceedingly classical educations, compared to our American standards, and they did not have to disregard serious scholarly writing in order to write their popular works. My own view is that their legacies speak not only to the Holy Spirit's unique ways of meeting desperate American evangelical needs—and not a little to both Anglophilia and cultural momentum—but also to the possibility that the best, most lasting popular writing comes when people don't strive too hard for relevance. The dispensationalist theologies Scot references—of which I read more than a few while growing up—were in a sense easy to digest, but to speak of their "rhetorical powers" may be a bit of a stretch. More to the point, their views of Baconian inductive methods (and the like) were inherently anti-elitist and popularizing. When we look across the landscape at other popular writers today—for instance, the "young, restless, and Reformed" phenomenon—we see that there is a modest market for fairly detailed versions of biblical truth even in somewhat dense packaging. Conversely, anecdotal evidence might suggest that, regardless of the packaging, some other evangelicals don't want to be troubled by seriously biblical theology.

So I think we need to have evangelicals writing at all three levels: serious academic scholarship, mid-level volumes of the sort Scot thinks are too numerous (and by the way, I'd love to sell 1,400 copies of most of my work!), and credible popular materials. These need not be viewed in either/or rather than both/and terms, and I suspect that the popular material of lasting value will be written by those who do not try too hard. Re-envisioning doctoral education is simultaneously a worthwhile endeavor and a struggle with the contingent arts of the possible.

Lewis, Chesterton, and the like did not see faith and reason in oppositional terms; they relished rather than resisted the mysteries of the faith that generate rational points of tension; and they had a lively sense of the staying power of God's gospel, whatever the latest cultural or churchly fads. They wrote simply because they understood so deeply, and because they mined the riches of traditional consensus Christianity rather than focusing primarily on internal divisions. Scot's positioning of the ancient creeds vis-à-vis Scripture itself offers important historical and pastoral resources for evangelicals to find that classic Christian healing. The creeds not only inform and regulate faithful, canonical interpretation; they enliven our cultural engagement by helping interpretation to orbit around the variously expressed central consensus to which they point. Thus, when I am inclined to despair, the creeds remind me of the biblical truth that Christ is Lord of the church, and even the gates of evangelical failure will not prevail against it.

7

Evangelicals and the Rule of Faith
Irenaeus on Rome and Reading Christianly

D. Jeffrey Bingham

Dallas Theological Seminary

ALLOW ME TO BE perfectly clear. I believe the future of evangelicalism is in jeopardy. My belief is linked directly to what I perceive as the subculture's movement away from, even rejection of, baptismal catechesis, particularly in its dizzying Free Church varieties. Such departures from baptismal catechesis, I believe, are at least in part responsible for recent concerns expressed about doctrinal weakness among evangelicals, the drift of "post-evangelicals" from such basic faith commitments as inerrancy and the unity of the Hebrew Bible and New Testament, and a growing openness among perhaps half of evangelicals to flirt with the idea that several religions, other than Christianity, could be salvific.[1]

Furthermore, Christine Wicker's book causes me some alarm. She argues that evangelicalism is progressively dying and being rejected by American society, partly because Americans are: "More thoughtful. More reasoning. *Less doctrinaire.* More changeable. More flexible. Less religious."[2] It seems to me irresponsible to completely reject her argument in an attempt to hold onto a nostalgic or triumphalistic notion of evangelicalism in America. If her thesis is even half true, we are facing the downward, potentially suffocating, pressure of a larger culture upon a subculture. This larger culture, to a significant degree, is, in part, "less

1. Spencer, "Coming Evangelical Collapse"; McKnight, "Ironic Faith of Emergents"; Pew Forum on Religion & Public Life, *U.S. Religious Landscape Survey*, 4.

2. Wicker, *Fall of the Evangelical Nation*, 56.

doctrinaire" and "more changeable." Here Wicker is dead right. And her analysis makes me break out in a cold sweat.

One of the ways evangelicalism continually relates to its culture is to imitate it. This suggests to me that the "less doctrinaire" and "more changeable" aspects of America will find stronger and stronger acceptance and expression within evangelicalism. No two characteristics of a society could be more in contrast to the words of Jude 3, which speak of the decisive, final, conclusive doctrine of Christianity handed down by the apostles as "the faith once for all delivered." American society in this vein is in conflict with Christianity and evangelicalism should not imitate it. Evangelicalism must not become less doctrinaire in order to become "more relevant, more practical, and more contemporary," to use the language of evangelical pop culture. The evangelical pragmatist must don the robe of ideologue. Evangelicals, at the very beginning of their spiritual journey, must be taught to embrace the essential faith claims of Christianity and they must be taught to see all of life, every text, in the light of these faith claims. They must be instructed in the art, the hermeneutic, of reading all things Christianly. Christians do not read the texts of their world as others do. They see everything through the vantage point of the apostolic teaching.

Perhaps a model from second-century Christianity will help us to understand how such a perspective works. The domination of contemporary intellectual life by the assumptions of both modernity and postmodernity prohibits our finding, I believe, a suitable model after the eighteenth century. We need to return to premodern thought, a renewed *ad fontes* journey, if you will.

In the late second-century context of Irenaeus of Lyons, a context flush with heretics, the bishop put forth a polemic in order to protect his community from the seductive, duplicitous teachings of his opponents. Against his opponents, who, he says, follow neither Scripture nor the apostolic tradition, he posits the church's singular, trustworthily preserved and received system of truth, the faith, the gospel.[3] It is this "truth," "faith," "this preaching," or "the body of truth," frequently referred to as

---

3. *Adv. haer.* 3 Pref. 3.4.2. The critical edition of *Adversus haereses* used throughout this study is *Contre les hérésies*, translated and edited by Rousseau et al. See the bibliography for a convenient, yet dated, English translation by Roberts and Rambaut. Further citations to these translations will reference the translator(s).

"the rule of truth," that the believer receives through baptism.[4] This rule
or body of truth is composed of different members, different elements of
the church's one faith.[5] Irenaeus usually only presents selected features
of the rule and it can be set forth, like Scripture, in different genres.
In one place it can be mainly didactic, while in another didactic and
narrative seem to join, with the narrative providing warrant for the didactic element.[6] A Trinitarian structure seems characteristic of the rule.[7]
In contexts more polemical, like *Adversus haereses*, Irenaeus seems to
prefer the term "rule of truth," while in catechetical contexts like the
Demonstration he seems to prefer "rule of faith."[8]

This rule is expressed in different summaries in *Adversus haereses*
1.10.1 and 1.22.1. In the first summary it is called the church's "faith,"
and in the second it is named "the rule of truth." In the second summary
a rule concerning God is expressed: "The rule of truth which we hold,
is, that there is one God Almighty, who made all things by His Word,
and fashioned and formed, out of that which had no existence, all things
which exist" (a statement of faith, it appears, inherited from Hermas).
Immediately this rule is substantiated by a network of biblical passages
which together testify to the rule: Psalm 33[32]:6; John 1:3, the Prophet
and Apostle.[9] Here we see that for Irenaeus Scripture functions as the
warrant or witness to the rule of truth. In effect, he says, we confess such
and such about God because Scripture says such and such. Indeed, to
use his words, the prophetic and apostolic Scriptures furnish "proof" for
the ecclesiological faith, tradition and practice, while the heretics have
no such "proof" for theirs.[10] Furthermore, in the mind of our bishop,
the "proofs contained in the Scriptures cannot be shown except from

---

4. *Adv. haer.* 1.9.4–10.2; 1.22.1; 2.27.1; 3.11.1; 3.12.6; 3.15.1; 4.25.1; *Dem.* 1, 3. The
critical edition of *Demonstratio* (*Epideixis*) used throughout the study is *The Proof of the
Apostolic Preaching, with Seven Fragments*, edited and translated by Mekerttshian et al.
Cf. the translations of *Démonstration de la predication apostolique* by Rousseau (1995)
and Froidevaux (1959).

5. *Adv. haer.* 1.8.1: "members of the truth."

6. E.g., *Adv. haer.* 1.10.1; 3.3.3; *Dem.* 6.

7. *Adv. haer.* 1.10.1; 1.22.1 (God and his Word); *Dem.* 6.

8. *Adv. haer.* 1.9.4; *Dem.* 3; Cf. Fantino, *La théologie d'Irénée*, 15–22.

9. See *Hermas, Man.* 1; cf. 2 Macc 7:28; Wis 1:14. Other biblical texts contributing
to the network through allusion: Col 1:16; 2 Cor 4:18; Gen 2:7; Matt 22:29; Exod 3:6.

10. *Adv. haer.* 2.32.5; 2.35.4; 3 Pref. 1; 3.5.1; 3.11.7; 3.12.9; 3.21.1, 3; 4.24.1; 4.34.5; 5
Pref.; 5.14.4; 2.28.8; 2.30.5, 7; 5.18.1.

the Scriptures themselves."[11] The church has its own belief about God and God's relation to creation. It has its own faith concerning the origin of creation, its nature, its corruption, and redemption. It has its own tradition about revelation. This faith, this tradition, has been preserved and handed down only within the church, and it is substantiated and validated only by the Scriptures.

The rule of truth and its scriptural proofs, in Irenaeus's community, were learned and received in the ritual of baptism, indicating a preparatory period with a catechetical structure.[12] Indeed, to deny the church's baptism is to renounce the church's entire faith.[13] Baptism in the church at Lyons must have involved instruction in the faith and confession of it. This baptismal reception of the rule of faith prepared the baptized believer, who retained the rule without change, to distinguish between an orthodox connection of biblical texts proving an orthodox faith-claim from an illegitimate linkage of biblical texts testifying to a corrupt and heretical faith-claim.[14]

Irenaeus's opponents frequently built their own competitive doctrines by connecting biblical passages into their own networks, which they argued gave witness to their own theses. To illustrate the heretics' perversion of the proper way to relate different parts of the Scriptures to each other, which the church alone possessed, Irenaeus employed two metaphors.[15] One was that of a mosaic. He tells a story of how a vandal can take the same individual tiles of a mosaic that an artisan used to configure a portrait of a king and rearrange them into an entirely different picture of a fox. The other metaphor was that of a Homeric cento, a literary composition using the words of Homer in connections that were not of Homer, so that Homer's words end up saying something not Homeric.

After his presentation of the illustrations of the mosaic and Homeric cento, Irenaeus provides a pivotal insight into the way in which he and his community read. Referring back to both illustrations, he argues that the ability to assemble accurately the elements of Scripture, to give the parts the proper fit, rests with the members of the community. He argues

---

11. *Adv. haer.* 3.12.9.

12. Cf. Fantino, *La théologie d'Irénée*, 20 n. 24.

13. *Adv. haer.* 1.21.1.

14. *Adv. haer.* 1.8.4.

15. *Adv. haer.* 1.8.1; 1.9.4.

that it is the baptized faithful who know how to read; the baptized who can detect and dismantle illegitimate systems:

> If anyone takes these verses [which have been removed and rearranged from Homer] and restores them to their original setting, he will make the system [created in the cento] disappear. And thus whoever keeps the rule of truth which he received through baptism, unchanged within himself, knows these names, phrases, and parables from the scriptures but does not recognize their blasphemous system. If he recognizes the stones (of the mosaic) he will not take the fox for the royal image. Setting each word in its context and adjusting it to the body of truth, he will strip it of their fiction and show their inconsistency.[16]

Reading well, in the thinking of Irenaeus, is a function of community. The reader owns and employs the fit that a community gives to a particular set of data. Ownership of this fit, or system, is received at initiation, at baptism, and should be faithfully and continually embraced and utilized. In first order, for this community, the data are the terms and passages of Scripture. These data, arranged properly, form a system, a whole, within which the parts are properly set: the canon of Scripture.

However, from Irenaeus's own exegesis, we learn that "setting each word in its setting" does not mean only placing a passage within its original literary context. That is certainly one dimension, but not the only one. As R. T. Mead wrote forty-five years ago, "'context' depends upon consensus."[17] Typically, in the community of Irenaeus, the rule of truth and all its component parts were proven, not by a single biblical proof text, but by a network of passages joined together through commonly shared terms or concepts. These networks, centos, collages, pastiches of biblical material testified to the elements of the rule of truth.[18] They formed, from different parts of Scripture, from prophetic, apostolic, and dominical words, a harmonious attestation to the church's faith. In the belief of the bishop and his community, Scripture explains Scripture. The sayings of the Lord provide commentary on the words of the apostles and prophets; the prophets shine light on the apostolic and the dominical words; the apostles illumine the Old Testament and the words of the Lord who appointed them. The immediate context of a passage provides

---

16. *Adv. haer.* 1.9.4; translation from Grant, *Irenaeus of Lyons*, 70.

17. Mead, "Dissenting Opinion," 288.

18. On these networks, centos as pastiches, see Osborn, *Irenaeus of Lyons*, 158–59.

some understanding of its testimony to the rule of truth, but other texts, from disparate parts of the canon, also bring understanding. Any text of Scripture is to be read within the larger context of the one Scripture. This is what the bishop means when he writes that the "proofs contained in the Scriptures cannot be shown except from the Scriptures themselves."[19]

Irenaeus, then, demonstrates his community's consensus that individual words and passages have connections to other biblical terms and texts.[20] These connections form intertextual networks within which different parts gain normative meaning. This should come as no surprise, for "intertextuality is built into the system" of the Christian Scriptures where the Old Testament anticipates the New and the New fulfills the Old.[21]

In some of Irenaeus's presentation of various biblical centos, which testify to the substance of the rule of truth, he manifests heretofore unrecognized relationships between texts. In other cases, he is passing on networks he has received. These relationships, for him, are implicit within the sacred text, though they are not explicitly laid out in Scripture. He displays these connections between texts, but does not replace the canon with them. They exist within the canon, which by its very nature is intertextual. His labor, then, supplements the networks of biblical texts he has received. This is necessary in every age. As new perversions of the faith arise, theologians display anew the biblical testimony that supports the church's faith and dismisses the heresies of false teachers.

For Irenaeus the rule of truth and its biblical testimony were received in baptism. Baptism does not only pass on to the baptized the rule of truth and its scriptural proof, but also the ability to recognize and shun the heresy of the community's opponents. Baptism passed on to them a way of reading. Baptism and what is received in it contains the spectacles through which they are to read Scriptures, the heretics, and the structures and events of their world. They are Christians of the rule and they read and comprehend by means of the rule. Allow me to demonstrate this dynamic at work in Irenaeus. As my example, I have selected Rome and the Roman Empire. His reading of these structures demonstrates helpfully the role of the rule of truth in his hermeneutic of life.

19. *Adv. haer.* 3.12.9.

20. I have developed this more fully in Bingham, *Irenaeus' Use of Matthew's Gospel*, 303–5.

21. Stroumsa, "Christian Hermeneutical Revolution," 19.

Reading the Roman Empire and Rome

Writing his *Adversus haereses* under Commodus ca. 180, Irenaeus employs his view of the city of Rome and the Roman Empire within his polemic against his opponents. We know from Eusebius, whose report was aptly defended by Paul Keresztes, that under Commodus Christians enjoyed a general peace common to the empire.[22] Commodus's reign was anything but just and anything but popular if we listen to Dio's account.[23] But, although some may have found life uncomfortable in Rome, the provinces experienced a peace rarely broken and the Christians experienced a calm only sporadically spoiled by persecution.[24] Irenaeus knew of the fierce persecution of 177 which had enveloped the Christian communities of Lyons and Vienne.[25] He had been a presbyter of Lyons and had barely escaped the terror. At the time of the persecution he was in Rome, having served as courier for a letter from Lyons to the Roman bishop Eleutherius.[26] But, under Commodus, he found relief from persecution and turned his attention fully to a polemic against his opponents. My question is: What does he have to say about Rome and the Empire within this context? And, how does his manner of reading Rome and the Romans help us come to grips with reading him?

In *Adversus haereses*, when Irenaeus speaks of "the Romans," he most often has Paul's epistle in mind.[27] His overwhelming usage of the phrase refers to the Christian community addressed by the apostle. Likewise, when he speaks of "Rome," he often has in mind the church of Rome founded and organized by the apostles Peter and Paul.[28] In addition, he speaks once of Paul's journey to Rome and of his being in Rome after the manner of Luke's account, and of Polycarp's coming to Rome where he turned many away from the heretics.[29] Otherwise, his interest

22. Eusebius, *Eccl. Hist.* 5.21.1; P. Keresztes, "Favourable Aspect of the Emperor Commodus' Rule, 368–77."

23. Dio Cassius, *Roman Histories,* 72–73.

24. Cf. Keresztes, "Favourable Aspect," 368–77; Weber, "Antonines," 384.

25. Eusebius, *Eccl. Hist.* 5.1–3. The letter might very well have been authored by Irenaeus himself (see *Nautin, Lettres et écrivains chrétiens,* 54–61).

26. Eusebius, *Eccl. Hist.* 5.4.1–2.

27. *Adv. haer.* 2.22.2; 3.16.3, 9; 22.1, 2; 4.21.2; 29.1; 34.2; 36.6; 37.1; 5.7.1; 10.2; 14.4; 32.1.

28. *Adv. haer.* 3.1.1; 3.2, 3.

29. *Adv. haer.* 3.14.1.

in the city pivots around the history of the heretics coming to Rome. He mentions, in particular, Marcellina, Cerdon, Marcion, and Valentinus.[30]

Irenaeus recounts the chronology of the heretics and their relationship to Rome by correlating the periods of the heretics' activities in the city with the corresponding periods of Roman bishops. He focuses upon this chronology in order to show that the doctrine the heretics brought to Rome was much later than the doctrine passed on to Linus by Peter and Paul. This lateness in the heretics' doctrine and its divergence from the apostles' doctrine passed on to Linus warrants its rejection. We shall return to this interest of his in some detail below.

The majority of Irenaeus's references to Rome or the Romans, then, have to do with the city as the locale of that great and ancient church founded by the two great apostles, Peter and Paul. Its earliest doctrine prior to the coming of the heretics is the true apostolic tradition and this tradition has been passed down faithfully and with integrity from Roman bishop to Roman bishop, who are in succession to the apostles. With this history the church of Rome functions as a model of true doctrine and has an exemplary role in the preservation of the truth within the Western church.[31]

But what of his view of the Roman Empire? Does he hold the same view, say, that we would find in a Cicero, whose Stoicism, with its confidence in reason and law, governs his high appraisal? A. B. Bozeman summarized that perspective this way: "Along with most other contemporary Romans, Cicero thought of [the Roman Empire] not only as an administrative unity, but also as that superior human association in which all individual aspirations could find expression."[32] Or is his view overwhelmingly critical due to his bitter experience with the persecution of 177? Neither, really, as we shall see. His theological construct of the divine economy reduced, for him, the prominence of the Empire so that it becomes a device by which he explains the catholic faith. The economy is that providential, "powerful, mysterious drama of change" through which the Father by his Word and Spirit orchestrates the history

30. *Adv. haer.* 1.25.6; 27.1; 3.4.3.

31. See *Adv. haer.* 3.3.2–3; and cf. N. Brox's interpretation of the hotly debated passage of 3.3.2 (N. Brox, "Rom und 'jede Kirche,'" 42–78. See Donovan, "Irenaeus in Recent Scholarship," 238–40, for a quick orientation to the debate.

32. Bozeman, *Politics and Culture*, 187.

of creation, humanity, salvation, revelation, and of nations.[33] It is a center point of Irenaeus's theology.[34] Compelled, then, by faith to see history in this light, the bishop understands the particulars of history always as parts of the whole drama conveyed to him in the apostles' teaching. My questions, then, are: What does he have to say about Rome and the Empire within the context of his polemic? How does his way of reading Rome and the Romans help us come to grips with his way of reading? And how does his manner of reading Rome and the Empire demonstrate the role of the rule of faith in all of his interpretative activity?

Reading the Roman Empire

"The best-known fact about the Roman Empire is that it declined and fell."[35] As Irenaeus thinks theologically about the Roman Empire, he seems to know something about this fact. He doesn't appear overwhelmingly impressed. In some cases he speaks of it in flattering tones, but the flattery is quickly replaced by the theological/polemical point for which, it becomes clear, he is merely exploiting the Roman Empire. His thoughts, at other times, instead of going to the glories of Roman history, go to redemptive history, and there the turn can be quite negative. He takes the reader back into pre-Roman history, a history that anticipates Christianity, and then forward into the history that is to come in the last days, a history that, at the very least, moves beyond that of Rome, and at most, might condemn it.

In *Adversus haereses* 2.6.2 Irenaeus is involved in refuting the Valentinian thesis of a Pleroma superior to the Creator-God.[36] He will raise the issue of the Empire to aid his polemic against the Valentinian view of the Father. The Valentinians believe that the Father of the Pleroma contains all things within himself, but that the material creation was formed by a Demiurge or angels distant from the Father.[37] Furthermore, they argue that this Demiurge or these angels were ignorant of the Supreme Father and indeed of all spiritual forms and es-

33. Osborn, *Irenaeus of Lyons*, 94. See for his entire discussion on "economy," 49–94. Also see Fantino, *La théologie d'Irénée*, 85–264.

34. Osborn, *Irenaeus of Lyons*, 78; Fantino, *La théologie d'Irénée*, 204–64.

35. Starr, *Roman Empire*, 3.

36. See 62.26–30.

37. *Adv. haer.* 1.5.1–6.

sences.[38] Irenaeus rhetorically questions these two beliefs: "How, again, could either the angels or the Creator of the world, have been ignorant of the Supreme God, seeing they were His property, and His creatures, and were contained by Him?"[39] Irenaeus reasons that if the Father of the Pleroma contains all things, then all things, including the distant Creator, must know something of him. Although in his spiritual superiority the Father would be invisible, by his providence, his extended dominion over all things, the Demiurge and angels would have some intuitive perception of the Father.[40]

As an illustration of his principle of knowledge of a ruler through the ruler's providential government, he offers the example of the Roman Empire. He writes,

> By way of parallel, shall not those who live under the empire of the Romans, although they have never seen the emperor, but are far separated from him both by land and sea, know very well, as they experience his rule, who it is that possesses the principal power of the state?[41]

From the rhetorical question to the analogy he draws between the Creator and Emperor a transition in his argument has occurred. He no longer simply refutes the heretics' thesis, but also presents the orthodox conception of God. The analogy between Emperor and Creator serves, then, to refute the Valentinian reasoning and to support the church's faith. Two points come forth: (1) the absurdity of a supreme divine being who "contains everything," yet is limited externally, that is, whose power is unknown to some; and (2) the reasonableness of the one true God who although separate from creation, still holds sway over all things and whose greatness is perceived by the creation.[42]

---

38. *Adv. haer.* 1.5.3, 4; 2.3.1; 6.1.

39. *Adv. haer.* 2.6.1 (Roberts and Rambaut, 365).

40. Ibid.

41. *Adv. haer.* 2.6.2; (Roberts and Rambaut, 365).

42. For further treatment of *Adv. haer.* 2.6.1–2 see Greer, "Dog and the Mushrooms," 159; Schoedel, "Enclosing, Not Enclosed," 80; Norris, "Transcendence and Freedom of God," 94–95. On the basis of Irenaeus's use of *Ratio* in 2.6.1 (Rousseau, 294:60.16) it seems that he is not offering a natural theology, but a revelation of God through the Word's (*logos*) operation in providence. The Word mediates God's containment of all things perceived by the creation. Cf. *Adv. haer.* 4.6.1–7 (Rousseau, 100.2:220); Escoula, "Saint Irénée et la connaissance naturelle de Dieu," 252–58; Audet, "Orientations Théologiques chéz Saint Irénée," 33–39; Ochagavia, *Visibile Patris Filius*, 77–80.

Here, Irenaeus's mention of the Roman Empire and emperor shows his recognition of that emperor's full and sovereign control of his territories. From it, he develops a commonality of principle between the secular government and the government of the divine Creator. His purpose, however, is thoroughly theological. His employment of this principle arises specifically within his anti-Valentinian polemic.

A similar exploitation of the virtue of the Empire takes place in his discussion of Israel and the spoils of the Egyptians.[43] Irenaeus praises the accomplishments of the Empire as he refutes an interpretation of Israel's leaving Egypt with the spoils of the Egyptians (Exod 3:21–22; 11:2; 12:35–36) held by the Marcionites and others among his opponents.[44] As Tertullian relates, the Marcionites used the event to substantiate their thesis of contradiction between the Creator and the good God, Christ's Father.[45] They charge the Creator with instituting fraud and injustice against the Egyptians, for their belongings are unjustly demanded of them. Too, they point to the antithesis between the Creator's command to spoil the Egyptians and Christ's command to his disciples that they take not even a staff (Luke 9:3/Matt 10:10).

Irenaeus, in particular, faces the heretics' charge that Israel in spoiling the Egyptians acted in an unjust manner.[46] In *Adversus haereses* 4.30.1–3 he counters the charge by arguing: (1) that the Egyptians were in debt to the Israelites and owed them much more than they took; and (2) that the Israelites were a type of the church, for the church also benefits materially from the society, culture, and business of the Gentiles.[47] Then, he continues in 4.30.3 to point out to the heretics that they too benefit from the material of others and it is against them that the Lord spoke his rebuke against hypocrites (Matt 7:5/Luke 6:42). By such a

43. *Adv. haer.* 4.30.3.

44. Cf. Orbe's insistence that Irenaeus's language of *gloriatur in sua scientia* ("boasts in one's 'gnosis'"; *Adv. haer.* 4.20.3) indicates that Irenaeus's accusation stands against both Marcionite and Gnostic. Orbe, *Parábolas Evangélicas en San Ireneo*, 2:214 n. 34.

45. Tertullian, *Adv. Marc.* 2.20.1–4; 4.24.1; see the commentary on 2.20 in *Contre Marcion*, edited and translated by Braun, 2:224–27.

46. Cf. *Adv. haer.* 4.30.2 (Rousseau, 10.2:776.42, 778.61). The editors apparently prefer the Armenian, which would translate into *injustus*. The essence of the charge remains the same.

47. See for commentary on this argument: Bacq, *De l'ancienne à la nouvelle Alliance selon S. Irénée*, 212–14; Orbe, *Parábolas Evangélicas*, 2:207–16; Clarke, "Irenaeus *Adv. haer.* 4.30.1, 95–97"

hypocritical charge against the church they show themselves unjust. And it was against this type of judgment that results in judgment of self that the Lord spoke the words of Matt 7:1–2: "Do not judge, in order not to be judged, for, in the manner which you judge, you will be judged yourselves."

His argument of the church's material benefit from the society, culture, and business of the Gentiles specifies the good fortune the Mediterranean territory experienced under Roman rule. He writes that through the Romans "the world is at peace, and we can walk without fear and sail where we wish."[48] He unabashedly recognizes the benefits of Roman rule experienced by all within the Empire. He is not, however, praising the Roman peace and order for the purpose of loyalty to the emperor. His purpose is to refute the heretics by causing them to see their hypocrisy. They accuse the Jewish God and the church of fraud and injustice when they too benefit without merit from the bounty of others. Again, his reading of the virtue of the Empire of the Romans is polemically motivated as he develops his theology in the face of the theses of his opponents. But his reading of Rome can also turn supercessionist. He minimizes the contemporary state by highlighting instead the catholic understanding of history's movement toward the church and history's movement toward the final state of things, which either merely anticipates the Roman Empire or supersedes it. Regardless, the catholic view of things causes the Empire of Rome to recede into the background.

In the third book of *Adversus haereses* he discusses the prophecy of Isaiah 7:14, which Theodotion the Ephesian, Aquila of Pontus, and the Ebionites understand to refer to a "young woman" who conceives.[49] The church, on the other hand, follows the Septuagint, which translates, not "young woman," but "virgin," thus supporting the faith in a virginal conception. Irenaeus provides a historical account of both the giving of the original prophecy and of its translation into Greek in order to counter any notion that "virgin" is a biased translation.

First, he points out that the original prophecy is old, given long before the founding of Christianity. Isaiah uttered the prophecy prior to the Babylon captivity and prior to the rule of the Medes and Persians. Second, the Jews, not the church, translated the prophecy, for the seventy elders sent to Ptolemy were Jewish. Third, the translation took

---

48. *Adv. haer.* 4.30.3.

49. *Adv. haer.* 3.21.2–3.

place under Ptolemy prior to the time of Christianity because (1) it was done "before the Romans possessed their kingdom while as yet the Macedonians held Asia," and (2) because "our Lord was born about the forty-first year of the reign of Augustus; but Ptolemy was much earlier, under whom the Scriptures were interpreted."[50]

In this reference to the Roman Empire, Irenaeus is concerned with establishing a chronological context in order to validate the church's faith. He gives no role of prominence to the Roman Empire, but rather insinuates that a central sacred event, the translation of the Septuagint, took place before it came to power. In Irenaeus's mind, several kingdoms have ruled the Holy Land: Babylon, the Medes and Persians, the Macedonians, and finally the Romans. The current empire is given no rank of prominence, for others have ruled the same territory before. Christianity may have sprouted up in the days of the Romans, but there is a sacred history that precedes their Empire, and the church's faith descends from that history.

In moving his thought from the past to the future, Irenaeus speaks of "the Empire which now rules"[51] This identity sets the Roman Empire within a procession of world kingdoms. The past kingdoms of Babylon, the Medes and the Persians, and the Macedonians he has already mentioned.[52] They were *before* the Romans. Now, in the present context he also thinks of the future kingdoms of the last times predicted in John's Apocalypse. In Irenaeus's understanding, the ten kings of Revelation 17:12–14 are the ten toes of the statue in Daniel 2 and the ten horns of the beast in Daniel 7.[53] In his understanding, these future kings and kingdoms arise through the division of the kingdom currently reigning in Irenaeus's day.[54]

This partitioning of the Roman Empire among ten other kings leads to its demise, for he also believes the Lord's word of Matthew 12:25 applies to the eschatological division of this kingdom. There the Lord had said: "Every kingdom divided against itself is laid waste, and no city or house divided against itself will stand."[55] The division of the kingdom

50. *Adv. haer.* 3.21.2; 3.21.3 (Roberts and Rambaut, 451, 452).
51. *Adv. haer.* 5.26.1.
52. *Adv. haer.* 3.21.2.
53. *Adv. haer.* 5.25.1—5.26.1.
54. *Adv. haer.* 5.26.1.
55. Ibid.

is a necessary step to the Lord's final destruction of the eschatological kings and beast when he returns after the manner of Revelation 19 and 2 Thessalonians 2. Therefore Irenaeus, in interpreting Matthew 12:25, writes: "For that kingdom must be divided, and thus come to ruin."[56] The Lord's destruction of the kings and beast in their divided state is the Lord's destruction of the Roman Empire from which they came. Irenaeus also sees this final destruction predicted in Daniel 2:44–45, where the kingdom that God raises up shatters and destroys all the previous kingdoms.[57]

The final destiny of the Roman Empire for Irenaeus is division and defeat. It merely stands as one of several kingdoms in procession, each of which has been or will be destroyed by a subsequent kingdom. As it was for Babylon, the Medes and Persians, and the Macedonians, so it will be for the Romans. In Irenaeus's reading of Daniel, Christ, will "destroy temporal kingdoms, and introduce an eternal one, which is the resurrection of the just; as he declares, 'The God of heaven shall raise up a kingdom which shall never be destroyed.'"[58] The Roman Empire is but one of several temporal, passing kingdoms. A greater one is coming.

Irenaeus's discussion of the Romans arises only within his polemic against the heretics. This time, he manifests, through the demonstrated continuity of message between the prophet Daniel, the apostle John, and the Lord himself, the unity of the one who is God of the prophets and God of the apostles and Lord. In so doing he reduces expectations for the current Empire and heightens an eschatological hope. This same strategy appears again in another discussion of the Empire.[59] The point this time, however, is a bit more negative. He moves from just de-emphasizing the ultimate historical importance of the Empire of the Romans to defaming (one might say demonizing) it.

In his treatment of the apocalyptic number 666 he advises that it is better not to speculate on the meaning or referent of the number, but to await the prediction's fulfillment. However, he can't resist offering a few examples of how mathematically one might identify some names whose letters total 666. One of these is the name *Lateinos*. He writes, "Then also *Lateinos* has the number six hundred and sixty-six; and it is com-

---

56. Ibid.

57. Ibid.

58. *Adv. haer.* 5.26.2 (Roberts and Rambaut, 555).

59. *Adv. haer.* 5.30.3.

pletely worthy of credence, since the last kingdom precisely possessed this name: because these are those Latin's who rule at this moment; however I will not boast in this credible solution."[60] Irenaeus thinks there is good reason to see the antichrist coming from the Romans, but he does not press his solution too far. It is credible, but not certain, for the prophecy awaits fulfillment. Here the bishop presents a view of the Roman Empire that places it in the center of apocalyptic eschatology. It is entirely conceivable that the Romans will give birth to the archenemy of God's people in the last days. Once again, the polemicist of Lyons sees his world through eyes apocalyptically tinged.

The catholic reads all contemporary history in light of a particular eschatological expectation, a peculiar view of history, and a distinct conception of the divine. These perspectives, forming together a unique vantage point and contained within the community's faith commitments, inform all that the orthodox believer sees.

Reading Rome

According to Eusebius, Rome, the imperial city, was under siege in the days of Claudius Caesar, during the time of the apostle Peter's preaching. The armies were not those of Carthage or the barbarians, of course, but of "the enemy of humanity's salvation" led by Simon Magus (*Hist. Eccl.* 2.12.1). Bringing Simon to Rome and strengthening him, this enemy, Eusebius tells us, "took possession of many people in Rome and led them astray." The historian's source for his claim was Justin Martyr, who in his first *Apology* (1.26) had described Simon and his activity as exemplary of a demonically orchestrated deception. Simon, notes the apologist, had been lifted up as a god by the residents of the "imperial city of Rome," who even honored the Samaritan magician with a statue in the Tiber.

Simon's first encounter with the Christian message took place within Samaria, either in the city of Sebaste or Gitta (Acts 8:4). From there, Eusebius says (*Hist. Eccl.* 1.2.14), he fled, embarking upon a long journey from "east to west," finally arriving at Rome where the demonic powers were waiting to begin their assault of duplicity by empowering

60. Ibid. This English translation influenced by the French of Rousseau, 4:381–83, and by Roberts and Rambaut, 559. Rousseau et al. provide "ce mot" as the referent of the Latin's *in hoc*. Roberts and Rambaut provide, in brackets, "coincidence." The point seems to be that the bishop will not press the probability too far, because the solution is unknown. Cf. Orbe, *Teologiá de San Ireneo*, 3:268.

Simon. However, maneuvering against Simon and the demons came Peter, outfitted in the armor of God, and brought to Rome in the time of Claudius, by the gracious and kind "providence of the universe." He too traveled from the East to the West, bringing with him spiritual light.

Unknown to Claudius, but recorded by the Christian apologists Justin and Eusebius, Rome was the location of a cosmic conflict between God and the fallen angels. This Western urban center found itself, in the Christian consciousness, as the field into which spiritual strategists had maneuvered their troops from the East to do battle.

This peculiar perception of Rome as the location of cosmic warfare in the time of Claudius is already anticipated in an early Christian interpretation of the city during Nero's reign. This ruler, we are told (*Hist. Eccl.* 2.23.1–3), "took up arms against the God of the universe" in his impious, murderous deeds, and became the first emperor to be "declared the enemy of the worship of God."[61] Tertullian, the Roman, Eusebius specifies, provided him the warrant for such an account of Nero's rule, a rule that especially manifested its cruelty "in Rome (*Apol.* 5)." Nero, then, as God's antagonist, expressed his hostility by murdering in Rome both the apostles Peter and Paul, whose monuments according to Gaius (*Dial.*) were still visible within the city during the third century.[62] Rome is the urban battlefield upon which the enemies of God enter into combat with God's forces. Again, Christian polemicists, Tertullian now being enlisted alongside Eusebius and Justin, read the story of Rome with spectacles tinted with shades of spiritual warfare.

This reading of mid-first-century Rome by the fourth-century historian, who employed Christian sources from the mid second and early third century, appears again as also characteristic of Rome under Commodus towards the end of the second century. As Eusebius gives a brief account of the peaceful times under Commodus and the conversions to "the God of the universe" that were are taking place among the upper-class within Rome, the positive narrative is unexpectedly disrupted (*Hist. Eccl.* 5.21), in the reader's mind, by Apollonius's martyrdom. But for Eusebius, the departure from the peace is expected, for "the demon who hates things and is by nature envious" is unable to bear this shifting of forces from his kingdom to God's. So the demon "strips" himself for combat and presses a multidirectional attack, which involves

61. Cf. *Hist. Eccl.* 3.17 on Domitian as Nero's successor.
62. Cf. *Hist. Eccl.* 3.1.3.

on one front the cruel arrest, trial, and death of the prominent Christian Apollonius in Rome.

Such perceptions of the city of Rome as a battlefield, or a coliseum, circus, amphitheater, or arena in which gladiatorial combat takes place, is quite different from the way in which Rome would have been seen by others. These early Christian perspectives, these readings of the urban center as the space of cosmological, spiritual conflict, are off center from the opinion of the Stoic Epictetus, who sees anthropology, defined by *polis*. Epictetus, a resident of Rome, saw humanness as interconnectedness with the urban:

> "What are you?" he asks. And then he answers, "A human being."
> If you see yourself as something separate, it is natural for you to
> want to live to old age, to be rich, and to enjoy health. But if you
> regard yourself as human and as a part of some whole, for the
> sake of that whole you may have to suffer illness, make a voyage
> and run risks, be in want, and even die before your time. Why
> then are you vexed? Do you not know that as a foot, if detached,
> will no longer be a foot, so you too, if detached will no longer
> be a part of humanity? For what is a human being? [A human
> being is] A part of a city; first that [universal city] of the gods and
> men and then that city which is very close to it, the city that is a
> miniature of the universal one.[63]

One of the fundamental principles of his philosophy, stressing the faculty of will, was that the citizen should create concord in the city (*Golden Sayings* 148). Despite his emphasis on the universe and universal citizenship, we still find him advocating the localized urban setting (*Golden Sayings* 15). And Stoicism laid the foundation for a Roman philosophy of cities in other ways. As Donald Engels has shown through Cicero's *De Legibus*, the Stoic notion of universal, natural law, which humans shared with the gods, is reflected by cities in their optimistic idea of a universal recognition of justice and virtue.

These Stoic ideals had important consequences for cities. They not only informed the law codes, but also the public policies that made classical cities unique. Supplies of clean water, often brought in from distances at great expense, paved streets, sewage disposal, public art, public baths, and numerous other public facilities, all reflect, however

---

63. Epictetus, *Discourses* 2.5.25–26; translation from Engels, *Roman Corinth*, front matter.

imperfectly, the Stoic ideals of public service and rational planning that embodied the will of God himself.[64]

Cities, then, for the classical Roman, were not "centers of evil," but, instead, as for Cicero, the city was "the highest creation of nature and reason."[65] The city is "the physical and institutional embodiment" of the Stoic virtues which reflect a life lived in harmony with what nature reveals.[66] Due to the natural reason and virtue that humanity shared with the gods, there was no collective sense of being evil, no perception of the urban as without virtue. To live in the city was to impart and receive the benefits of reasonable virtue, for within the city one finds the opportunity and means for health, justice, and beauty through, in addition to sources mentioned earlier, gymnasiums, markets, public physicians, participation in government, punishment of crimes, architecture, public entertainment and other pleasures.[67]

The city of course was by no means perfect.[68] Police matters could, at times, just as well be the responsibility of private citizens. Justice frequently needed to be pursued by the victim, and private contractors were available to hurry along the process. Although elements of the military would, particularly with Augustus, perform police functions, "if a rich man went out at night, he took private body guards with him. The poor man took his chances."[69] Medical care, of course, in the ancient city sometimes was based upon superstitions, sometimes upon a variety of folk remedies. Such haphazard approaches resulted in an urban environment filled with the open display of wounds, illnesses, and misery. But whereas sickness was widespread and visible, education was usually privileged. The pupil, normally a male child of the upper class, was schooled by a slave, hired educator, the colleagues of his father, or within a club.

The ideal of the city as the incarnation of virtue endured despite such harsh realities. In order to provide the desired benefits, planning for outlays of streets, use of space, and urban infrastructure was given

64. Engels, *Roman Corinth*, 7.

65. Ibid., 135.

66. Ibid., 88–89.

67. Ibid., 88.

68. The following discussion is informed by Stambaugh, *Ancient Roman City*, 123–41.

69. Ibid., 126.

its just due. In keeping with the Stoic ideal, urban planning sought to provide services, amenities, and facilities in optimal placement for the most advantageous quality of life for the citizens.[70]

Of first importance, of course, were the walls, especially before the *pax Romana*, and terrain that provided natural defensive properties frequently determined location. In addition to providing security, walls were symbols of independence, of prestige, and served also as civil monuments. Walls and their gates could be important also for determining placement of forums, shops, and markets, but could not be said to limit urban occupation. Suburbs were intimately related to cities and could serve as typical locations for cemeteries, industrial establishments, stadia, amphitheaters, circuses, gardens, temples, schools, baths, libraries, gymnasia, and for the elite, country homes.

Though the walls provided security, symbolism, and certain limits, facilities and social structures, both urban and suburban, existed to provide and express community. Although communication by message outside the city could be dreadfully slow, in some cases taking a letter a month to reach its destination as it was carried by a slave or acquaintance, inner-city communication was quite efficient. Social networks, formal state announcements, postings within the forums, public presentations, signs, graffiti, temple inscriptions, sculptures, and inscriptions on various monuments throughout the city all sped the passing along of information.[71] Forums with their enclosed areas served as commercial, religious, and administrative centers. Temples, theaters, and public buildings all serving the community's religious interests could be found throughout the Roman city. Under Augustus, the baths featured lectures and readings and public libraries were opened. Rome's citizens profited from these public opportunities for further education.[72] Even more than in the Greek city, the Roman city recognized the benefit the population received from entertainment. Roman urban life included normative baths, games, and shows as spaces for relaxation and social networking opportunities. In his description of the Roman baths, Stambaugh writes:

> The grand scale, the imposing technology, the marble revetments,
> the Greek architectural details applied to Roman concrete walls,
> the copies of Greek sculpture distributed throughout, made of

70. Owens, *City in the Roman World*, 149–63.

71. Stambaugh, *Ancient Roman City*, 139–41.

72. Ibid., 139.

such baths a museum, a cultural center, a political statement that declared the glory of Rome and its emperors as eloquently as the monuments in the Forum.

For a minimal admission fee, all this luxury was available for anyone who wanted to enjoy it. In these "villas of the poor," the commoner found opportunities for exercise, swimming, steam baths, saunas, sex, gossip, lectures, and poetry readings. The towel-draped nudity of the bathers must have contributed considerably to a perception of social leveling . . . (Petronius, *Satyricon* 27–28).

Customers had a wide variety of exercises to choose from, from lifting weights and playing ball to swimming and receiving a massage. . . . Service personnel were available to give massages, to pluck hair, and to sell cakes, sausages, and bath oil (Seneca, *Epistulae Morales* 61.1–2).[73]

Roman hydraulic technology not only allowed for survival, but nurtured, as a civic amenity, the urban population's well-being physically, emotionally, and psychologically. Fountains, gardens, baths, and even public latrines were social facilities, yes, but they were also adorned to be pleasing to the eye and spirit as well. Pliny was so impressed with Rome's sanitation system that he "managed to express the thought (*Natural History* 36.104) that of everything in Rome, the sewers were 'the most noteworthy thing of all.'"[74] The city in all its aspects, with all the planning put into it, existed not by accident, but by design and purpose, in order to provide an urban setting of communal welfare, felicity, and harmony. Although Rome exhibited a collection of social levels ranging from the impoverished to the wealthy, the public areas were open to all and provided all Romans "a share in their grandeur."[75]

Yet, in the polemic of Irenaeus of Lyons, the city of Rome is not presented as a haven of communal well-being. Christopher Kelly, in his essay "Empire Building," might refer to Rome as "the most important place in the Roman Empire" prior to the dedication of Constantinople in 330, but the bishop of Lyons was not so impressed.[76] E. J. Owens could write that for both the Greeks and Romans, "city was synonymous with civilization and in opposition to barbarity and chaos," but Irenaeus is

73. Ibid., 204–5.
74. Ibid., 133.
75. Ibid., 141.
76. In Bowerstock et al., *Late Antiquity*, 170.

not so sure.[77] And Thucydides might argue that the city is the structure that can guarantee safety and order, yet Irenaeus is skeptical.[78] In
the thought of Irenaeus, the urban environment of Rome is a breeding ground for heresy and doctrinal corruption. In his essay on the role
of physicians in cities of the Roman Empire, which helps us, perhaps,
understand Irenaeus's concern with a megalopolis, R. Jackson, making a somewhat obvious point, writes: "cities, as places of concentrated
population, facilitate the spread of disease."[79] For Irenaeus, the same was
true of unorthodox teaching. It flourished in areas of high population
density. Furthermore, Jackson says, the city also provided for a larger
"market," and this in turn allowed for a patient to "shop" among several
different physicians with different specialties.[80] Rome, in the eyes of the
Gallic heresiologist, provided a similar "*supermarché*" for a variety of
false teachers. Continuing his discussion on physicians within the ancient urban setting of Rome, Jackson goes on to point out that such a
context also contributed to the survivability of hoaxers and imposters.
"Galen paints a gloomy picture of Rome in his day," he notes, "where the
anonymity of the big city allowed incompetents to prosper and charlatans to avoid exposure."[81]

The idea of charlatans who can hide and skirt detection within the
bustling, crowded city runs parallel to one of Irenaeus's main ideas about
heresy's characteristic features. Immediately in his preface to the first
book of *Adversus haereses*, and then also later in the same book (1.3.6;
1.8.1; 1.9.4), Irenaeus describes his opponents as those who with duplicity and seduction draw the simple away from the apostles' teaching with
their plausible falsification of the Scripture's words.[82] Their error has a
disguised nature. Only by concealing its falsehood through cleverly, but
deceitfully, devised presentations of the church's terminology does it
survive, prosper, and captivate those who are unaware. He explains that
error does not present itself in open display, for if it is exposed or dis-

77. Owens, *City in the Roman World*, 1.

78. Thucydides, *History of the Peloponnesian War* 1.2.

79. Jackson, "Role of Doctors in the City," 202.

80. Ibid.

81. Ibid., 208; Galen, *On Prognosis* 14.621–3K, 178–80.

82. See Bingham, *Irenaeus' Use of Matthew's Gospel*, 13–15, 18–21; cf. Le Boulluec,
La notion d'hérésie dans la littérature grecque, 1:218–24; Hefner, "Theological
Methodology and St. Irenaeus," 297–99.

robed it will be detected as untrue. Instead, error must wear an attractive costume so that through its fraudulent exterior it may dupe the simple. To illustrate and ground his perspective in the tradition he brings up the words of an elder and of the Lord (Matt 7:15) which provide metaphorical embellishment for the reality: error is like a counterfeit, glass emerald, a silver alloy, or wolves cloaked in the skin of sheep. Someone skilled must come along and debunk the charade or the heretics will lead away those not strong in the faith. Later (*Adv. haer.* 1.8.1; 1.9.4), as we noted above, he will originally introduce two additional metaphors that are informed by the earlier metaphor from the Lord's saying, but which more picturesquely portray the rearrangement of the elements of Scripture. The first is the one of a mosaic. Irenaeus's opponents are pictured as those who plausibly adapt or transfer the words of Scripture from their true, catholic order into a fable. The second is a Homeric cento. The Valentinians have likewise transferred the names and sayings of Scripture into their own composition and formed a different system from the orthodox one. The astute orthodox believer would recognize the parts of Scripture, but not the foreign motif, theme, or system.

Although in these contexts Irenaeus does not specifically link the density of the city to the effectiveness of the duplicity of his opponents, it seems it is not far from his thinking and we can see a parallel with Justin's comments in *1 Apology* 1.26 discussed above. We may catch a glimpse of this line of thought when, in his introduction to the father of all heresy, Simon the Samaritan, citing Acts 8:9–11, he seems to highlight the origin of heresy in *the city* of Samaria through the popularity of his witchcraft among the urban populace. He writes:

> Simon, the Samaritan, was the famous magician of whom Luke, the disciple and follower of the apostles, said: "But there was a man, named Simon, who had previously practiced magic *in the city*, and led the people of Samaria astray, proclaiming that he himself was some great person. The residents of the city, from the least to the greatest, gave careful attention to him saying, this man is the power of God, which is called great. And they gave careful attention to him, because over a long time he had cast a spell over them with his sorcery."[83]

Furthermore, he goes on goes on to say that Simon "feigned faith" and that he did not truly believe in God but rather "intended to contend

---

83. *Adv. haer.* 1.23.1. Emphasis mine.

against the apostles, in order that he himself also might *appear renowned.*
So he devoted himself the study of all sorcery, so that he might *thoroughly bewitch and overpower the crowds of people.*" Simon is presented
as inaugurating his error within an urban setting in which he sought to
be received as a famous, powerful sorcerer by the city's residents, while,
in fact, he was nothing more than a charlatan.

Furthermore, his connection between the charlatans of heresy and
the city comes forth particularly as he develops the history of heresy in
Rome in other portions of his work. Because of that history, for him, the
city falls short of the stoic ideal.

For instance, in his account of the doctrines of Carpocrates, who
lived under Hadrian either in Asia Minor or Alexandria, we find him
telling us, with obvious distaste and disapproval, about a group who
branded their disciples on the inside of the right ear lobe (*Adv. haer.*
1.25.6).[84] This same group also employed their own icons in their devotions, perhaps including ones of Christ, and exalted them alongside images of the world's philosophers.[85] This group, he says, labeled themselves
Gnostics, and within his description of their peculiarities he names one
Marcellina, a teacher among the Carpocratians, and the leader of the
Marcellians, known to Celsus (Origen, *Con. Cels.* 5.62). A disciple of
Carpocrates, she established the western extension of his school with its
syncretistic iconic worship in Rome during the episcopate of Anicetus
(155–66), perhaps around the same time that Polycarp arrived to discuss
the date of Easter (*Adv. haer.* 1.25.6; 3.3.4; Eusebius, *Hist. Eccl.* 4.14).

Before Marcellina, there was Cerdo, who Irenaeus says took his beliefs from Simon's followers (*Adv. haer.* 1.27.1). He arrived in Rome during the episcopacy of Hyginus, and was succeeded in Rome by Marcion
of Pontus. Marcion, Irenaeus says, developed Cerdo's doctrine, which
distinguished the Father of Jesus Christ from the God of the law and
the prophets. (*Adv. haer.* 1.27.1–2: cf. 3.4.3). He, we are told, flourished
under Anicetus. Valentinus, too, Irenaeus tells us, came to Rome while
Hyginus was bishop. He flourished under Hyginus's successor, Pius, and
remained in the imperial city until the episcopacy of Anicetus.

---

84. For Carpocrates see Hippolytus, *Philos.* 7.32; Clement of Alexandria, *Stromateis*
3.5; Epiphanius, *Panarion* 25; Eusebius, *Hist. Eccl.* 4.7.

85. Cults of images were somewhat popular within other Gnostic groups as well.
See Rudolph, *Gnosis*, 225–26.

The years, then, of Anicetus, 155–66, for Irenaeus were years filled with the arrival, settlement, and growth of false teachers, mainly from the East, within Rome. The city became not the locus of well-being, but the locus of heresy's productivity. And we are able to see that for him the city is only of concern in so far as it relates to the history of Christianity.

Rome also became in that time, while Anicetus was bishop, a city of conflict. Polycarp of Smyrna also came to Rome while Marcellina, Valentinus, and Marcion are there (*Adv. haer.* 3.3.4). During his time there, according to Irenaeus, Polycarp reduced some of the effect of the heretics' teaching and redirected many to the church by proclaiming the apostolic teaching. Such days of conflict hardly call up images of close-knit Roman families or neighbors at the forum, coliseum, or baths. Rather, they call up scenes like that which Polycarp related about John's day in the baths of Ephesus. Entering into the Ephesian bathhouse one day, John spied Cerinthus and without taking time to bathe, he ran out and exclaimed, "Let us flee, just in case even the bath-house collapses, because Cerinthus, the enemy of truth is inside" (*Adv. haer.* 3.3.4). Such hostile encounters in Rome are not difficult to imagine, for even Polycarp, upon meeting Marcion, is said to have replied to his question, "Do you know me?," with, "of course I know you, first-born of Satan" (*Adv. haer.* 3.3.4).

The cosmological conflict portrayed by Eusebius in the fourth century predates him, for it was with Irenaeus in the second. For Irenaeus also, the Christian history of the city begins with Peter and Paul who founded, within the city, the church with its doctrine, which, down to his own day, had remained faithful to the apostles' teaching. But the city's early original simplicity in its doctrine, concerning the newness of Christ, had become more complicated, more diverse. For Irenaeus, the Roman church had remained pure, as its episcopal history demonstrated, but not the city. Rome, as the arena of Christian life and history, became, particularly in the days of Anicetus, but even before him under Hyginus, an urban center of Christian communal conflict. Once and originally it had been catholic, but no longer. No longer was Epictetus or Cicero the author of the words that provided the paradigm for the city. Now, instead, as Irenaeus records, the words informing the bishop of Lyons and his mentors are the words of Paul: "If a man is a heretic, after the first and second admonition, reject him" (Titus 3:10; *Adv. haer.* 3.3.4).

So it appears that it was, as Richard Lim has said, "Clustered in isolated small groups, sometimes in semi-autonomous house churches, early urban Christians easily accommodated a variety of different beliefs and practices."[86]"Now, we must be careful in drawing unwarranted distinctions between the rural and urban in antiquity, particularly those that repeat the belittling characterizations by the urban elite of the rural as simple, old-fashioned in its morality, traditional, and unchanging, but the urban as sophisticated and cautious in superstition.[87] And while we note the importance of location in Roman paganism, we need also appreciate that ancient religious loyalties seem to have crossed the borders between town and country.[88] However, still, MacMullen does have a point. He reminds us that the city provided a more appropriate context for change and experimentation in contrast to the village, which normally "hovered so barely above subsistence level that none dared risk change."[89] Furthermore, with a population density of perhaps 200 persons per acre, cities provided the ideal setting for the planting of Peter and Paul's universal message with its exclusivist claims and demands. But the favor was also provided to a dizzying number of competing interpretations of Jesus and his teachings.[90] The city, and especially Rome, Tacitus told us, in his denigration of the Christians, is the space "where every kind of infamy converges."[91] Irenaeus would have agreed.

The urban accommodation noted by Lim was by no means performed willingly or without objection. The city was an environment of claim and counterclaim. The idea of the city, seen in Irenaeus, as an arena in which one particular group's history is played out, and the prevalence of ideological conflict in that history, has reconceptualized the city. Stoicism, with its more universalistic and anthropologically oriented perspective of the city, has been replaced. Harmony has been

---

86. Lim, "Christian Triumph and Controversy," 200.

87. Cf. North, "Religion and Rusticity"; Starr, *Roman Empire*, 93.

88. North, "Religion and Rusticity," 142–47.

89. MacMullen, Roman Social Relations, 27.

90. See Fowden's characterization of Christianity's universal address in "Religious Communities," 84–85; and MacMullen, *Roman Social Relations*, 63, for population estimates.

91. Tacitus, *Annals* 15.44, in Turcan, *Cults of the Roman Empire*, 11; "where all things hideous and shameful from every part of the world find their centre and become popular" (*Complete Works of Tacitus*, 381). Cf. Seneca, *Consolation to Helvia* 6.2; Juvenal, *Satires* 3.62; Turcan, *Cults of the Roman Empire*, 11.

overcome by conflict, and Paul's more stern view of human nature has taken the place of Cicero's more optimistic view.

But, perhaps the romantic view painted by Stoicism hasn't been replaced, but shown by Irenaeus to be what it always was: a wishful, idealistic, but unfortunately, unreal interpretation of the city. Martin Goalen, in his rehearsal of the history of studies of Pompeii, has shown that although there is a reality to the continuum between the elements of the city—its design, architecture and amenities—and civilization, between microcosm and macrocosm, between decoration and the imagined, even desired, urban community or world, historians, archeologists, and architects have imported their own worlds into their interpretations of the ancient.[92] While the amenities linked to urban living are difficult to deny, it seems that Irenaeus's way of reading brings the perceived costs to the foreground, much like Galen's comment that characterized the city as a vehicle that, through its consumption of resources, leaves the rural areas impoverished.[93] The city of Rome in the second century was not as the Stoics had dreamed it. Urbanization sometimes included visions more appropriate to a nightmare.[94] Amenities did not secure wellbeing. Micro-societies, sects, and other marginal groups substituted for the growing disconnect between the typical Roman and affairs of the city. Urban crowding, while aiding the dissemination of information, also contributed to an atmosphere of alienation and anonymity. Such an atmosphere could help, as Robert Turcan has suggested, explain the success of Gnosis, in its various sectarian expressions, with their myth of the exile who must escape the world, at Rome, Lyons, and other cities.[95]

What Irenaeus and his future admirer see in second-century Rome manifests an inescapable feature of the idea of the urban in that period. The city is a fertile field for the planting of a message, but argument, contest, and combat inevitably result between competing groups seeking to establish a universal vision within an environment that can breed particularization. When Irenaeus's contemporary, Athenaeus of Naucratis, described Rome as the *Uranopolis*, the universe-city, he was espousing

92. Goalen, "Idea of the City," 181–202.

93. Galen, *On Good Food and Bad Diet* (*Claudii Galeni Opera Omnia*, 6.749–50); cf. Starr, *Roman Empire*, 101–2.

94. The following brief analysis of the costs of urbanization in the Roman world is dependent upon Turcan, *Cults of the Roman Empire*, 17–18.

95. Ibid., 18.

an interpretation that neither Irenaeus nor his opponents could embrace.[96] For them, the city's light was somewhat dim.

Reading Christianly

The rule of truth then, forms the lens through which all things are to be read. The baptized see not only the Scriptures by means of it, but also the systems of the heretics, and, as Irenaeus has shown us, also the structures of their world. This is what it means to read Christianly, in a manner distinct from that of the pagans and the heretics. Christians see all things in the light of the rule. At this point I wish to make clear why I have chosen the structures of the Empire and the city as my subjects in Irenaeus. I selected them because they are obviously central aspects of his world and precisely because they are *not* biblical texts. He employs the hermeneutic I have described to read biblical texts. But he also employs it in the larger dimension of life, which encompasses reading other texts, people, art, social and political structures, nations, events, experiences, emotions, lectures, poetry, and clouds. It is the way he interprets everything. And so I propose it as the hermeneutic he entrusts to his readers.

It seems, then, that Irenaeus has set before us the way he wishes for the baptized to read. In his mind, to read, at the most basic level is to see the texts of his world in light of the rule of truth. When he reads Rome, he relates the Empire and the city to perspectives and texts never imagined by the Romans. However, these Irenaean connections are governed by the rule. Such reading is not arbitrary. The rule restricts what is seen. The reading is ruled. And, since the Scriptures prove the rule, the Scriptures, of course, are restricting the reading. Baptized Christians are to see all things in light of the Scriptures. To read Christianly is to read confessionally, in line with the members of the rule of faith. And to read Christianly is to read scripturally. The confession does not exist independent of the Scriptures, it only can exist because of them.

This is the manner in which, for instance, Irenaeus himself reads Hermas. In one of the summaries of the rule we mentioned above (*Adv. haer.* 1.22.1) he cites Hermas's words on God in the context of his polemic. Immediately, after providing this statement of faith, this confession, this member of the body of truth, he adds to those words

---

96. *Deipnosophists* 1.36.20, cited in ibid.

of Hermas the cento comprising words of the psalmist and evangelist. When the rule is spoken, the Scriptures that prove it are spoken too. Doctrine and exegesis must not be separated. Without the Scriptures the rule is unproven. Without the rule Scripture can be easily exploited to unorthodox ends. And where the Scriptures and the rule are spoken, light pierces the darkness of heresy, and the baptized see all things after the manner of the apostles.

So, may I invite evangelicals to join me in my concern for evangelicalism's less doctrinaire future? May I ask evangelicals, particularly those of the Free Church tradition, to embrace a new baptismal catechesis in which the common confession of historical orthodoxy with its Scriptural attestation is passed on to the baptized? May I request that evangelicals recognize more fully the complementary relationship between confession and exegesis, between doctrinal assumptions and biblical interpretation? May I invite evangelicals to return to the *euangelion* in the sense in which Irenaeus refers to gospel as the church's faith? May I encourage the baptized to look at everything through the vantage point of the scripturally founded rule of truth of the apostles? If evangelicals learn to read the culture Christianly, they will be less apt to imitate it and more apt to engage it courageously and lovingly with scripturally warranted, immovable faith claims.

A Response to Jeffrey Bingham

BRYAN LITFIN

Moody Bible Institute

D R. JEFFREY BINGHAM HAS devoted many years to the study of Irenaeus, and in the process he has come to resemble the bishop of Lyons. Their learned approach to theology, their piercing intellects, and their eloquence of expression make them kindred spirits across the ages. However, the point of similarity that most obviously emerges here is their concern to offer a Christian apologetic to an increasingly non-Christian, or even anti-Christian, culture.

If the evangelical world is becoming increasingly "less doctrinaire" today, so too was the Christianity of the second century. That statement, somewhat surprising on its face, only holds true if we define both "Christianity" and "doctrinaire" in a certain way. It has become common in scholarly circles to let any movement from the ancient world go by the name "Christian" so long as it called itself Christian. In this way of thinking, various Gnostic groups and heresies would be included in the term. If we understand "Christianity" in this light, and if we also define "doctrinaire" as reflecting a concern for doctrine received from the apostles, then we find a remarkable parallel between Irenaeus's situation and our own. The bishop of Lyons faced opponents who claimed to speak for "the Christian church," yet whose fundamental ideas and concerns were distinctly out of step with the basic axioms of the faith. So too, there are those today who wish to speak for Christianity, but whose doctrinal commitments ring hollow when measured by the standard of historic orthodoxy.

Dr. Bingham has diagnosed the underlying cause of this doctrinal malaise within evangelicalism: lack of traditional baptismal catechesis. He does not elaborate on what a robust catechetical endeavor should look like today, though one suspects he intends more than a new member's class offering a PowerPoint presentation of the church's doctrinal statement. I suspect Dr. Bingham even intends more than a brief doctrine course prior to a baptismal service, although that would be a good start. No, at the heart of his message, Dr. Bingham is talking about a core commitment to doctrine, the kind of commitment that finds its way into the fundamental DNA of a church, and from there into the broader Christian subculture. In other words, Dr. Bingham is calling for a return to *theology* within evangelicalism.

The spirit of our age is anti-propositional, anti-rational, and anti-traditional. Fixed and indubitable propositions that have come down to us from the past are about as fashionable today as leisure suits and disco shoes. The problem is, it's impossible to function as human communicators without making propositions supported by rational thought. And, as Irenaeus would certainly agree, it is impossible to make *Christian* propositions without also appealing to the catholic church's Holy Scriptures and her received doctrines. If evangelicalism cannot recover what Bingham calls "the decisive, final, conclusive doctrine of Christianity handed down by the apostles as 'the faith once for all delivered,'" then we may very well go the way of the Gnostics before us. And that prospect leaves Dr. Bingham deeply concerned.

Irenaeus, like other church fathers (particularly of the ante-Nicene period), offers us the *regula fidei* or rule of faith as a theological lens through which to read Scripture. In other words, the rule served as an organizing principle so that the individual *tesserae* of the biblical mosaic would be properly assembled into the known and recognizable pattern. In the rule of faith, the fathers possessed a useful tool that always kept before their eyes the essentials of Christianity, the metanarrative of God's great plan. Though the rule could not solve every exegetical conundrum, it certainly could guide the interpreter toward the bigger picture. It was an interpretive key to unlock the meaning of the Bible. Bingham emphasizes how the rule itself is drawn from Scripture, and how it forces the exegete to make biblical connections until a matrix or network is formed. Of course, Irenaeus's commitment was not to the text *per se*, but to the apostolic faith to which the text is a witness. In other words, Irenaeus was a little more *ecclesial* and a little less *biblicist* in his outlook than we might imagine. Yet who would want to dispute that Irenaeus had an extremely high view of Scripture? He was a biblical theologian, and for him the rule of faith was a vital tool with which to do exegesis.

Perhaps the most intriguing aspect of Dr. Bingham's paper was his treatment of Irenaeus on Rome and the Roman Empire. His paper opened up a new arena of Irenaean thought. And yet, I must admit I did not completely like what I found. I had always perceived Irenaeus as one of the first systematic theologians. Though he was not speculative like Origen, I knew the bishop of Lyons as one of the earliest patristic thinkers to reflect on a grand scale about Christian doctrine. We can see this in the way he linked the two Testaments into an organic whole, and also in his recapitulation theory, wherein Christ summed up salvation history by his perfect obedience. In other words, Irenaeus was, in my mind, a constructive theologian who thought positively about how he might arrange the data of Christian doctrine into a new, organic whole.

However, the Irenaeus I encountered in today's paper was far more defensive and reactionary than I had supposed. I knew he was an apologist; but somehow I had put him in a different category than folks like Epiphanius with his dogged pursuit of heresy. Yet the Irenaeus who views the city as a hothouse for every kind of noxious intellectual weed, or as a breeding ground for theological disease, is, of necessity, a theologian on the *defensive*. Heresy as urban blight was a new concept for me. I found myself uncomfortable with this fundamentalist wall-builder I seemed to be meeting. I had thought Irenaeus was more constructive than reactionary—more *urbane* in the fullest sense of that word. Truthfully, this new Irenaeus sounded a lot more like my old friend Tertullian! (though without the sarcastic wit).

In the end, the paper leaves Irenaeus in his defensive position. He is, like Dr. Bingham, "breaking out in a cold sweat." I share many of these same concerns. I look around and see a culture going to hell. Worse, I see that hellish culture making deep inroads into the church. The white linen of the Bride is stained—and she doesn't even know it. What are we on the inside to do about these incursions of a post-Christian culture?

Dr. Bingham proposes a return to a more ecclesial, more historic, more catholic, and for these very reasons, more *biblical* catechesis. Christian confession rests on exegesis; doctrine rests on interpretation of the sacred and authoritative text. To aid us in understanding the meaning of the Bible, thinkers such as Irenaeus have provided a rule of truth through which to view aright the fuller revelation of God's Word.

Such a "back to the Bible" approach might be construed as fundamental-ist retrenchment: stake out territory, defend it with vigor, and keep the heretics off our backs until Jesus returns. I do not think this is what Dr. Bingham was trying to say, nor do I believe it worthy of Irenaeus. I do believe there will be some who respond to evangelicalism's drift with precisely this approach. We must resist that temptation. Why? Because in the Lord Jesus, we already have the victory, even if proleptically. We are not a people on the defensive, but the people of the risen King. Our theological task is not to hang on by our nails until we're rescued, but to go forth into the culture and remake it in the image of Christ. To do this we need what Bingham describes in his closing line as "scriptur-ally warranted, immovable faith claims." Modernity did not invent this; indubitable truth was around a long time before Descartes. The truth claims of the Christian faith, as expressed in the Bible, are more than just *tesserae* with which to build a delicate mosaic. They are solid *bricks* with which to construct a sturdy Christian edifice—an edifice whose chief Cornerstone binds it together and causes it to stand.

8

Evangelicals, the Bible, and the Early Church

Michael W. Graves

Wheaton College

THE PRIMARY TOPICS THAT I wish to discuss are the Bible and the early church. These topics are of obvious interest to evangelicalism as it exists today, since evangelicals place great emphasis on the Bible, and many within the evangelical world desire to connect more significantly with the early church. As a result, it is natural for evangelicals to ask how the Bible relates to early Christianity and whether understanding the early church might aid in the interpretation of Scripture. My goal will be to set forth some major points where I think that the Bible and the early church illuminate each other.

By way of introduction, I would like to say something about the study of the Bible as a document of the past. There is an ancient tradition of studying classical texts with the recognition that they come from a distant time and context. Starting in the third century BCE, scholars such as Aristarchus of Samothrace and Aristophanes of Byzantium wrote commentaries, compiled critical editions, discussed the authenticity of various works, and produced specialized studies on the vocabulary of earlier Greek authors in order to preserve and explain their literary heritage.[1] Among their many astute observations, these scholars saw that the vocabulary of Homeric Greek was different from their own, and so they self-consciously attempted to determine the meanings of words as

---

1. On classical scholarship in antiquity, see Dickey, *Ancient Greek Scholarship*, 3–17; and Pfeiffer, *History of Classical Scholarship*, 171–279.

they would have been understood in Homer's time, not their own—they sought to identify "Homeric usage" (*homērikōteron*), and more generally they endeavored "to interpret Homer from Homer" (*omēron ex omērou saphēnizein*).[2] This tradition of scholarship came into the Greek church and then eventually into the Latin church, and had a significant impact on patristic exegesis, as recent books on Origen, the Antiochenes, Jerome, and Augustine have shown.[3] Although this tradition never died out, it took on fresh wings in the Renaissance, added a new twist in the Enlightenment, and has been a prominent feature of biblical studies in the twentieth century.

As evangelicals have entered into the world of biblical scholarship, they have devoted much effort to studying the Bible as an ancient document that comes from a time and place different from our own. I think that this work is extremely valuable and has genuine theological significance. The cultural and historical distance between us and the writers of the Bible was also recognized as significant by the church fathers. For example, in his discussion of the polygamy of the patriarchs, Augustine argues that certain behaviors that were acceptable in the past are no longer acceptable today (*Doctr. chr.* 3.12.19–20; see also 3.17.25; 3.18.26–27; 3.22.32; cf. Jerome, *Helv.* 20). Similarly, I have not met any evangelicals who think that everything about the culture of the biblical world should be revived today. By studying the Bible as a collection of books from the past, evangelicals have learned to see how God's working in the world has been rooted in particular historical contexts, and as a result they have become more responsible interpreters of Scripture.

Of course, evangelicals also recognize that Christians should study the Bible as more than just a collection of documents from the past. We may contrast the present position of the Bible with that of the *Code of Hammurabi*. Hammurabi's code is a fascinating text that tells us about

2. On Aristarchus and Homeric usage, see Pfeiffer, *History,* 227; and Sandys, *History of Classical Scholarship,* 1:132–33. The phrase "to interpret Homer from Homer" comes from Porphyry, *The Homeric Questions* (third century CE). Pfeiffer, *History,* 226–27, is skeptical that it goes back to Aristarchus, even if it generally accords with his opinion. James Porter, on the other hand, connects the phrase more closely to Aristarchus, and appealing to Aristarchus's connection to Aristotle he argues that the concept of elucidating Homer from Homer went beyond linguistic usage to interpretation at a broader level; see Porter, "Hermeneutical Lines and Circles," 73–77.

3. Neuschäfer, *Origenes als Philologe*; Schäublin, *Untersuchungen zu Methode und Herkunft*; Graves, *Jerome's Hebrew Philology*; and Marrou, *Saint Augustin et la fin de la culture antique.*

people who lived long ago and who were both like us and different from us in many ways. The primary interest for people today who read the *Code of Hammurabi* is to learn what the text said back then to whatever sort of audience the writer had in mind. The text may be meaningful today if the contemporary reader perceives within it some helpful insight, but that is very much up to the individual reader. The Bible can be studied in this way, too. But Christians have traditionally believed that reading the Bible went beyond a merely historical engagement. We may ask: How has the Bible continued to speak and remain relevant to successive generations of Christians?

A key element of the Bible's enduring ability to be meaningful and authoritative is the ongoing existence of a community that recognizes its authority and continues to interpret it. Even if one believes in the possibility of strictly historical exegesis (which I do), and also believes in the value of historical exegesis (which I do), it must be remembered that the results of this kind of exegesis are necessarily past tense, as in, "This is what Amos said to them back then" or "This is what Paul said to that church back then." In order to ascertain what a biblical text "says" (present tense) to us today, we need some kind of interpretive stance towards the text. This stance comes from the Christian community of which we are a part.

Consider the difference between the *Code of Hammurabi* and the U.S. Constitution: in the case of Hammurabi's code, there is no surviving community that continues to appeal to it as authoritative, and so it is read by individuals primarily as a document of the past, with appropriate historical and literary interests; but in the case of the U.S. Constitution, there is a living community that continues to appeal to it as an authority, and so there surrounds the interpretation of the Constitution a system of hermeneutics that is vastly more complicated than anything done with the *Code of Hammurabi*.[4] Scriptural interpretation is complex and sophisticated precisely because the church continues to recognize the authority of Scripture.

While it is true that a text needs a living community to preserve it and apply it to new circumstances, living readers by no means do all the work of mediating the text to their community. Tradition is the record or memory of what the community has practiced in the past, and tradition can be said to mediate the text to the living community. Tradition

4. Cf. Pelikan, *Interpreting the Bible*.

significantly affects how individual readers perceive the text, and it also impacts what interpretations others within the community are willing to accept. Because of the closeness of the early church to the events of the New Testament and the foundational role of the early church in establishing Christian doctrine, practice, and scriptural canon, the literature and history of the early church represent the most significant deposit of tradition available to the contemporary church. It is essential that Christians today be aware of these traditions. We need to know where we have come from, and we also need to know how to move forward in essential continuity with historic Christianity.

I believe that the early church can inform every aspect of our engagement with Scripture. I will try to demonstrate this briefly below. First, I will give a few examples of how early Christian traditions can help us better understand the historical or literal subject matter of the biblical text, that is, Scripture as seen as a document from the past. Then, I will give some examples of how early church traditions aid us in perceiving how Scripture is meaningful for us today. After this, I will address the problem of how to identify and utilize early Christian traditions in relation to Scripture. Finally, I will suggest a few ideas as to how the study of the Bible and the early church together can benefit the evangelical community.

Early Christian Tradition and the Historical or Literal Subject Matter of Scripture

In studying the history of biblical interpretation, it would be possible to see all of the different ideas that have been attached to the Bible and to conclude that the Bible can be made to say almost anything, and so has no real meaning at all. No one could accept all of the interpretations that have been assigned to a given biblical text, and it is surprising how confidently many past interpreters held to their own sometimes-idiosyncratic views. Nevertheless, although a measure of caution is certainly warranted, I believe that there is also a convincing case to be made that studying ancient Christian exegesis of the Bible—and the history of exegesis in general—can lead to a greater recognition and appreciation of the genuine subject matter of biblical texts. When I see a particular point being made from a biblical text by numerous authors from different times and contexts, then I can see all the more readily that the point in question represents a tangible idea that is really expressed in that text. Each writer may have a peculiar way of making this point; but in the end, the repeated testimony of multiple, learned, faithful Christian witnesses serves as a strong indication that we are reading the text well. Here is the big-picture payoff for this first section: careful attention to the history of interpretation can help us to identify what is really there in the text, because one can see it emerge in the writings of careful readers from diverse contexts.

Let me illustrate this with a few examples of patristic interpretations that at least partially confirm certain observations that have been made by modern biblical scholars. For nearly two hundred years modern scholarship on the Pentateuch has worked under the auspices of a "documentary hypothesis," which has attempted to identify different sources for the Pentateuch by paying attention to (1) the different names for God, especially *Jahveh* and *Elohim*, (2) repetitions, and (3) contradictions in the narrative. Since most of the church fathers read the Old Testament in translation, they have little to say about the names of God, as that information did not come through clearly in translation (although the rabbis have something to say about this topic). But as for the details identified by modern critics as repetitions or contradictions, many of the plausible examples were noticed by patristic commentators.

Origen, for example, noted the difficulty in Genesis 1 of having three days with mornings and evenings before the creation of the sun, moon, and stars on day four (*Princ.* 4.3.1), taking this as evidence that the text was not meant to be taken literally (cf. *Hom. Gen.* 1.5–7). Augustine, who also favored a non-materialistic interpretation of Genesis 1, took notice of the problem of God's speech in 1:3, since there could be no physical voice before the creation of matter (*Gen. litt.* 1.3.9; 1.9.16; 1.10.20–22). Augustine also expends considerable energy in his largest commentary on Genesis admonishing Christians not to argue with learned non-Christians about the creation of the world (*Gen. litt.* 1.18–21; 2.1.4; 2.9.20–21). John Chrysostom observed that a second description of creation follows after the first one, a phenomenon he takes to be indicative of Scripture's custom of giving both detailed and summary accounts of events (*Hom. Gen.* 12.3–5).[5] Jerome, like modern

---

5. Cf. *Hom. Gen.* 21.3–5, where Chrysostom gives a moral exposition to the fact that Gen 5:1 seems to go back to the beginning of the creation of humanity (Gen 5 is the "P" account of Adam's posterity).

critics, identifies the "book of the law" found by Josiah as the book of Deuteronomy (*Jov.* 1.5; cf. 2 Kgs 22:8), although he sees in this no evidence that the book had only recently been composed. He also points out that the name of Moses' father-in-law changes "suddenly" from Reuel in Exodus 2:18 to Jethro a few verses later in 3:1, "without any reason given in advance for the change." Jerome regards this as part of the style of Scripture and gives a host of similar examples (*Helv.* 13). There is actually a well-attested tradition among the church fathers that Ezra was responsible for the editorial restoration of the Pentateuch. The general idea is that during the exile the Law was lost either in part or in whole, and Ezra came along and by God's guidance rewrote it or restored it from fragments (e.g., Clement of Alexandria, Irenaeus, Tertullian, Basil the Great, John Chrysostom, Theodoret, and Jerome).[6] This is reminiscent of the modern idea that the Pentateuch was compiled for the first time during the period of Ezra; yet, for the church fathers this is simply a textual transmission theory that takes seriously the role of Ezra the scribe as described in the books of Ezra-Nehemiah.

What is one to make of such parallels between early Christian thinking and modern scholarship? For one thing, they help to confirm the reality of at least some of the observations upon which modern theories are based. It would be helpful for any commentator to explain the relationship between Reuel and Jethro in Exodus; and at a broader level, there are indeed linguistic and thematic parallels between Deuteronomy and the literature associated with Josiah's reforms. At the same time, there are numerous features of modern scholarship on the Pentateuch, as expressed in its classic JEDP form, that find no parallel in the church fathers. For example, modern scholars claim to have found distinctive strands of material throughout the Pentateuch, so that they identify a particular creation narrative, a particular sister-wife story, and a particular call of Moses story as all belonging to a single source. Furthermore, modern scholars claim to be able to establish a basic chronology of the pentateuchal sources; thus, they assign a late date to the priestly material based on their particular theory of how religions develop. It is precisely

6. Clement, *Strom.* 1.22; Irenaeus, *Adv. haer.* 3.21; Tertullian, *Cult. fem.* 1.3; Basil, *Epist.* 42; John Chrysostom, *Hom. Heb.* 8; Theodoret, *Comm. Cant.*, preface; and Jerome, *Helv.* 7. A similar theory circulated regarding the postexilic restoration of the Psalms; e.g., see Diodore of Tarsus, *Comm. Ps.*, prologue; and Origen, *Selecta in Psalmos* (PG 12.1076). Cf. 4 Ezra 14:21–26, 39–48.

at these points of greatest innovation that modern critical commentaries on the Pentateuch are least plausible.

Other examples of this kind could be given. John Chrysostom acknowledged that there were many discrepancies between the Gospel accounts of the life of Jesus, but he took this as confirmation that the writers had not simply met together to concoct their stories; according to Chrysostom, this makes them all the more reliable in the vast number of places where they agree (*Hom. Matt.* 1.6). Jerome regards Hebrews as non-Pauline because it differs from Paul's style—although this is not too surprising since Hebrews is formally anonymous (*Vir. ill.* 5.10; cf. 15.10). Jerome also reports that 2 Peter is considered by many not to belong to Peter because it differs in style from 1 Peter (*Vir. ill.* 1.3), although he appears less sure of what to make of this. Another striking parallel between modern scholarship and the church fathers can be seen in Theodore of Mopsuestia's identification of the subject matter of certain Psalms. In his *International Critical Commentary* on the Psalms written in 1906–1907, Charles Briggs, who perceived a great deal of editorial activity in the composition of individual Psalms, assigned verses from Psalm 44 (vv. 9, 11, 20–21), Psalm 69 (vv. 32–33, 35–36), Psalm 74 (vv. 4b-6, 9), and Psalm 80 (vv. 16–17) to the Maccabean era, on the grounds that the references to oppression and the cries for help fit best in the second century during the persecution instigated by Antiochus IV.[7] Theodore of Mopsuestia dates the subject matter of all these Psalms to the Maccabean period,[8] drawing parallels with many of the same verses as Briggs to the persecution of the Jews inflicted by Antiochus IV.[9] I suspect that Theodore recognized the importance of Antiochus's persecution of the Jews as a paradigm for Israel's suffering for God, just as the New Testament does when it applies imagery from this event to the church.[10] Unlike Briggs, however, Theodore maintains the literary coherence of the Psalms in his exposition and refrains from chopping them up.

7. Briggs, *Critical Commentary on Psalms*.

8. In terms of authorship, Theodore regards all of the Psalms to have been written by David, who spoke prophetically about future events; see Manlio Simonetti, "Theodore of Mopsuestia (CA. 350–429)," 2:814–15.

9. See Theodore of Mopsuestia, *Commentary on Psalms 1–81*.

10. E.g., with regard to the "abomination that makes desolate," see Dan 9:27, 11:31, 12:11; 1 Macc 1:54; Matt 24:15; Mark 13:14; Luke 20:20–21.

In sum, we may note that sometimes early Christian commentators run on the same track as modern critical interpreters, and often we may take this as confirmation that the track they have discovered is actually present in the text. The best commentators from the patristic period were men with literary training, and so it should not surprise us that they observe many of the same textual phenomena as modern scholars. Yet, we saw that in the early Christian interpreters, alongside of their critical sensibilities there was a consistent concern for the theological nature of the biblical text. They tended to give "faith-based" explanations for textual details rather than purely secular explanations. This would seem to make the church fathers excellent conversation partners for contemporary evangelicals who want to be critically aware but also faithful to the Bible as Scripture.

Early Christian Tradition and the Meaningfulness of Scripture

Tradition as it relates to biblical interpretation moves beyond the literal sense of Scripture into the sphere of the Bible's significance to later situations. We will consider an extended example in this section that demonstrates how early Christian tradition can help us to identify the abiding meaningfulness of the biblical text.

In his *Life of Moses,* Gregory of Nyssa interprets the book of Exodus as a paradigm for how Christians ought to live and how they can draw near to God. Gregory begins by giving a "history" of Moses, a summary of the literal account of Moses' life. After this literal overview, Gregory starts over again at the beginning of Exodus with his spiritual contemplation, which often refers back to the history and always presupposes its basic framework. Gregory quite plausibly regards Moses as the central figure of the story of Israel from Exodus through Deuteronomy. Gregory's spiritual contemplation is based on his belief that the lives of noble men have been set forth in Scripture as a pattern for those who come later to follow (2.48, 1.77). Gregory recognizes, of course, that later people cannot experience the identical literal events that Moses experienced; therefore, one must discover the moral teaching contained within the literal account. This moral teaching transcends the specific unrepeatable situation of Moses and allows the text to help those striving towards virtue to live a virtuous life (2.49). Such an approach to interpreting the biblical text finds support in the New Testament in 1 Corinthians 10:1–13, which says that the narratives about the exodus and wilderness wandering were written for the instruction of later people, and also in passages such as Hebrews 11 on examples of faith, James 5:10–11 on the prophets and Job as examples of patience, and Galatians 3:1–9 on Abraham as an example of one who believes in God. Furthermore, it is difficult to see how historical narrative could "teach" anything if it could not be interpreted in a way that transcends the unique events that it recounts—and according to 1 Timothy 3:16 all Scripture is useful for teaching.

Since it is impossible here to give a complete account of Gregory's spiritual contemplation, we will limit ourselves to just a few events in Moses' life. In Exodus 2 Moses strikes down an Egyptian who was beating a Hebrew. Gregory sees this in a positive light, since Moses is resisting those who oppose Israel, or true religion. "We may see this same conflict in us," he says. Moses teaches us to take our stand with virtue, and to side with true religion against idolatry, with self-control against licentiousness, with righteousness against injustice, and with humility against arrogance (2.14–15). Afterwards Moses encounters two Hebrews fighting, and their charge against him causes him to flee. Gregory notes that at this point Moses is not able to resolve the wicked conflict (2.16), but later, after he has met with God, he is able to address all of the Israelites and (at first) they pay attention to him. According to Gregory, the historical narrative "all but cries out to you not to be presumptuous in giving advice to your hearers when you teach, " (2.55) but to wait until the ability has been perfected in you after long training with God.

In Exodus 3, Moses meets God from within a burning bush, since now Moses is living a quiet, peaceful life and is therefore ready for the truth to shine upon him (2.19). Moses has taken a foreign wife, but this simply expresses the reality that what is profane may be redeemed; thus, when we desire to give birth to virtue, certain things derived from profane education, such as moral and natural philosophy, should not be rejected (2.37). Of course, their son needed to be circumcised, which shows that what is profane must have its foreign elements removed; for example, pagan philosophy teaches the immortality of the soul, which is a pious offspring, but the idea of the transmigration of souls must be cut away (2.40–41).

According to Gregory, the details of the Passover meal in Exodus 12 must have some greater significance, since it means nothing to virtue or vice if you eat this way or that (2.105). For example, the traveler's equipment signifies transiency, and for us it shows that this present life is fleeting. God sets us out on a divine course of life, and we must not be hindered by the likes of a flowing tunic (2.106, 108). As for the plundering of the Egyptians (Exod 12:36), Gregory insists that this should not be taken as a command to wrong one's neighbor; rather, he takes this as another example of the valid appropriation of pagan philosophy, geometry, astronomy, dialectic, and so forth (2.113–16).[11] Israel sets out like those who are newly established in the faith, and God leads them by a pillar of cloud, which represents the Holy Spirit (2.117, 121). God leads them through the water of the sea, drowning the Egyptians, who are the various passions of the soul, such as covetousness, wrath, malice, and envy (2.122, 125). This army of evil is put to death when the Christian passes through the mystical water in baptism (2.125). But some Christians do not make the complete break that this deliverance in baptism requires; instead, they bring along with them the Egyptian army, or, referring to Paul's metaphor in 1 Corinthians 5:6–8, they mix in the old leaven with the new (2.127). The manna is the Word, Jesus, who is the Bread from Heaven (2.140; cf. John 6:32–35). The falling of the manna teaches that those who make their living in material things should not exceed what they need, so that each can share equally (2.141). When Moses raises his hands in the battle with Amalek he is symbolizing the contemplation of the Law through lofty insights (2.149).[12] Finally, Moses ascends Mt. Sinai in order to receive the ineffable knowledge of God (2.152). He purifies his life from sensual and irrational emotions (2.157) and moves towards the contemplation of God who dwells in thick darkness (2.162; cf. Exod 20:21), since God transcends all knowledge (2.163). This ascent of Moses is the climax of the book.

Gregory of Nyssa's exposition points out numerous ways that the text of Exodus can and should relate to Christians. When we are saved,

11. On this motif, see Allen, *Despoliation of Egypt*.

12. If this seems fanciful, it should at least be acknowledged that "up" is the direction of God in Scripture. Thus, Moses went up the mountain to God, who lives in the "sky" (*shamayim*, "heavens"), and Jesus ascended "up" (Acts 1:9–11), not because he was flying to outer space, but because that is a symbol of where God is. For Gregory, the raising of Moses' hands is a symbol of divine assistance and not a practical battle strategy.

it is through Jesus. When we are led, it is through the Holy Spirit. Just as with Moses' calling in Exodus, we are called in Christ to walk in the Spirit and according to its fruits, which Gregory describes through the Greek terminology of virtues. What enslaves us is sin, and it is from sin that Christ sets us free. As Moses is brought near to God by ascending the mountain, so we also approach God by ascending spiritually, which starts with baptism and involves a continuing life of storing up treasures in heaven. Gregory explains to us that we should not rob people on the basis of the plundering of the Egyptians, and that we should not kill people in imitation of the killing of the firstborn in the tenth plague or the destruction of the Egyptian army (2.91–93, 122–25).

The book of Exodus has always been regarded as Scripture by the church, but this status has been accompanied by frameworks of interpretation such as we find in Gregory of Nyssa. Thus, Christians have almost universally understood that they do not need to slaughter a lamb as described in Exodus 12, but they do need Christian baptism. Christians today could appreciate these points better by reading Gregory's *Life of Moses* or many other patristic treatments of Exodus.[13] Similarly, most early Christians did not understand the wars of biblical Israel as paradigms for literally fighting people.[14] Therefore, when Oliver Cromwell

13. Tertullian (*Bapt.* 9), Ambrose (*Myst.* 3.13; *Sacr.* 1.6.22), Cyril of Jerusalem (*Catech. Lect.* 19), Aphrahat (*Dem.* 12), Basil (*Spir.* 14) , Theodoret (*Quaest. Exod.* 27) and many others give typological descriptions of the Exodus as salvation through baptism, where Moses is Christ, the Egyptians are the devil or guilt, the pillar of cloud is the Holy Spirit, etc. This follows the trajectory of 1 Cor 10 and allows for a directly christological reading. Gregory of Nyssa also reflects this tradition in his sermon *On the Baptism of Christ.*

14. Most early Christians addressed the issue of war by looking to the New Testament, especially the teaching of Jesus. See Bainton, *Christian Attitudes toward War*, 66–89; and Cadoux, *Early Christian Attitude to War*, 49–160. When Christians did consider this issue in light of the Old Testament, they tended to relegate the wars to a former dispensation (e.g., Origen, *Cels.* 7.26; Tertullian, *Marc.* 4.16), point to prophetic passages that promise peace, such as Isa 2 and Mic 4 (e.g., Justin, *1 Apol.* 39; *Dial.* 109–10; Tertullian, *Marc.* 3.21; Irenaeus, *Adv. haer.* 4.34), or read allegorically as Gregory does (e.g., *Barn.* 12.1–11; Justin, *Dial.* 90, 111, 113, 115, 131; Origen, *Hom. Josh.* 8.7, 12.1, 13.3; Tertullian, *Marc.* 3.14; *Adv. Jud.* 9; and Hilary of Poitiers, *Tract. Ps.* 137.15; cf. Augustine, *Doctr. chr.* 3.11.17). Yet, Tertullian (*Idol.* 19) suggests that some Christians served in the military and cited the Old Testament as justification. Moreover, Ambrose later appeals to Abraham and Moses as models for virtuous behavior in war (*Off.* 1.28.135; 2.15.74; see also 1.27.129). It should be noted, however, that Ambrose describes just war in terms of defense, justice, and self-sacrifice, and the actions of Cromwell and Mather are not justifiable on these criteria.

described his revolution in terms of the exodus and decided to treat the Catholics of Ireland as the Canaanites, or when Cotton Mather encouraged the colonists to fight against Native American tribes and branded them as "Amalek annoying this Israel in the wilderness,"[15] they were reading the traditional biblical text, but they were not perceiving its meaningfulness in conversation with early Christian tradition. They would have been well served to read Gregory of Nyssa's exposition of the book of Exodus.

Gregory's *Life of Moses* stands in a tradition of biblical interpretation stretching back to Origen, Clement of Alexandria, and Philo the Jew, whose positive reception in the church led to his being identified as "bishop Philo" in many Byzantine *catenae*.[16] Since the time of its composition the *Life of Moses* has been very influential on the spiritual life of the church.[17] The enduring value of Gregory's approach is shown by the long and wide reception his work has enjoyed throughout the centuries. Of course, Gregory's reading is culturally situated, is not equally "traditional" in every aspect (e.g., his notion of *apokatastasis* ["final restoration"] at 2.82), and is not above criticism. But as Christians our perception of the meaningfulness of Exodus has been shaped by ideas such as Gregory expresses, and we will understand how best to express the book's meaningfulness if we attend to what Gregory and other representatives of the early church have said.

Identifying and Interpreting Early Christian Traditions

So far I have been speaking about tradition without identifying clearly how I think one comes to learn tradition. I stated above that tradition is the record or memory of what the community has practiced in the past. If we follow these analogies, how does one gain access to tradition as a record or a memory? Is there an elder from whose memory we can learn tradition, so that our task is simply to ask? Are there written records that we should consult in order to learn tradition? What does one do if the

15. Collins, *Does the Bible Justify Violence?*, 19–20.

16. See Daniélou, *From Shadows to Reality*, 202–26. On Philo in the Christian *catenae*, see Runia, *Philo in Early Christian Literature*, 3.

17. Gregory's influence on Greek Christian thought was direct, while his influence on the Latin west was more indirect; see Meredith, *Gregory of Nyssa*, 99–101, 138–39; McGinn, *Foundations of Mysticism*, 140–42; and Jaeger, *Two Rediscovered Works*, 174–230.

elders do not all agree, or if the records are in conflict? While I believe that tradition is indispensible, I also recognize that receiving tradition is not as straightforward as it might appear. As an example of the complexity involved in appropriating tradition, let us consider one subject area where early church tradition directly impacts the interpretation of Scripture, namely, the "rule of faith."

One obvious way that early Christian tradition could guide us in our interpretation of Scripture would be if the tradition provided specific information about the content of what we are meant to derive from Scripture. If an interpretation deviated from this content, or perhaps even if an interpretation failed to produce this content, then that interpretation could be identified as illegitimate. Such an appeal to tradition can be found in Irenaeus, who refers to a "rule of faith" received from the apostles and accepted by all authentically apostolic churches everywhere (*Adv. haer.* 1.10.1; 3.4.1–2; 4.33.7–8). Irenaeus clearly believes that the heretics against whom he is writing have twisted the meaning of Scripture and can be rebuked by citing Scripture, but even without Scripture the "rule of faith" is enough to distinguish the heretics' errors from the apostolic truth. Augustine also appeals to church tradition with reference to Scripture, and he explicitly says that if an interpretation of Scripture violates the "rule of faith," it must be rejected.[18] It would seem that knowing such a "rule of faith" would be extremely important for any Christian who wanted to interpret Scripture faithfully. Our question is this: How does one actually identify and appropriate the "rule of faith"?

Since traditions are handed down (*traditum*), one obvious answer to this question would be to ask the caretakers of the tradition to hand down to us the content of the rule of faith. The first difficulty arises, however, with identifying who are the caretakers of the Christian tradition. Should we rely on a tradition-oriented Protestant church such as the Episcopal Church? What about the Roman Catholic Church? Or the Greek or Russian Orthodox Churches, which recognize seven normative councils? Or the Syrian Orthodox, Coptic Orthodox, or Armenian Apostolic Churches, all of which are non-Chalcedonian? Or the Assyrian Church of the East, which represents an ancient stream of Syriac Christianity and recognizes only two councils? How is one to know which group represents the true church founded by the apostles,

---

18. E.g., Augustine, *Doctr. chr.* 3.2.2–5; *Sermon* 7.3. See Litfin, "Rule of Faith in Augustine."

and which are the deviants? Moreover, another difficulty arises when comparing the practices of these churches with the literature of the early church. How does one resolve the conflict if what is handed down by a given church seems not to agree with what the church fathers actually said?

Another way to approach the question of tradition is to posit that the church, considered broadly, has handed down its traditions in the form of records that can be consulted. These records consist mostly of written documents, produced both by individuals and by groups, and they become part of the tradition not only because of their foundation in Christian experience in their own day but because they have continued to speak with meaning and authority to some part of the church in later times. On this paradigm, the tradition of the church is the actual life and history that the church experienced, and it is kept alive by people who hand it down and interpret it. We make it our own by learning it, and then interpreting it and handing it down ourselves. Our responsibility towards tradition is not exhausted when we find someone to tell us what the tradition says. Rather, our responsibility is to go back and learn from the long and deep experience of the church throughout time and to receive this tradition in communion with other Christians. If we were to apply this thinking to the rule of faith as it relates to the interpretation of Scripture, we would desire to know what the church fathers actually said about the content of the rule of faith.

In his fullest statement of the rule of faith that the church throughout the whole world received from the apostles and their disciples, Irenaeus gives this description:

> [The church believes] in one God, the Father Almighty, who made the heaven, and the earth, and the seas, and all that is in them, and in one Christ Jesus, the Son of God, who was made flesh for our salvation, and in the Holy Spirit, who through the prophets proclaimed the dispensations of God—the comings, the birth of a virgin, the suffering, the resurrection from the dead, and the bodily reception into the heavens of the beloved, Christ Jesus our Lord, and his coming from the heavens in the glory of the Father "to sum up all things" [cf. Eph. 1:10], and to raise up all flesh, that is, the whole human race, so that every knee may bow, of things in heaven and on earth and under the earth, to Christ Jesus our Lord and God and Savior and King, according to the pleasure of the invisible Father, and

every tongue may confess him [cf. Phil. 2:10–11], and that he
may execute righteous judgment on all. The spiritual powers of
wickedness [cf. Eph. 6:12], and the angels who transgressed and
fell into apostasy, and the godless and wicked and lawless and
blasphemers among men he will send into the eternal fire. But
to the righteous and holy, and those who have kept his commandments and remained in his love, some from the beginning
[of life] and some since their repentance, he will by his grace
give life incorrupt, and will clothe them with eternal glory.[19]

Irenaeus' account is briefer elsewhere:

[The church believes] in one God, maker of heaven and earth and
of all that is in them, through Christ Jesus the Son of God, who
on account of his abundant love for his creation submitted to be
born of a virgin, himself by himself uniting man to God, and
having suffered under Pontius Pilate, and risen, and having been
received up into splendor, is to come in glory as the Savior of
those who are saved, and the Judge of those who are judged, and
will send into eternal fire those who alter the truth, and despise
his Father and his coming.[20]

One can see from these quotations the basic shape of the rule of
faith according to Irenaeus. Very similar statements are made about
the "rule of faith" by Tertullian (*Prax.* 2; *Praescr.* 13.1–6; and *Virg.* 1.3),
Hippolytus (*Noet.* 17–18), Origen (*Princ.,* "preface," 4–10), and the
Didascalia apostolorum (15.26), with shorter statements in Cyprian
(*Epist.* 73.5.2), and Novatian (*Trin.* 9). The essential content of the rule
of faith based on these sources is clearly discernable, although individual
authors have their own peculiarities: for example, Irenaeus alone mentions that Christ "sums up all things," which fits his understanding of
recapitulation (*anakephalaiōsis*); Tertullian is unique and in character
when he includes the idea that Christ "preached a new law"; Hippolytus
is distinctive in his description of the "heavenly part" and "earthly part"
of Christ; and Origen alone mentions free will and includes as part of the
church's "rule of faith" that the Scriptures have two meanings, the second
of which can only be understood by those who have wisdom and knowledge from the Holy Spirit. It is noteworthy that none of these writers in

---

19. Irenaeus, *Adv. haer.* 1.10.1. See Richardson, *Early Christian Fathers,* 360 (slightly
modified).

20. *Adv. haer.* 3.4.2. See Richardson, 375.

their accounts of the rule of faith say anything about the church.[21] Each one has their own specific way of describing the rule, but the essential agreement between these various authors makes it very believable that the shared content of their statements really does represent what the apostles taught the churches.

What can we say about these earliest accounts of the rule of faith? First, I would think that any Christian would be comfortable to interpret the meaningfulness of Scripture in accordance with these fundamental Christian beliefs. From a historical perspective, the basic theological narrative told by the rule of faith would have served in the second century as an effective means for distinguishing between the genuine gospel preached throughout the ancient world by the churches started by the apostles, and gnostic mythologies based on supposed secret teachings and taught only in specific regions. We can understand why the church has preserved these early Christian writings and has continued to make use of them throughout the centuries.

Second, these rule-of-faith statements are much simpler than what many later writers came to regard as the authoritative teaching of the church. For example, in the second and early third century, Justin Martyr, Tatian, Theophilus of Antioch, and Clement of Alexandria each speak of the divinity of Jesus in terms of Jesus being the *logos* or "thought" of God which always existed with God but which came forth from God for the purpose of creation.[22] This does not contradict the rule of faith as given by any early figure, and so there is no reason to doubt that it was one sensible way for Christians to interpret the divinity of Jesus in keeping with Scripture and tradition as understood at that time. Later formulations that revise this notion and expand the church's teaching on Christ also become part of the tradition, but they constitute interpretations of both Scripture and the rule of faith; these later formulations cannot legitimately be regarded as "apostolic teachings."

21. See Hanson, *Tradition in the Early Church*, 91–92.

22. Justin, *Dial.* 56.4, 60.2, 61.1–5 (regarding Justin's reference to the *logos* as "another God," cf. Origen, *Cels.* 5.39, "a second God"); Tatian, *Orat.* 5 and 7; Theophilus, *Autol.* 2.10, 2.22; and Clement, *Strom.* 5.3.16. Tertullian (*Herm.* 3) argues that prior to the Son, God was not yet "Father," and prior to creation, God did not yet have the title "Lord." This reflects some sense that the Son came forth at a certain point, perhaps in connection with creation. Irenaeus, (*Adv. haer.* 2.28.4–5) describes Jesus as the *logos* or "thought" of God but is hesitant to speak about the Son's generation.

As another example, when Augustine says that interpreters of Scripture must agree with the church's rule of faith, he has more in mind than simply what we saw in Irenaeus. Thus, Augustine defends his particular understanding of original sin by appealing to the rule of faith; and elsewhere, he even acknowledges that the rule of faith as known to him was different from what was known to Cyprian one hundred years earlier.[23] To suppose that Augustine's rule of faith was equivalent to that handed down by the apostles is unhistorical, and it does not respect the actual testimony of the second-century church as tradition has given it to us. Besides, once Christian tradition branches off into different regional, ethnic, and political divisions, it becomes not only unhistorical but also uncharitable to ascribe all of the later material from only one's own tradition to the rule of faith. The evidence for a rule of faith in earliest Christianity would better serve as a basis for broad communion across the whole spectrum of Christianity.

In order for tradition to function as an evolving norm for the interpretation of Scripture, it would need to be grounded either in principles by which true development could be distinguished from error, or in a historical argument for the authority of a single branch of Christianity to authorize (only its own) doctrinal growth. Roman Catholic scholars have made such arguments thoughtfully, but I have not found them convincing either historically or theologically. I think it wiser to stay receptive to the whole of Christian tradition, East and West, Greek and Oriental, Catholic and Protestant.[24] In my view, to read Scripture in conjunction with the rule of faith means, first of all, to read in accordance with the teaching of the apostles as found in the New Testament and as confirmed in the earliest fathers, and second, to read under the counsel and instruction of the whole Christian tradition, but not in rigid conformity with any one historical branch of the church.

Scripture, the Early Church, and Evangelicals

I would like to conclude by pointing out a few ways that evangelicals can better position themselves to learn from patristic biblical exegesis.

23. On original sin, see Augutine, *Grat. Chr.* 2.34.29; on the rule of faith in Cyprian's time, see *Bapt.* 2.1.2. At times, Augustine appears simply to defend his own interpretations of Scripture by appealing to the rule of faith, e.g., *Tract. Ev. Jo.* 105.8, *Trin.* 15.28.51.

24. It is possible to see the Spirit at work in the evolving life of the church in all its manifestations without affirming the claims of exclusivity made by any particular branch.

1. *When studying the historical sense of Scripture, we should place a higher value on tradition than on novelty.* The training of a modern Bible scholar focuses on writing a dissertation, the goal of which is to say something that no one has ever said before about some part of the Bible. This is not a helpful way for a young scholar to learn how to read Scripture. It is not impossible that a person might come up with a new insight in the course of their research, especially if they are looking at newly discovered material (for example, Ugaritic literature); but in general the requirement that young scholars prove themselves by making an "original contribution" to our understanding of the Bible promotes novelty for its own sake at the expense of trying to understand the text correctly for the text's sake. I think it would be better if the qualifications for teaching Scripture focused more on mastery of the received tradition: knowledge of biblical languages and the transmission history of the Bible, knowledge of the commentary tradition as much as possible (including the best of modern scholarship), and competence in the disciplines of hermeneutics and theology. Reading the church fathers on Scripture will help us to make tried and true observations about the Bible, and thereby perceive the literal sense of what the text said in a way that respects the subject matter.

2. *In looking to discover the Bible's meaningfulness, we should contemplate how our understanding of Scripture relates to our understanding of God.* We should ask the questions: What can the text tell us about God? What does the character of God tell us about how to organize the ideas of the text? The church fathers read Scripture to hear what God was saying, so they naturally kept their doctrine of God at the center of their hermeneutic, and some (such as Origen) regarded prayer to God and illumination by the Spirit as crucial for discovering the "higher sense." While they were generally willing to talk about a "past tense" sense of Scripture, they focused on how Scripture spoke to the present, and as Christians they did not usually seek to apply the "principles" of Scripture apart from Christ, since it is through Christ that the literature of ancient Israel has come to be meaningful and authoritative for the church. One of the most important benefits that can come from reading Scripture with the church fathers is the emphasis they place on Christ and the doctrine of God.

3. *In seeking to identify and utilize early Christian traditions that relate to the interpretation of Scripture, we should respect historical diversity and we*

should focus on the gospel. The historical diversity of patristic literature is an essential part of its importance. The church fathers do not simply offer one way to read Scripture, but they present numerous paradigms and open up a wide range of insights into how best to interpret the Bible. Issues of development and variety should be studied and valued. At the same time, within this diversity one can recognize throughout early Christian tradition a distinctive sense of Christian identity, as can be seen in the earliest statements of the rule of faith. However much variety may have existed in the patristic church, all Christians of this period were united by their belief in the core gospel of Jesus Christ. The reality of diversity along with this common grounding in the gospel make the early church an obvious conversation partner and teacher for contemporary evangelicals.

A Response to Michael W. Graves

Timothy Larsen

Wheaton College

Dr. Michael Graves has insightfully and honestly mapped the possibilities, limitations, and questions that arise when thinking about the interaction of evangelicals, the Bible, and the early church, and therefore my purpose here will be primarily to underline some of Dr. Graves's observations.

If you will forgive it, I would like to begin illustrating one of Dr. Graves's points by speaking autobiographically. I was raised as a low-church evangelical Protestant. My idea of ecclesiastical architecture has always been folding chairs in a gymnasium. I went to a private Christian school for kindergarten through high school, but do not recall ever hearing of any Christian figure between the New Testament and Martin Luther. (Luther, however, got a full day all his own annually in which normal classes were disrupted to aid learning about Luther's life and thought). Therefore the first time I ever read anything by a church father was during my first semester as a freshman at Wheaton College, when I was assigned Augustine's *Confessions*. It was the Penguin edition and I still have my original copy. The cover image depicted St Augustine in ostentatiously rich vestments and full ecclesiastical attire including prominently what appeared to my untrained eye to be opera gloves. This cover image seemed to me to speak of the kind of dead, formal, Christianity that my evangelical spirituality had taught me to distrust, if not despise. But you can't judge a book by its cover. David Bebbington has taught us to think in terms of four markers of evangelicalism: conversionism, activism, biblicism, and crucicentrism. I think I was probably most won over by Augustine's clear testimony of his conversion experience.

Nevertheless, in line with Dr. Graves's comments, Augustine's attentiveness to Scripture also struck me forcefully. My freshman self was asked to write a short reaction paper to the *Confessions*, and one passage that I focused on would surely be seen as incidental and insignificant to most scholars: it is in book 4, chapter 4, when Augustine comments: "How I cried out to you when I read those Psalms! How they set me on fire with love of you!" Here was a living, personal, intimate relationship with God nourished by reading the Bible—something an eighteen-year-old evangelical Protestant could identify with.

I also remember being gripped by books 10–13. In my first year of teaching I assigned the *Confessions*, but was stunned when the edition I had carelessly ordered for my students came in and I discovered that it did not even include the last three books. It had not occurred to me that an editor and publisher would assume that there would be readers who would track with Augustine when he was expounded on themes such as the errors of Manichaeism or the nature of memory, but would draw the line when he started commenting on Holy Scripture—particularly as prominent, resonant, and inviting a biblical passage as the first chapter of Genesis. All that goes to say that I agree with Dr. Graves that an ideal way for evangelical Protestants to join the patristic conversation in a way that is the least disorienting for them is to read the fathers commenting on the Bible.

Dr. Graves also rightly reminds us that the Bible is a collection of books from time periods and cultures very different from our own and therefore its appropriation by believers today can be done in deeply misguided ways—a potential danger, as he also demonstrates, that the fathers well understood. Dr. Graves wisely commends to us the patristic pattern of reading Scripture in the light of the rule of faith. In the last few years I have spent a fair amount of time reading nineteenth-century Unitarians who believed in the plenary, verbal inspiration and truthfulness of the Bible. If these Unitarians had learned to read with the rule of faith, it would have saved them many errors. Evangelical Protestants have been relearning this lesson in recent decades. Perhaps most symbolically, the Evangelical Theological Society decided that its sole confessional point on the nature of Scripture was insufficient and so added an affirmation of the doctrine of Trinity as well. Wheaton College, where Dr. Graves and I teach, of course, has its own statement of faith. Dr. Graves has noticed that Irenaeus, Tertullian, and Origen had a basic rule of faith in common, even though they all also incorporated a few special themes of their own, and perhaps one can say as well that the Wheaton statement of faith is an expression of the rule of faith, its own idiosyncratic touches notwithstanding.

This emphasis on the rule of faith is vitally important because it seems to me that the main evangelical Protestant temptation in biblical interpretation and theological reflection is still to attempt to reinvent the wheel from scratch and thereby to end up going off the rails. The sixteenth-century Radical Reformers in the town of Münster serve as a perpetual warning of what can happen when people try to interpret the Bible without reference to what the church has believed and practiced throughout the centuries. Such a go-it-alone effort reflects a fundamental arrogance that disdains to make use of the resources that God has given to us—one primary such resource being patristic biblical, theological, and ecclesial reflections.

Still, as an evangelical Protestant, I would like to strike a note that some other Christians might not sound. It is precisely because we have the Bible and the rule of faith that it is possible for new theological and ecclesial insights to arise today. Gregory of Nazianzus taught:

> The Old Testament preached the Father openly and the Son more obscurely. The New Testament revealed the Son, and hinted at the divinity of the Holy Spirit. Now the Spirit dwells in us, and is revealed more clearly to us. It was not proper to preach the Son openly, while the divinity of the Father had not yet been admitted. Nor was it proper to accept the Holy Spirit before [the divinity of] the Son had been acknowledged. . . . Instead, by gradual advances and . . . partial ascents, we should move forward and increase in clarity, so that the light of the Trinity should shine.[1]

As a Protestant, I would posit the possibility of the continuation of this process during the life of the church through the centuries; that a time can come when another area of doctrine or practice—for example, justification by faith or the priesthood of all believers—would come into increased clarity. Of course, Luther himself was keen to show how the ideas he was championing were present in the writings of church fathers. To conclude, therefore, a Protestant view of the development of doctrine places its weight differently from a Roman Catholic or Eastern

1. Gregory of Nazianzus, *Theological Orations*, in McGrath, *Christian Theology Reader*, 192.

Orthodox one in that Protestants are more willing to posit the possibility that the church might have wandered into error on a certain point or set of points and need to be restored to faithfulness to the Bible and the gospel in those particular areas. It cannot be stressed too much, however, that it is a very rare person in the history of the church who is ordained by God to restore a neglected truth—and it is not only a presumptuous but a spiritually dangerous and destructive act to take up such a role without a genuine divine call. Therefore, when the rest of us are tempted to interpret a biblical text (or, as Dr. Graves has remembered us, pursue our little pet point of novelty in a PhD thesis) in a way not in line with the consensus of historic Christianity, but rather in our own eccentric manner, we would do well to quote to ourselves a line from T. S. Eliot: "I am no prophet—and here's no great matter."

9

Evangelicals

Are They the Real Catholics and Orthodox?

GERALD L. BRAY

Beeson Divinity School

What's in a Name?

How CATHOLIC AND HOW orthodox are evangelicals? Those who belong to the great historic churches that call themselves Catholic and Orthodox may be friendly, hostile, somewhere in-between or indifferent to evangelical Christianity, but they all think that it is at best a truncated and inadequate version of the faith they profess. Catch them in an ecumenical mood and they may admit that evangelicals share important elements of Catholicism and/or Orthodoxy, and some of them are generous enough to recognize that individual evangelicals often put others to shame with their knowledge of the Bible and their eagerness to spread the gospel as they understand it. But however positive towards evangelicals they may be, they cannot accept that evangelicalism is a form of apostolic Christianity equal to their own beliefs, or that it could ever be authentically catholic or orthodox. To their minds, evangelicals must join the Catholic or the Orthodox church in order to perfect their faith and give it a maturity and depth that it otherwise lacks.

In recent years, a few high-profile converts from evangelicalism to Roman Catholicism or Eastern Orthodoxy, as well as a growing awareness among evangelicals of the riches of the wider Christian tradition, have brought this question to the fore in a way that has seldom if ever been seen before. For the first time in living memory, many evangelicals are now asking themselves whether the great churches of Rome or the East have something we need in order to be faithful soldiers and servants of Jesus Christ. What substance do the claims of those churches have, and how should evangelicals respond to them?

As Christians, evangelicals, Catholics, and Orthodox have a good deal in common. In fact, each group applies all three of these terms to itself, even if it prefers one of them as a convenient way of distinguishing it from the others. For example, Roman Catholics believe that their church is the touchstone of both orthodox and evangelical Christianity, but nobody ever speaks about the "Roman Orthodox" or the "Roman Evangelical Church"! The Eastern churches likewise think of themselves as being fully catholic and evangelical, but the term "Eastern Catholics" refers to churches of the Eastern rite in communion with Rome, and "Eastern Evangelicals," if it is ever used, can only refer to Protestants living in traditionally Orthodox countries.

Catholics and Orthodox do not often use the word "evangelical" in the context of their own churches, but when they do, they are usually speaking about a form of spirituality that seeks to return to the life and practice of Jesus and his disciples. Thus, it is not uncommon to hear Catholics say that St. Francis of Assisi advocated a life of "evangelical poverty" in direct imitation of Christ.

This usage is important, because evangelicalism is essentially a spiritual movement found mainly in Protestant churches, but having an ambiguous relationship to them. It is doctrinally conservative in the sense that it holds to the central beliefs of both the ancient creeds and the sixteenth-century Reformation confessions, but it generally sits light to the theological distinctives that created and have maintained the separate identity of the different Protestant denominations. Indeed, there have always been some evangelicals who have been prepared to look beyond Protestantism and recognize kindred souls among both Roman Catholics and Eastern Orthodox. If the latter regard evangelicals as potential converts who are already in possession of important elements of the truth, evangelicals see them as members of corrupt denominations who have become true believers in spite of that. To Catholics and Orthodox who may be puzzled or offended by this, it should be said that evangelicals think the same way about the mainline Protestant churches. The difference is that whereas Protestant evangelicals can reconcile their spiritual experience to their church's official doctrine, even to the point of claiming to be the only ones who take it seriously, evangelical Catholics and Orthodox are forced to turn a blind eye to aspects of their church's teaching that contradict their spiritual experience.

We have forgotten it now, but in the eighteenth century, Protestant evangelicals came across as liberals because they put their spiritual experience before their church organization or confession of faith, and traces of that attitude can still be found in some traditionally minded Protestant denominations like the Lutheran Church Missouri Synod or the Southern Baptist Convention. Evangelicalism is transdenominational and transconfessional, having emerged in the context of a divided Protestantism as a spiritual movement determined to put the basic principles of the gospel, as these had been rediscovered in the Protestant Reformation, into practice. Roman Catholics and Eastern Orthodox, with a different ecclesiology and historical experience, often find this difficult to understand. They are puzzled to discover that liberal Protestants, with whom they have much less in common, are often more willing to engage in dialogue with them than many evangelicals are, and that those evangelicals who do talk to them are usually disowned by some of their fellows, for whom any pre-Reformation church is virtually un-Christian.

Leaving such prejudices aside, we must recognize that there is a real question of theological method at stake here. To put it bluntly, how can we compare evangelicals with Catholics and Orthodox when evangelicals are a part of a spiritual movement lacking a central authority or clear boundaries, and the others belong to highly structured ecclesiastical institutions? Is there any common ground that would make a genuine comparison possible?

To test this, let us begin with the term "orthodox," which evangelicals appropriate more readily than "catholic," and which is probably easier to define. The word originally meant "right worship," but that can only be the fruit of right belief, which is how the word is now used in both secular and religious contexts. An orthodox Christian believes that the Holy Scriptures are God's revelation to humanity and confesses the faith expounded in them. Any teaching that contradicts what they say must be rejected. Of course, there are times when Scripture is not clear, and problems arise that a simple appeal to the text does not resolve. When that happens, the church must either decree what is to be believed or say that the disputed issue is a matter of indifference that can be left to private judgment. The first of these options was taken by the great ecumenical councils, which decided complex matters of Trinitarian belief and Christology in a way that has been accepted by most of the Christian world ever since. There are churches in the Middle East that did not accept the two-natures Christology of the council of Chalcedon, held in 451, but modern ecumenical discussions have shown that this has more to do with the technicalities of theological expression than with the substance of belief, and so the non-Chalcedonian churches of the East are usually accepted today as being orthodox in intention, if not always in expression.

Allowing for that exception, the Eastern Orthodox define themselves as the church of the seven ecumenical councils, the last of which was held at Nicaea in 787. In their eyes, the claim of a Christian church to be called "orthodox" is determined by its attitude to them. Rome accepts all seven, but its claim to orthodoxy is rejected because it adds a further fourteen councils which it insists are ecumenical because they were summoned by the pope and their decisions have been ratified by him, even though the Eastern churches have not accepted them. There is also the problem that Rome has never ratified the council *in Trullo*, so called because it was held in the imperial palace of Trullum in Constantinople in the winter of 691–692. That council promulgated disciplinary canons to supplement the doctrinal pronouncements of the fifth and sixth ecumenical councils, which Rome does recognize. Many of the practical differences that distinguish the Eastern from the Roman church, like the use of leavened bread in the Eucharist and the right of married men to be ordained as priests, derive from the canons of the council *in Trullo*. Some Orthodox insist that these disciplinary canons have the same divine sanction as the doctrinal decisions of the other councils, but opinion within the Eastern churches is divided on this. There are also a number of canons promulgated at other councils that were not ecumenical, but which Orthodox tradition has absorbed into its understanding of the faith and which would be almost impossible to abolish or even modify now. The difficulty the Eastern churches face is that any attempt to do so is liable to split their own communion without achieving reunion with Rome, as the sorry tale of the calendar has demonstrated. In the early twentieth century, some Orthodox churches abandoned the Julian calendar for the Gregorian one, but this produced schism within the Orthodox world and has led to a situation in which all Orthodox churches still adhere to the Julian date of Easter so as not to cause further division, and those that have changed the calendar are under constant pressure from conservative elements to return to the traditional Julian usage.

The Eastern churches also reject Rome's claim to orthodoxy because they say it turns the mystical and spiritual nature of the faith into a legal code that covers everything and leaves precious little freedom to the individual believer. In their eyes, Protestants are just as bad, because they also use juridical categories to define their understanding of the faith. The validity of this Eastern perception can be debated, but suffice it to say that the Eastern church's claim to have greater spiritual freedom is not always what it appears to be. Take for example, the double procession of the Holy Spirit, a doctrine that Western Christians are obliged to believe but that Eastern Christians are not. Theoretically, this means that Eastern Christians are free to believe it if they wish, but in practice the Eastern churches expect that their members, and especially their official representatives, will *not* believe it, if only because it was defined by Rome without consulting them. It is therefore misleading to say that the Eastern churches allow freedom on this point, and the same must be said for other doctrines that are regarded as characteristic of the Western churches. For instance, when asked by the Lutherans whether he believed in justification by faith alone or not, Patriarch Jeremias II of Constantinople replied that he did not understand the question and would therefore have to say no. Some Orthodox go to the point of saying that Western Christians must renounce more than a millennium of theological thought and go back to the eighth century, but Catholics and Protestants both reject that idea as unrealistic. To them, Eastern Christianity may be fine as far as it goes but it got stuck in the early Middle Ages, and by discounting so much of the Western tradition has effectively made itself incapable of setting the standard of orthodoxy for the rest of the Christian world.

Where do evangelicals stand in relation to this? As Protestants, they accept the decisions of the early church councils in so far as they reflect the teaching of Scripture. In practice, this means that they have little trouble with the first six ecumenical councils, apart from the canons made at the council *in Trullo*, which they generally ignore. They do, however, have problems with the seventh council because of the way in which that council authorized the veneration of icons. Evangelicals do not deny that Jesus Christ was a real human being whose physical features could have been painted during his lifetime, but point out that this did not happen. Furthermore, there is no encouragement given in the New Testament or in the very early church period to make pictures of him or of anyone else, and certainly no suggestion that such pictures should be venerated as an integral, not to say essential, part of worship. Here the Eastern churches have gone beyond the teaching of Scripture and evangelicals cannot follow them. What is more, the veneration of icons is not peripheral but central to Orthodox worship and devotion, which makes the evangelical rejection of them more serious than it would otherwise be.

On other matters however, evangelicals are generally at one with Catholics and Orthodox on the great doctrines of the Christian faith as the ancient councils expressed them. For example, evangelicals do not regard Jehovah's Witnesses as Christians any more than Catholics or Orthodox do, because their Christology is not that canonized by the early church. Here the difference between evangelicals and Catholics or Orthodox lies not in the content of orthodoxy but in their attitude towards the sources to which appeal is made to justify it. Whereas for both Catholics and Orthodox it is the reception of the conciliar decisions by the church that makes them authoritative, for evangelicals it is their conformity to Holy Scripture—the criterion, we may add, on which the councils themselves based their decisions. In other words, evangelicals decide what is orthodox in the same way as the ancient councils did, and not on the ground that those councils possessed some special divine insight or authority of their own. We can therefore argue that evangelicals are closer to the mind of the early Christians than either the Orthodox or the Catholic churches are, because their principles and theological methods are closer to those of the church fathers. Like them, we respect our forbears and walk in their footsteps, but without canonizing their decisions as infallible and therefore immutable. Orthodoxy remains fundamentally the same in every age, but its expression can change and grow if circumstances so demand, as the fathers of the ecumenical councils knew very well.

The word "catholic" is seldom claimed either by evangelicals or the Eastern churches, probably because the Roman church has so successfully appropriated the term to itself that to do so would only cause confusion. A century ago, G. K. Chesterton wrote a book called *Orthodoxy*, which was a defense of Roman Catholicism. Readers might disagree with his definition, but relatively few would be surprised to discover that the book is not about the Eastern churches. Around the same time however, W. H. Griffith Thomas wrote a book of Anglican evangelical theology, which he called *The Catholic Faith*, but most people today are surprised when they discover that it is a refutation of the teachings of the Roman church and not an exposition of them. Rightly or wrongly, the Roman claim to exclusive use of the term "catholic" has been accepted by the general public and if Griffith Thomas were writing today, he would probably have to change his title to something less misleading. In the eyes of Rome, to be catholic is to be in communion with the bishop of Rome, whom it claims is the vicar of Christ on earth, the successor of St. Peter and the chief pastor of the universal church, which he is called to govern as "the servant of the servants of God." Other churches may use the word *papa* as a term of endearment for their heads, but the bishop of Rome has succeeded in appropriating it to such an extent that even the Eastern Orthodox now use it primarily of him. For a Catholic, to be orthodox is above all to submit to the pope as its universal head on earth. Those who fail to do this have lost their catholicity and compromised their orthodoxy, because they are out of communion with the one who is privileged to embody that catholicity and to determine what its orthodoxy should be.

The papacy likes to insist that its claims to universal ecclesiastical jurisdiction go back to Jesus, who told Peter that he was the rock on which the church would be built and that he would be given the keys of the kingdom, allowing him to decide who was and who was not part of that church. Peter is then supposed to have been the first bishop of Rome and to have passed on his authority to his successors, the two hundred and sixty-third of these being Pope Benedict XVI. It is claimed that no pope has ever fallen into heresy, and that when he speaks in his official capacity, his pronouncements are held to be infallible and binding on the church as a whole. This gives him the power to define new doctrines, like the perpetual virginity of Mary and her bodily assumption into heaven, which then become matters that we must believe if we want to be saved. Allowance is made for what is called "invincible ignorance" and for people like Thomas Aquinas, who lived centuries before these doctrines were defined and who explicitly rejected them, but such indulgence is not available to modern believers. The truth is that the church whose proudest boast is that it is always and everywhere the same has changed over time as new revelation has been given to it, and Catholics today are not at liberty to subscribe to what was acceptably catholic in the thirteenth century.

That is just as well, because the further back one goes in Christian history, the less solid the evidence is for the claims that the modern Roman church insists upon. There is no indication that Peter was Rome's first bishop, though it is probable that he was martyred there in the time of Nero, nor do we know anything about his supposed successors until more than a century later. Rome's prominence in the Christian world was due to its position as the imperial capital, and it was only when that was threatened that its claims to spiritual jurisdiction began to be advanced. Even then, the seven ecumenical councils of the ancient church were all held independently of the Roman bishop, who was expected to ratify their decisions just like any other church leader of the time. It would not be until the eleventh century that the papacy would start to claim jurisdiction over the rest of Christendom, a claim that has always been strongly resisted by the Eastern churches. The popes had more success in Western Europe, but even there it was by no means always plain sailing. Remote places like Ireland resisted papal control until after the Reformation, and in the fourteenth century the kings of France managed to hijack the papacy and install the pope at Avignon. The return to Rome two generations later provoked a schism that at one point led to the creation of three different popes. Even when that difficulty was finally overcome, it took another generation for the papacy to re-establish its control over the church, a process that involved a good deal of underhanded diplomacy and some vigorous prosecution of dissenters like Jan Hus. Since then, every advance in papal power has provoked schism, the most recent one being that of the so-called Old Catholics, who refused to accept the proclamation of papal infallibility in 1870. Far from being an instrument of unity, the papacy became and has remained one of the main stumbling blocks to the achievement of what it officially stands for.

But quite apart from its failure to persuade Protestant and Eastern Orthodox Christians to accept its claims, the modern papacy is also faced with widespread rebellion and disarray within its own ranks. To be blunt, it is only outsiders who think that all Roman Catholics are genuinely submissive to the pope. Many Catholic observers of their own church accuse its members of evading papal decrees (on birth control, for example) rather than implementing them, and the gap between the huge numbers of people who are officially recorded as Catholics and the relatively few who practice their faith is wider than in any other church. The superstructure looks impressive, but take a closer look and you will soon find that the foundations are weaker than they seem and crumbling, not least in places like Spain, Quebec, and Ireland, where Catholicism enjoyed a virtual monopoly for centuries but is now in serious danger of disappearing as the younger generation turns its back on an institution that has insisted on remaining excessively hierarchical in an increasingly democratic age.

Having said that, it remains true that the Christian gospel is one message of salvation that is valid for all people, and so the sense of universality embodied in Catholicism is an intrinsic part of the church's identity. Can any other branch of Christianity plausibly claim the kind of catholicity that Rome has always regarded as its hallmark? The Eastern Orthodox churches do make such claims, but only up to a point. It is not widely understood that they have always recognized the Petrine primacy of the Roman church and been willing to accord a presidency of honor to the pope, provided that he ceases to claim universal jurisdiction over the church as a whole. As a result, although the Eastern churches claim to be catholic in the sense of holding the fullness of the faith, they do not claim to embrace the whole of Christendom in the way that Rome does. In a reunited church, they would not replace the papacy but re-establish it along what they believe are the correct lines so that true catholicity can be achieved. How realistic this is may be questioned, but it is fair to say that the Eastern churches as they now stand do not think of themselves as being the universal church in and of themselves.

Evangelicals are in a different position altogether. Unlike the Eastern churches, they are not a historical institution challenging the papacy's self-conceptions of its role and authority in the Christian world. Their approach to Catholicism is part of a wider challenge to all forms of institutional Christianity, including those of their own churches. Evangelicalism does not rival Rome in institutional terms but offers an alternative understanding of what the church is. As they will tell you themselves, evangelicals belong to the church because the gospel of Jesus Christ has changed their lives. They may have been brought up in a Christian environment and even believed the fundamental truths of the faith, but it was not until they heard the gospel, were convicted of their sinfulness, and repented and surrendered their lives to Christ in a direct and personal way that they became living members of the body of Christ. There is a particular kind of conversion narrative associated with evangelicals, but evangelicals are not usually too bothered about the details of how people have become Christians. They recognize that God works in mysterious ways; what matters to them is the fact that God *has worked* in your life and that you really *are* a believer right at this very moment. The rest is history and the precise details are irrelevant as far as having fellowship with them now is concerned.

Evangelicals are people of the present and the future more than of the past, and in this respect they differ significantly from many Catholics and Orthodox, who are steeped in tradition and regard it as authoritative for their faith and practice. Evangelicals are not entirely indifferent to tradition, but to them it is a tool to use and not an object to revere. If you can show an evangelical that he has something to learn from Augustine, Aquinas, or John Calvin, he may be interested in them, but in evangelical circles the great saints of the past are liable to find themselves competing with modern preachers like Mark Driscoll or Tony Campolo for attention. It is easy to be dismissive of this attitude, but in thinking the way they do evangelicals are probably closer to the mindset of those great saints than are many of the more historically minded. Men like Basil of Caesarea, Bernard of Clairvaux, and Martin Luther were dynamic and enthusiastic innovators who did all they could to stir the church into action, but it has to be said that their memory often seems to be cultivated most by those who are least inclined to imitate them. Evangelicals rarely make that mistake, believing instead that the Holy Spirit who inspired them is alive and working in us today for the same basic purpose and with equal or perhaps even greater effect.

As a spiritual movement, evangelicalism lacks a clear institutional identity. There are some small denominations that are entirely evangelical, but many evangelicals belong to mixed churches, where they are often a barely-tolerated minority. This situation is sometimes painful for those caught up in it, but it has the great advantage of making evangelicals see that they cannot tie their faith to the institutional church. That in turn means that they are open to the possibility that people who do not belong to their particular denomination may be brothers and sisters in Christ, whom they will recognize as such even if they differ from them on many secondary matters. You cannot be either Catholic or Orthodox without being received into membership of one of those churches, but you can be an evangelical regardless of your church affiliation, even when the church in question is officially opposed to evangelical beliefs. In claiming to be both catholic and orthodox, evangelicals are referring to the substance of those terms, and not restricting themselves to formal or institutional definitions, which they regard as secondary. Seen from that perspective, evangelicals can reasonably claim to be at least as catholic as anyone else, and probably more so. Not only do they see no need to abandon an evangelical church for a Catholic or Orthodox one, but they think that their own understanding of the Christian faith does greater justice to the true meaning of catholicity and orthodoxy than do the churches that go by those names. Indeed, someone who abandons an evangelical church for a Catholic or Orthodox one may actually be diminishing his catholicity and orthodoxy because he will be forced to break communion with those who are not members of his new church.

That is a bold claim to make, especially at a time when it has become fashionable for some American evangelicals to convert to Rome or to one of the Eastern churches and then to become missionaries to their former brethren. It should perhaps be said that this phenomenon is largely confined to the United States and would be almost incomprehensible in the European countries where these different churches originated. In the USA, there is a free market in religion and people can usually choose whatever they want. There is competition for adherents, and all kinds of claims are advanced in support of one church or another. Rome or the Eastern churches can say that they are ancient and authentic in a way that Baptists or Presbyterians are not, and many will find that a plausible and persuasive argument. Europeans think differently. Most European Protestants think of Catholics and Orthodox as coming mainly from parts of the continent that are backward, corrupt, or both, and are not persuaded by any claims to spiritual superiority they might make. Conversions do occasionally occur, but Protestants who cross the line seldom become evangelists to their erstwhile coreligionists. A good example is the case of Tony Blair, the former British Prime Minister, who became a Roman Catholic six months after leaving office in 2007. Many people regarded this as just another stunt from the stunt master himself, but not even those who took him seriously imagined that he had changed his personal convictions, whatever they might be. The all but universal perception among believers and unbelievers alike was that it was more a case of Rome opportunistically relaxing the rules for new converts than of a Damascus road experience on Tony's part. At least nobody need worry that he is about to write a book about it or go on the lecture circuit to extol the virtues of his newfound faith, as he might have done had he been a former American president instead.

This is not just because Europeans tend to be more skeptical about religious matters than Americans; it is also because they sense that so much more is involved in conversion than simply going to a different church next Sunday. History and daily experience tell us that there are profound differences separating the major Christian churches and that these differences have important social and cultural consequences. My own Church of England has spread its wings to the ends of the earth, scooping up everyone from native tribes in the South Pacific to the lesbian and gay tribe in North America, but it has never gone to France. Why not? It is not simply that we do not want Frenchmen in heaven—we do not expect to see them there in any case—but because we feel that somehow we are not meant to preach the Gospel to them. They have a Christian heritage of their own to deal with, and creating French Anglicans seems to be pointless and even wrong. In that context, what it means to be an evangelical, and how we relate to Catholics and Orthodox, takes on another dimension that is of great practical importance at the level of everyday mission.

I have painted this as a difference between Europe and America, but although there is some truth in this, the two continents are closely connected and relations between evangelicals and Catholics or Orthodox in the United States are in reality just as complicated as they are elsewhere. The great Christian churches have become what they are for theological reasons that have developed distinct traditions and created lasting social and cultural differences. Only a clear understanding of how the Christian church has developed and differentiated itself theologically can make us fully appreciate this, and it is to that development we must now turn.

Understanding the Christian Tradition

Christianity is essentially a monotheistic faith in the Holy Trinity—three distinct Persons in the one Being of God. The doctrine of the Trinity sets us apart from Judaism and Islam, the other so-called religions of Abraham. In many ways, Judaism and Islam have more in common with each other than Christianity has with either of them, despite our obvious kinship. A Christian minister will go to seminary to study theology, whereas a Jewish or Muslim one will specialize in religious law. To put it in simple terms, there is no Christian equivalent to *kosher* or *halal* food, and no Jewish or Muslim equivalent to the bread that came down from heaven in the person of Jesus Christ.

That Christianity would never be just a variant form of Judaism was clear from the start. When Jesus called God his "Father," he made himself equal with God in Jewish eyes and forced his followers to think about their inherited monotheism in a new and different way. Calling God "Father" is so commonplace today that we forget how strange it seemed to those who first heard Jesus talking like that. In the New Testament, "Father" is not just another title given to God but the name of a person who lives in relation to the Son and to the Holy Spirit within the Godhead. It took some time for the precise nature of that relationship to be clarified, but its main outlines were presupposed from the start by identifying the one God of Abraham as being somehow also three.

Once the identity of the Father was secured, the next stage was to clarify the nature of his work. This meant identifying him as both the Creator and the Redeemer. In the late first and early second centuries it was not uncommon to say that the Father of Jesus Christ was the Redeemer God, and that the material world had been created by an inferior deity, known as the Demiurge. Christianity however, could not tolerate such a distinction between the Creator and the Redeemer, because it called into question the incarnation and bodily resurrection of the Son of God, who could not have assumed sinful matter and remained fully divine.

This way of thinking, which modern scholarship has labeled "Gnosticism," was finally overcome by the third century and is now known only to specialists. No sooner had that happened though, than the next theological controversy broke out, this time over the identity of Jesus Christ. When that first became an issue is hard to say, but it went back at least to Paul of Samosata, who was condemned in 268 for saying that Jesus was a human being whom God had adopted as his son. Adoptionism never got very far, but it was quickly supplanted by more sophisticated theories of how God and man were related in Christ, and it took two centuries of debate to resolve the question to most people's satisfaction. The definition adopted at the council of Chalcedon in 451, which has become standard in most churches, says that the Son is a divine person who became a man by assuming a complete human nature in addition to the divine one he already possessed. Resistance to this continued in the East and led to further councils that had to clarify the implications of Chalcedon, but although the schisms caused at that time have not been resolved, it is fair to say that for most Christians the issue was settled and has never been seriously challenged.

The next great controversy to erupt was over the work of Christ, which was expounded in depth by Anselm of Canterbury in the eleventh century and remained a theological battleground until the Reformation. Before Anselm's time, the doctrine of salvation, or soteriology, was subsumed under Christology; in the words of Gregory of Nazianzus, "what has not been assumed has not been healed." Even Anselm couched his discussion of the saving work of Christ in incarnational terms—he did not ask why Christ died, but why God became man, the question that is the very title in Latin of his famous book (*Cur deus homo?*). Anselm's answer was to say that on the cross, Jesus paid the price for the sins of the whole world, which he then took up into heaven. From the mercy seat at the right hand of the Father, he now dispenses grace from the merit he earned by his death and through the sacramental system of the church, and he applies it to each individual sin, as when sinners draw on him for help.

This so-called satisfaction theory of the atonement eventually gave rise to the system of indulgences, which was fully developed in late medieval theology and against which Martin Luther protested so strongly. Luther might have gained more sympathy if he had stuck to criticizing abuses of the system, rather than the system itself, but his protest moved from being a current within the Western church to becoming a revolt against it because he came to realize that Christ had not died for sins, as abstract things, but for sinners—for people who had been chosen from before the foundation of the world to receive the adoption as sons proclaimed by the apostle Paul in Romans and Galatians.

Before that was clarified though, a further controversy had already broken out over the identity of the Holy Spirit. From the fifth century onwards, the Western church had said that the Holy Spirit proceeds from both the Father and the Son. The Eastern church had no clearly formulated view of this, but whenever the subject was raised, its spokesmen inclined to the view that the Spirit did not proceed from the Son, because the Father alone was the fountainhead of deity. The difference of opinion grew sharper as the centuries wore on, but did not become a source of theological conflict until the Western church tried to impose its authority on the East. There were attempts made to reach an understanding at the second council of Lyon in 1274 and again at the council of Florence in 1439, but they both failed, and after the fall of Constantinople to the Turks in 1453, West and East went their separate ways.

In the Western church, that led to the next stage of theological development, which concerns the Holy Spirit's work. The Protestant Reformation became what it was because it combined a certain understanding of the work of the Spirit with a certain understanding of the atoning work of Christ to produce a new kind of Christianity. Luther and his followers based their case on the Bible alone, a method that was to be characteristic of their followers. In essence, what it amounted to was the belief that the work of the Spirit was primarily spiritual—the Holy Spirit bears witness with our spirit that we are children of God. If that is so, then it must also be primarily personal. A Christian believer is not someone who has been cleansed of his sins but a sinner who has been justified before God by the shed blood of Christ. This justification is not measured by the number of sins he has committed, but is defined by his status as a sinner. In other words, whether you have sinned a lot or a little makes no difference; you still need the saving grace of God because you are sinful whether you have expressed this outwardly or not. The grace of God does not remove your sins but unites you to Christ, who pleads with the Father to forgive you on account of his sacrifice, and not because of anything you have done.

According to Anselm, Christ died for the sins of the whole world, and his sacrifice was universal both in intent and in efficacy. Evangelical Christians agree with him that no sin is too great for the blood of Christ to be able to pay for it, but we also believe that Christ died for specific people, whom he has united to his death and atonement by uniting them to himself. His saving work is effective only for those who are so united to him by the work of the Holy Spirit, and it is over the nature of that union that evangelicals differ most profoundly from Rome.

In the Roman view, the Holy Spirit works primarily through institutions of one kind or another. Jesus chose disciples, laid hands on them, and empowered them to do the same to the next generation. Today, those who are called to minister the gospel are the direct descendants, through the laying on of hands, of the apostles. It is true that mistakes are sometimes made—even Jesus had to put up with Judas—but the authority of the teaching office, or *magisterium*, is protected by Christ's promise to Peter and his successors that the gates of hell will not prevail against them. The continuity of sacramental administration guarantees that even if the minister is defective, the message will continue to have its saving effect. Just as a medicine ought to be given by a qualified doctor but does not lose its healing power merely because it is administered by an unsuitable person, so the sacraments remain valid even when the minister himself is suspect. The Roman system does not depend on subjective experiences like conviction of sin or the indwelling presence of the Holy Spirit. Those things may of course be present, but they are not essential to salvation in the way that receiving Christ's sacramental gift of himself in the Eucharist is. Of course, the communicant must be prepared to receive the sacrament in the right way, since otherwise it will harm him. That involves confession and penance, which are equally sacramental and efficacious. For every sin confessed to the priest there is an appropriate penance, and when he has done what is required of him the sinner will be absolved of his guilt and restored to favor with God.

How different all of this is from the evangelical view. Evangelicals have the same theological framework and use the same vocabulary, but invest them with a different meaning because their understanding of the work of the Holy Spirit is different. We believe that the Holy Spirit works primarily in the hearts of those who have been chosen for salvation. It is possible, indeed it is easy and very common, to administer the sacraments to people who have no faith and no desire to submit to Christ. The belief that a person is born again simply by being baptized is untenable, as two well-known examples will illustrate. Adolf Hitler was baptized a Catholic and Josef Stalin as an Orthodox; indeed, Stalin even went to seminary! Were either of them born again? Who would make such a claim? Admittedly these are extreme cases, but they make the theological point: it is not enough to receive the outward sacramental signs to become a Christian. If there is no faith in the heart, external actions of whatever kind will fail in their purpose. You do not become a Christian by having water poured over you but by being born again, a spiritual reality to which baptism bears witness but with which it cannot be identified.

In sum, it was the discovery of the supreme importance of the inner working of the Holy Spirit, who draws us to Christ by grace and not by works, that caused the sixteenth-century Reformation. From the beginning the Reformed churches called themselves evangelical, and some still do. But it is clear to everyone nowadays that if Protestantism and evangelicalism were once synonymous, that is no longer true. Something has happened to make the modern evangelical a very distinct kind of Protestant, so much so in fact that many evangelicals feel closer to Roman Catholics and Eastern Orthodox Christians than they do to non-evangelical members of their own churches. Why is this so and what are we to make of it?

The Protestant Reformation had many positive features, but there were negative ones as well and we must not be blind to them. Because it was not a centrally organized movement but a spontaneous outbreak in different places, differences appeared from the very beginning. Martin Luther did not see eye to eye with Huldrych Zwingli, for example, and before long there were many different kinds of Protestant, each of them claiming to be in exclusive possession of the truth and determined to defend it, regardless of the consequences for the unity of the church. As time went on, these groups consolidated themselves and drew up confessions of faith in order to emphasize their own distinctiveness as much as anything else. These confessions tend to follow a discernible pattern, starting with the faith of Christendom as a whole, proceeding to the Reformation doctrines of justification and sanctification and then continuing with their own doctrinal distinctives. Examination of these denominational distinctives shows that they seldom have much to do with the gospel and are usually focused on secondary matters like church government, Sabbath observance and the like. Unfortunately, the churches of the Reformation divided over such things, with all sides relying on inadequate Scriptural support for their own position and preferring to exclude others rather than compromise.

The different denominations, as we now call them, gradually settled down, but much of the life that had been present in the early days of the Reformation was lost, and for many people churchgoing was just as formal and meaningless as it had been in the Middle Ages. Faced with this situation, some godly people began to wonder what had gone wrong, and whether the Protestant world could be spiritually revived and re-united by finding common ground among the different confessions. This was the climate in which modern evangelicalism was born. It began in Germany as pietism, and spread from there to the other Protestant countries of Europe, notably the British Isles, where it took the shape we now recognize. It did not seek to overturn the official confessions of faith but to probe more deeply into their spiritual meaning and make that a part of everyday experience. In Germany pietism was essentially a revival of Bible reading, prayer, and devotional singing that transformed the worship of the church. In England it became in addition a movement of popular evangelization, which eventually spilled over into foreign mission work as well. Wherever it went, it was rooted in a personal encounter with God that had many antecedents in Christian history but had been obscured by the legalism of the institutional churches. Above all, evangelicalism was a faith for the masses. The preaching of the gospel extended to everyone, rich and poor, learned and ignorant. Those who repented were born again by the indwelling presence of the Holy Spirit given to all true believers, which made them a spiritual elite within, but often on the margins of, the institutional church.

And there we have what was and still is the problem with evangelicals, as far as other Christians are concerned. They are in the institutional church in one sense but not in another. Their loyalty to a denomination may be real but it will not come before the sense of fellowship with evangelicals from other churches. In some cases it will mean leaving the institutional church and starting a new one, or even subsisting in some kind of parachurch organization, of which there are many in evangelical circles. It is the long-term viability of this ambiguous relationship of evangelicals to the institutional church that is the main cause of the current anxieties and explains the appeal of Roman Catholicism and Eastern Orthodoxy to some. Whatever else one may say about the Catholics and Orthodox, they are strong on the doctrine of the institutional church, and many evangelicals are drawn to this when they realize how weak their own tradition can be in this area. It is therefore to the nature of the church and what it means for us that we must now turn.

Understanding the Nature of the Church

Defining it has never been easy, but the church is a reality that we cannot escape. We may preach that it is individual faith that matters and think that a living relationship with God in Christ will keep us safe from what may be going on elsewhere. Yet if the Roman Catholic Church is racked by pedophile scandals, or if Eastern Orthodox Christians are being persecuted in the Middle East, we cannot remain indifferent. We may have no responsibility for these things and feel no personal connection to them, but if the name of Jesus Christ is being attacked we cannot pretend that it is none of our business or ignore it. In an increasingly secular world, Christians of all kinds are being thrown together as never before and we cannot afford the comfortable mixture of ignorance and polemic that we were too often content with in the past.

In this globalizing world, it must be said that evangelicals have been among the first to adapt to changing circumstances. Unencumbered by any notion that their denomination is the only true church, they have associated with others without fuss and usually without compromising their beliefs either. On the evangelical mission field, people do not worry whether you are Episcopalian, Presbyterian, or Congregationalist, even if the local church has necessarily adopted one of these systems of church government. Infant versus believers' baptism does not seem to present much of a problem either, at least not in parachurch missions to students and other subgroups in Western society. Evangelicals maintain their differences in such matters, but learn to live with them in a way that would be impossible for Roman Catholics or Eastern Orthodox. For them, the church is a complete whole and you must be converted to it in its entirety. It is true that many individual Catholics and Orthodox adopt a kind of "pick and mix" attitude to their own church, picking up what suits them and mixing it with influences that may come from almost anywhere. But such people do not represent their church's teaching. When they are confronted with that, it is their duty to submit, and most of them at least tone down or conceal whatever it is that they really think or do. This explains why, for example, a Roman Catholic country like Poland can have the highest rate of illegal abortions in Europe, why the Italian prime minister can live in open sexual relationships with just about any woman he can lay his hands on, and why the rulers of Russia can seek the Orthodox patriarch's blessing while at the same time engineering the assassination of selected political opponents. It is worth remembering that none of these things would be possible in a Protestant country, despite the apparent weakness and fragmentation of the churches.

This is because for Protestants, and especially for evangelicals, the impulse for Christian behavior comes from the indwelling presence of the Holy Spirit who bears witness that we are members of the spiritual body of Christ, and not from some external church authority. Evangelicals do not want to turn nominal Catholics and Orthodox into good Protestants but into active, believing Christians. If they then leave the church of their birth and join or form an evangelical one, that is a secondary development. It may be a good thing and even necessary for them to do so, but creating evangelical churches is not the primary motive of evangelization. If a man or woman has been born again in Christ, evangelicals can be (and often are) remarkably flexible about what church they then join. Some will press the claims of their own denomination, but many will not, leaving it up to the people concerned to decide what is best for them. Many evangelical converts attend an evangelical fellowship of some kind without formally cutting links with their church of origin, and in some cases they may even be led back into it as witnesses to others who are still there. Admittedly, not all evangelicals like this approach, but we can handle it more readily than a Catholic or Orthodox could, because of our different understanding of what the church is.

Is this a good thing? We live in an imperfect world, but although the evangelical solution to the challenges posed by globalization cannot claim to have solved every problem, a case can surely be made for saying that it offers the best way to achieve genuine Christian unity at the present time. The reasons for this are as follows:

1. Evangelicals put first things first. To know Christ and to make him known is our aim, and if that is achieved then other differences fade into the background or cease to matter very much, even if they continue to exist.

2. Evangelicalism is based on the teaching of Scripture, which is common to all Christians. Others may add different things, and it is perfectly true that nobody can apply the doctrine of "Scripture alone" to the life of a church, which requires something more than that to form a coherent worshipping community. But evangelicals recognize that these additions

to Scripture are external variables, to which they can adjust in spite of their own personal preferences but which they do not canonize as immutable tradition. Only what is clearly taught in Scripture is imposed on everyone, a doctrine that focuses on universal principle rather than on cherished local practices, making cross-cultural adaptation much easier that it would otherwise be.

3. Evangelicals hold firmly to the coherence of the Bible as a body of truth, which has been expressed in the ancient creeds and in the confessions of the Reformation churches without being infallibly defined by them. We hold to "basic" or "mere" Christianity, to that which everyone must believe in order to be a member of the body of Christ. We can argue over the secondary issues but on the essentials we are agreed. We stand for traditional orthodoxy not because it is traditional but because it corresponds to the revelation of Scripture and continues to function as a reliable interpreter of its message.

4. Evangelicals accept a wide variety of practices in church life without trying to impose an artificial uniformity on them. Not everyone is equally accommodating of course, and there have been cases of so-called cultural imperialism in the history of evangelization, but these phenomena are aberrations and evangelicals are usually the first to be self-critical in this respect. An infallible church is unlikely to be wrong in its own eyes, but evangelicals are generally open to the leading of the Spirit, even if this means a radical change in their direction and approach. We have never hesitated to go out into the highways and byways to bring people under the sound of the gospel, and are in the forefront—sometimes notoriously so—when it comes to using modern technologies as aids to spreading the Word of God. Since the church is a missionary society, this characteristic is both essential and admirable, and it has done more to keep the church alive in the modern world than any of its proposed alternatives has achieved.

5. Evangelicals deal with scandals better than others do. We are not perfect, and it is relatively easy for a charlatan to set himself up as an evangelist and deceive many. But the evangelical world is sufficiently decentralized and open that such behavior does not go unchallenged for long. Contrast this with the way in which pedophilia among Roman Catholic priests has been covered up by the hierarchy, sometimes for

many years. That kind of thing could never happen among us, and we must be grateful for the institutional chaos that democracy brings. An evangelical pastor who falls from grace is dealt with promptly, even if not always lovingly. But however it is handled, the situation is dealt with, and you can go into most evangelical churches reasonably confident that however awful it may be in other respects, the leadership will be accountable to the people and therefore likely to be morally and spiritually upright. Perfection is not attainable in this life, but as far as it is possible to cope with the sins of believers, it can be said that evangelicals have a track record that compares favorably with what we find in other parts of the Christian world.

There is much more that could be mentioned but time is limited and we must draw to a close. Evangelical Christianity is not perfect or infallible, but it is basic gospel truth, common to all the great churches of the Christian world. By prioritizing what is essential, it crosses entrenched denominational lines and reaches to the ends of the earth, making it in practical terms the most catholic form of Christianity that there is. By concentrating on the basics, it has a doctrinal structure that keeps it firmly within the bounds of orthodoxy, leaving freedom to develop new insights and ideas as appropriate, but at the same time never deviating from the foundations of our faith.

Its success in doing this is due not least to its willingness to question its own traditions and rework them as new light is discovered in God's Word. There are dangers in this certainly, as the current tendency in some evangelical circles to bow the knee to the goddess of feminism makes clear. Other evangelicals like to reinvent the wheel, claiming on the dust jackets of their books that they have discovered something that will completely change our way of thinking about God, the church, and our mission in the world. We suffer these aberrations, but in the end we know that if they depart from our core beliefs, they will fade away. A hundred years ago, prohibitionists captured the evangelical world with their promise of social improvement. That ended in tears, but while the prohibitionists have disappeared, evangelicals continue to thrive and move on as if that particular folly had never existed. Some of our forbears were slave traders, but others were leading abolitionists and today everyone recognizes that they were the ones who were truly faithful to the Word of God.

In preaching the gospel to the nations, we proclaim that we are sinners forgiven by divine grace, whether we are members of an ancient church or not. We change over time and so do the churches we belong to, but the Word of our God stands forever. If we build on it as we say we do, we can rest assured that the Spirit of the Lord is in our midst and that eternal life is our inheritance. Surely nothing could be more catholic or more orthodox than that.

Before the Same Lord

A Response to Gerald Bray

KEITH L. JOHNSON

Wheaton College

GERALD BRAY'S PAPER PRESENTS a challenge to a respondent, both because it is a substantive piece and because it offers several different theses moving in a variety of directions. I am going to interact with what I take to be its most interesting claim: the notion that the very same "principles and theological methods" that distinguish evangelicals from Catholic and Orthodox believers reveal an intrinsic connection between evangelicals and the church fathers.

A brief summary of how Bray arrives at this claim will put us in position to assess his argument. He makes the case that while it is true that "evangelicals are generally at one with Catholics and Orthodox on the great doctrines of the Christian faith," a key difference remains: the Catholic and Orthodox accept these doctrines on the authority of "conciliar decisions by the church" while evangelicals accept them because of their "conformity to Holy Scripture." Since conformity to Scripture is the same "criterion . . . on which the councils themselves based their decisions," this means that evangelicals are "closer to the mind of the early Christians than either the Orthodox or the Catholic churches are, because their principles and theological methods are closer to those of the church fathers."

This correlation between the "principles and methods" of the early church and evangelicals reveals key areas of convergence between the beliefs, attitudes, and practices of the fathers and those of evangelicals. Bray sees evangelicalism primarily as a "spiritual movement" whose central commitments revolve around the way that the gospel changes people's lives. This makes evangelicals flexible on matters of church practice, because their focus is upon how to live out the gospel in the present and the future rather than to stay rooted in past loyalty to institution or de-nominational structure. In this sense, Bray argues that evangelicals have an "alternative understanding of what the church is"—and, by extension, an alternative pneumatology. Evangelicals do not believe that the Holy Spirit "works primarily through institutions of one kind or another" as the Catholic and Orthodox do. Instead, they focus on the "indwelling presence of the Holy Spirit," who "works primarily in the hearts of those who have been chosen for salvation." The Holy Spirit, in other words, works in Christians rather than in institutions. On the basis of this view of the Spirit's work, Bray argues that evangelicals share the same "mindset" as the great saints like Basil, who liked to "stir the church into action" in the same way evangelicals do. Indeed, the same Holy Spirit who inspired church fathers like Basil inspires evangelicals today "for the same basic purpose and with equal or perhaps even greater effect."

The payoff of this argument is that Bray is able to claim that evan-gelicals are the "real" heirs of the early tradition while the Catholic and the Orthodox are not. That is, because evangelicals focus on the "sub-stance" of the terms "catholic" and "orthodox" rather than "restricting themselves to formal or institutional definitions," they do "greater justice to the true meaning of catholicity and orthodoxy than the options that go by those names do." By "prioritizing what is essential," evangelicalism transcends denominational lines and become the "most catholic form of Christianity that there is" while also staying within the "bounds of orthodoxy." In this sense, Bray makes the case that, today, true catholic-ity and orthodoxy is found primarily in evangelicalism.

What are we to say about this argument? My first reaction is to say that it is simply another form of the same kinds of arguments that Catholics and Orthodox have been making against one another for a thousand years. Both the Catholic and the Orthodox churches insist that their respective traditions are the rightful heirs of the early church, and they justify their claims by pointing to specific ways in which their par-ticular church reflects the beliefs, practices, and attitudes of the fathers. Bray simply does the same thing: he believes that evangelicalism is the rightful heir to the early church, and he justifies this claim by pointing to specific ways that evangelicals reflect the beliefs, practices, and attitudes of the fathers. The difference is that, while the Catholic and Orthodox point to their respective *institutions* to establish this continuity, Bray establishes it by pointing to *individuals* who, through lives changed by the Holy Spirit, reflect the same "principles and theological methods" found in the fathers. The effect, however, is the same: the Catholic, Orthodox, and Bray all point inward to their central characteristics of their own respective traditions and then insist that these characteristics reflect the work of the Holy Spirit and stand in continuity with the early church.

We see the effect of this inward focus near the end of Bray's paper, where he seeks to establish the link between the early church and evangelicalism by listing some specific ways that the beliefs, practices, and attitudes of evangelicalism bear witness to its own catholicity and orthodoxy. Catholics and Orthodox, of course, could issue their own alternative list. Bray's list focuses on how evangelicals are orthodox on matters of God, Christ, and salvation; maintain the authority of Scripture; are flexible in ecclesial matters; and deal with scandals better than other churches. But we have to ask: Are these things really true *in practice*? Do we really want to point to the beliefs and actions of the average evangelical as the harbinger of our faithfulness? Should we really hold up our ecclesiology—influenced, as it so often is, by the sacred traditions of consumerism and individualism—as a model? And what about scandals? Professor Bray argues that evangelical decentralization helps to prevent scandals like those that plagued the Roman Catholic Church. But is that really the case? One could argue that evangelicals' decentralization presents the mirror image of the problem found in the Catholic hierarchy. To give an example (and since I'm a Baptist, I'll use a Baptist example): consider the organization Stop Baptist Predators.[1] It is dedicated to exposing dozens of Baptist ministers who have used their positions to commit heinous acts against their church members, including children. The problem is that Baptist churches are *so* decentralized that many of these ministers have been able to move from church to church to church over the course of decades—often recommended for these positions by denominational leaders unaware of their misdeeds—because there was no common database where information about their past crimes could be collected and made known.

All of this is to say: pointing to ourselves for evidence to support our own catholicity or orthodoxy will not get us anywhere, because we present a tarnished image at best. This is true for Catholics, Orthodox,

1. See the website at http://www.stopbaptistpredators.org.

and evangelicals. This tells us that the question of who is the "real" catholic and orthodox is precisely the wrong question to be asking, because it inevitably leads us to look to ourselves for evidence, and we can only do that when we talk about the Holy Spirit as if the Spirit's primary work in the world is to invest in *us*—either in our institutions or our own spiritual well-being. But a mistake is made either way. We have to be wary of construing the Spirit's work too directly with our own lives, so that the work of the Holy Spirit becomes nearly identical with *our* work, either in the context of the church or in our personal spiritual life. As Basil argues in *On the Holy Spirit*, we not only have to affirm that the Spirit works in us, but we also have to say that he works apart from us (23.54). The "Spirit blows where he wishes" (John 3:8), and indeed, throughout the New Testament we see that the Spirit's work is not centered primarily upon *us* at all. The Spirit's chief task is to bear witness to Christ (John 15:26–27; Acts 5:32; 1 Cor 2:14, 12:3). So, even when we talk about our lives *in* the Spirit, we point not to our own spiritual being or moral standing but to Christ. Paul makes this point in Romans 8 when he says that "Spirit himself bears witness *with* our spirit that we are children of God, and if children, then heirs—heirs of God and fellow heirs with Christ" (Rom 8:16). We are not heirs of a tradition; we are heirs of God with Christ. And we are not heirs because of what *we do*; we are heirs because of what *Christ has done for us*. The Spirit does not bear witness to our moral standing but to our status in Christ, and our task is to bear witness along with the Spirit by pointing not to ourselves but to Christ (John 15:26–27). "For in *this* hope we were saved. Now hope that is seen is not hope. Who hopes for what he sees? But if we hope for what we do not see, we wait for it with patience. Likewise, the Spirit helps us in our weakness" (Rom 8:24–26). If we look to ourselves, we will see only our sin and weakness; but if, by the power of the Spirit, we look to Christ, then we see his righteousness and our hope.

The question we should be asking is not, therefore, who is the "real" catholic and orthodox Christian, because that will only lead us to focus on ourselves. Rather, our question must be about the "hope" found *outside* of us. We find that hope in the same place the church fathers did: in the crucified and risen Jesus Christ revealed to us in Holy Scripture.

Athanasius points to the manifestation of this hope when he talks about how the risen Christ works "every day" by "invisibly persuading numbers of people all over the world . . . to accept this faith and be obedient to his teaching." He asks: "Does a dead man prick the consciences of men, so that they throw all the traditions of their fathers to the winds and bow down before the teaching of Christ?" (*On the Incarnation* 30). This statement gives us insight in to why evangelicals should read the church fathers. We read them because they bowed before the risen Jesus Christ, the same one who is present and active now in the entire world through the illuminating power of the Holy Spirit.

·Here I think Bray, at several points in his paper, offers some intriguing hints about some ways we are similar to the fathers. It would be helpful for evangelicals to explore the nature of this similarity in more depth, but not so that we can claim to be the church fathers' rightful heirs. That only takes us back to the same circular debates of the past thousand years. Rather, it would be helpful to explore how they, like us, were sinners saved by grace who tried their best to live faithfully in the midst of messy and challenging times; and how they, like us, turned to scripture so they could preach the gospel accurately and help the church stay faithful to it. The pay off of this story wouldn't be a claim about how we are their rightful heirs; it would be to join together with them in the chorus of believers who, by the power of the Spirit, look to Jesus as the hope of our salvation.

Epilogue

The Radical•ness of the Evangelical Faith

GEORGE KALANTZIS

Wheaton College

"An evangelical with an ahistorical faith is a superficial Christian."

—Bernard Ramm

WHEN WE WERE PLANNING this discussion (both as a gathering at Wheaton College and in this, its written form) our hope was that we could explore the challenges posed to confessional evangelicals on the grounds of history, tradition, and rootedness. We asked the question, "Why is it that the evangelical movement—especially in its North American multiformity—has often been described as an ahistorical peculiarity, and why have the various attempts of the last thirty years or so to give voice to the essentially historical character of the faith been received with a lingering suspicion?" The answers explored, the discussion engaged, and the conclusions to which we come are not for us a simple academic curiosity. This is, at the end, a call *ad fontes*. But any such call, any such engagement, is deeply personal. So, let me begin with a personal story: Relatively recently I had an experience that was somewhat perplexing to me. I happened to be on a panel discussing the relationship between evangelicalism—or rather, Protestantism—and Eastern Orthodoxy. With me on that panel were three other quite informed, articulate, and very generous persons. One was Protestant, the other two Eastern Orthodox. After about an hour's worth of discussion in which we touched upon Scripture, tradition, the foundational role of history and communal memory, the church fathers and the creed(s)— all the customary loci of such exchanges—one of my Eastern Orthodox interlocutors turned to me and said: "Truly, George, I have never met an evangelical like you before!"

I found that statement particularly troubling at the time, and I still do. In his attempt at generosity, my interlocutor—himself one who earlier in life was part of evangelical communions—was stepping right into the middle of the conversation we have had in this book. His comment stemmed from a genuinely held belief that my argument that the history and tradition of the church is not the birthright of any one Christian communion but a shared heritage that has been, is, and must continue to be integral to all Christian communions, was a novel idea—one he had not encountered before!

It took me a few days to figure out why that statement troubled me so much. After all, both by ecclesial affinity and academic training, as well as collegial relationships, that is exactly the kind of evangelical I was raised to be: rooted in the Scriptures and in history, neither I nor my friends and colleagues understood ourselves as standing outside the long tradition of Christians—from the earliest times to our own—who strive to be faithful witnesses to the saving grace of God through Christ. Along the way, it was abundantly evident that we all, Protestant, Catholic, or Orthodox, drink from the same well of a common Christian tradition whose spring is in the early Christian centuries.[1]

The Idiom of Ahistorical Evangelicalism

Yet, I have come to recognize that my interlocutor was also speaking truth. For, as our discussions in this volume have highlighted, this was a kind of a "particular" truth claim that is based mostly on personal experience. As Ken Steward has argued in an essay (and as the contributors to this volume have shown), the majority of those arguing that Protestantism has systematically neglected the early church for the past five hundred years have reached their conclusions "on the basis of perceptions gleaned within the strands of Evangelicalism in which they

1. For a more developed argument on this point, see Walker and Bretherton, *Remembering Our Future*.

were nurtured. While this is of foundational importance (they are, after all, eyewitnesses of the movements of their lifetimes), it is also limiting. Their judgments," argues Steward, "have involved a readiness to extrapolate from the evangelical movement as they have experienced it to the whole of it. And such an approach contains a rather wide margin of error. Evangelicalism sampled or experienced in one region cannot be simply equated with the global evangelical movement or even with evangelical movements elsewhere in the English-speaking world. It is possible therefore that the neglect of early Christianity which is complained against—for example in North America—exists primarily there and primarily in the environs of fundamentalist or parachurch Protestantism."[2]

Idiomatic—to the North American context—as those organizations and experiences might be, they nonetheless continue to be seen (at least in popular lore) as representative of twentieth-century evangelical ethos. Consequently, the complaint against "ahistorical evangelicalism" has become so common in the narrative of the latter part of the twentieth century as to escape from its fundamentalist and parachurch antecedents and be embraced as self-evidently accurate with no burden of proof demanded of those who are pressing the charge. Sometimes, even those of us who work in Patristics and early Christian studies in the North American context often feel like Elijah—our patron saint—and cry out, "I alone am left!" (1 Kgs 19:10). We often forget the 7,000 laboring along with us (1 Kgs 19:18)! As an evangelical with an accent, I can attest to the fact that such experiences of evangelicalism are neither universal nor axiomatic; but they are indeed influential, especially when they are exported as normative expressions of faith.

Our discussions in this gathering have shown so clearly that the current resurgence of interest in early Christianity among evangelicals ought not be understood as a wholesale rejection of the Reformation enterprise, for it is not "a swing of the pendulum towards something neglected for five centuries of Protestantism's existence."[3] Rather, it ought to be seen as a much-needed return to an emphasis *regularly* present in historic Protestantism. Since the dawn of the Reformation, countless theologians, historians, biblical scholars, preachers, teachers, and laity alike have engaged the early church and the church fathers in diverse

2. Steward, "Evangelicals and Patristic Christianity," 308.

3. Ibid., 321.

ways. Some exhibited that love-hate relationship we see in Luther, who—never lacking in passion—often seems to reject their biblical exegesis almost wholesale: "What good it does to rely on the venerable old Fathers, who have been approved through such long succession of ages. Were not they too all equally blind, or rather, did they not simply overlook the clearest and most explicit statements of Paul?"[4] While, on the other hand, as Chris Hall has reminded us, he also "listens to their voices and praises them when he feels they interpret Scripture correctly."[5] Others, like Calvin, were deeply influenced by Augustine's understanding of the "religion of the heart," of the love *of* God—not simply the love *for* God—and God's captivating and gracious pursuit of his people. It was Augustine who opened up for Calvin a reappropriation of predestination, a doctrine passed over in silence (for the most part) even since the council of Orange (in 529 CE). And of course John Wesley, who, as Frances Young notes, "Though a man of 'one book,' the Bible, Wesley early determined that a sure rule for its interpretation was the consensus of the ancients."[6] The influence of the Greek fathers upon John Wesley is "incontestable."

The Need for Radical Faithfulness

That having been said, however, does not mean that the dominant streams of *contemporary* Protestantism have been faithful to their own historical rootedness. For years Protestant theologians and historians—including those from the Free Church traditions, such as Bernard Ramm, Daniel H. Williams, and Everett Ferguson—have warned us of the danger of allowing the claims of ahistorical narratives and approaches to Scripture and theology to become the dominant paradigms of evangelicalism. This is no less than the danger of capitulating to the modernist insistence on the individual as the locus of authority and the acquiescence to that particular understanding of "the priesthood of all believers" that has served to make Scripture so often an artifact, isolating the Writings from the body to which they are addressed, authorship from reception, interpretation from faithful witness. The result, I would propose, is to domesticate Scripture's revolutionary message for the community/ies

4. Steward, "Evangelicals," 321.

5. Hall, *Reading*, 12.

6. Kimbrough Jr., *Orthodox and Wesleyan Spirituality*, 164.

whose lives it is meant to transform, whose path it is supposed to enlighten (Ps 119:105). *Sola Scriptura* has become *nuda Scriptura*.

Bernard Ramm famously warned, "To hold evangelical faith without a minimal knowledge of its history is theologically unhealthy if not precarious. Without question," Ramm argued, "a number of fundamentalists and evangelicals, have deserted the camp because, lacking any real historical knowledge of their heritage, they did not see their heritage in its proper light nor did they have an appropriate vantage point from which to assess the alternative view to which they capitulated."[7]

I think Daniel Williams puts it best when he states that, "Any oxymoron between Protestantism and the whole of the Church's history is artificially self-imposed. It is not necessarily built into the original fabric of Protestant spirituality."[8] The consequences of such a self-imposed incurvation are not hard to imagine. As Jeffrey Bingham warned us in chapter 7, we all live through them in our churches, where we seem to have divorced the function of the *ekklesia*, its *leitourgia* and *catechesis*, from its proper *telos* (which is the formation of the people of God to *be* God's people, called *out of* the world to live *in* the faith of the One whose name we confess, in whose name we are baptized, and whose body and blood nourish us in a life of service) and replaced it with commodities of satisfaction and entertainment, guided more, it seems, by our consumerist appetites and need for psychotherapeutic validation. And this, I am afraid, is not limited to the evangelical culture alone. Inarguably it has become the affliction of all of our ecclesial traditions, Protestant and Catholic and Orthodox alike on this side of modernity—can we blame this, too, on the Enlightenment, or could it be our own complacency?

Ross Douthat made the point in an op-ed piece in the *New York Times* during Lent in 2010. Quibbling with the perception that mysticism, and religion with it, is on the path to extinction, Douthat argues that, "In a sense, Americans seem to have done with mysticism what we've done with every other kind of human experience: We've democratized it, diversified it, and taken it mass market." The result, as we know, is not all that pretty: "By making mysticism more democratic, we've also made it more bourgeois, more comfortable, and more dilettantish. It's become something we pursue as a complement to an upwardly mobile existence, rather than a radical alternative to the ladder of success.

7. Ramm, *Evangelical Heritage*, 14. Emphasis original.
8. Williams, *Evangelicals and Tradition*, 12.

Going to yoga classes isn't the same thing as becoming a yogi; spending a week in a retreat center doesn't make me Thomas Merton or Thérèse of Lisieux. Our kind of mysticism is more likely to be a pleasant hobby than a transformative vocation."[9] It is the infernal, "I am not religious, I'm just spiritual" slogan of the ecclesially alliterate.

"Remembering the Past Is Essential for Facing the Future"[10]: A Not-So-Idealistic Proposal on Teaching about and Learning with the Early Church

Assuming, as this volume has shown clearly, that this temporary suspension of interest was neither normative for Protestants nor desirable for our future, how are we evangelicals to engage the early church? For, to quote Williams again, "far worse than suspicion or opposition, however is ignorance."[11] How, are we to undertake this seemingly monumental task of reintroducing the history of the church *to* the church? How can that be done in and through our institutions of higher learning that yearn to be faithful to the faith while educating young men and women to be Christians in the world?

Creating more centers like The Wheaton Center for Early Christian Studies throughout the CCCU and seminaries and endowing chairs of Patristics and early Christian studies (such as Gordon-Conwell's Robert E. Cooley, Chair of Early Christianity) would be the only reasonable answer, but since this is not Wonderland—or even Narnia—let me propose a more plausible alternative.

Eastern Orthodox theologian David Bentley Hart tells us how *not* to do it. Hart begins his essay titled "The Mirror of the Infinite: Gregory of Nyssa on the *Vestigia Trinitatis*" by reminding us that for the most part, "in our weaker moments, [we] prefer synopsis to precision [and] find in it a convenient implement for arranging our accounts of doctrinal history into simple taxonomies, under tidily discrete divisions."[12] Well, I propose that quite often this also holds true in our approach to and in the teaching of early Christianity in most of our schools.

---

9. Douthat, "Mass-Market Epiphany."

10. Walker et al., *Remembering Our Future.*

11. Williams, *Evangelicals and Tradition,* 17.

12. Hart, "Mirror of the Infinite," 541.

Increasing curricular constraints and an abundant emphasis on the "usefulness" of the end product—which, of course, is not ἀρετή, or the formation of character but marketability—have forced most of our colleges and universities to abandon traditional models of liberal arts education, where the student was expected to read within the so-called classical corpus with ever increasing facility and engage persons, movements, and ideas in a sustained dialogue with teachers and peers, for more fragmented exotic "specializations" that can attract the eye of future employers. And in these troubled economic times, as our students try to fit a four-year education into three or three-and-a-half years, it is not uncommon anymore for them to carry sixteen to eighteen or even twenty credit hours each semester in this mad dash to get out into "the real world." The teaching of any tradition, or movement, or subject that is not immediately within the life experience of our students is, therefore, bound to be hindered by those constraints. And the teaching of Patristics and the early church falls squarely within this discussion.

As I venture into this proposal, then, I want to borrow a phrase Wheaton's president used recently in his charge to the faculty of the College. Philip G. Ryken reminded us that

> *a liberal education prepares a person for anything and everything in life*. It prepares someone to be a better citizen, a better colleague, a better husband or wife, a better father or mother, a better friend. A distinctively *Christian* education does more: it centers every intellectual pursuit on Jesus Christ, "in whom are hidden all the treasures of wisdom and knowledge" (Col. 2:3). Properly speaking, such a Christ-centered education does not involve the integration of faith and learning, as if "faith" and "learning" were two separate and equal entities, but integrates learning with faith as the foundation for life.[13]

In our curricula, for the most part, early Christianity is treated as an idiosyncratic particularity within historical overviews of European history or Russian history or—in a best-case scenario—Byzantine history. Most of our students cannot be expected to have a grasp of the complexities of the national, historical, linguistic, even confessional diversity within early Christianity. Even those who work in denominationally oriented environments, or in schools with a particular theological and historical identity, find that our students may know the differences

---

13. Philip G. Ryken, address to the Wheaton College faculty, 20 February 2010.

between varying groups within their own traditions—to be able to recognize, for example, some diversity between United Methodists and Free Methodists, or Northern Baptists and Southern Baptist, PCA and PCUSA—and to know that Roman Catholics differ from Protestants in both doctrine and practice, but the various expressions of Christianity thriving in the East fall completely outside the realm of their experiences. As such, they cannot be expected to differentiate between Greek and Russian, Assyrian, Coptic, and Armenian, Ethiopic or Oriental Christianity. Nor have they had an opportunity to participate, or even observe, the traditional practices that undergird those communities.

And so, the question remains: How are evangelicals to relate to the tradition and history of the church diachronic? Especially if we are not to surrender to the lure of *synopsis* that forces us to collapse all differences into artificial monoliths that, at the end, trivialize—if not vulgarize—the multivalency of early Christianity?

It seems to me that one *first* step may be to recognize that the Hellenization thesis and the resultant collapse of the teaching of early Christianity as a prequel to the Reformation has outlived its purposes. The paradigmatic act of charity is patience and attention. What the early church demands of us is nothing less. We (North American evangelicals of the twenty-first century) need to take our time and live with the beauty of (re-)discovery; we need time and intentionality to engage with integrity the idiolect of early Christianity without creating category confusions that result in unrecognizable simulacra. We need to take the time to explore what seems arcane and opaque. We need to create curricular space where we can hear with attentiveness and engage critically, understanding the "dynamic nature of tradition as a living activity and process."[14]

In addition to the historical component, *second*, the development of the doctrinal character of early Christianity also needs to be presented with the same attention to the multiplicity of the claimant communities. A collapse of early Christian studies into "simple taxonomies, under tidily discrete divisions" is neither just to those long-standing communities nor historically and theologically true. Of course, one needs to be always conscious of the diachronic claims of the faith, but I contend that more often than not such synoptic presentations create a paradox of extremes and a retreat to a fictitious historical past that is worse than

14. Williams, *Evangelicals and Tradition*, 13.

naïve. And that is because, on the one hand, they lead to binary divisions into elements of radical opposition—Scripture *or* Tradition—while on the other, they tend to fall squarely into what Harvey Cox called the "mythicizing" of the fathers and other first Christians.[15] Any such attempt to make the study of early Christianity more appealing as the cost of nuance will be only Pyrrhic and continue to contribute to the undifferentiated theological anomie.

Otherwise we do a great disservice to our students, denying them the thrill of new discoveries in the meaning of those unfamiliar terms and concepts and practices, and reinforce the delusion of academic consumerism. What we owe our students and ourselves is to recognize what Justo González calls the difference between "innocent readings," of history in this case, and "responsible remembrance."[16] Innocent reading of history is selective forgetfulness, a heuristic device for our agendas and power struggles. Responsible remembrance leads to responsible action. In this exciting new period of our history, the period so aptly called, post-Christendom, instead of lamenting the loss of political and state power and influence, responsible remembrance encourages greater mutuality as it recognizes the futility of trying to excise the "other" from our doctrinal and ecclesial and historical accounts and, in mutual repentance, moves us towards embodied communities of grace.

Which leads me to my *last* suggestion, namely, to demand from ourselves and our students—let alone our institutions—the investment of *time* necessary to move beyond curiosity to truthful engagement with the unfamiliar. In the opening essay of this collection, which was also the inaugural address of The Wheaton Center for Early Christian Studies, Prof. Robert Louis Wilken challenged us to allow the fathers to help us go more deeply into the Bible and teach us how to read it more slowly.

This is not a new idea for evangelicals. I still remember my grandmother's Bible that was so worn from years of being read slowly that no one would confuse it for another library book, sitting ornamentally at the nightstand—it never was at the nightstand; it was always at the kitchen table, and it was always open. Somehow we have surrendered this "participation in the spiritual reality of the text," to use another of Prof. Wilken's exhortations, to the professional commentary writers, to

---

15. Cox, *Turning East*, 160: "As we avoid mythicizing other periods of history, we should also spare the first Christians this fate."

16. González, *Mañana*, 79.

whom we now turn for new wisdom. If it is true that "when all is said and done orthodoxy is the hard discipline of learning to say what needs to be said and no more,"[17] then taking the time necessary to learn what can be said and what the limits are of what can be said is of the utmost importance. Examples abound of what happens when we approach theology with an intuitive, if even pietistic, attitude.

I propose that as we move rapidly towards post-Christendom, we need to reclaim the teaching of Christian theology and practice from the classroom and guild-focused books and move it back where it belongs: the living, breathings, acting communities of faith. One of the axioms of Christianity, Eastern and Western alike, is that there ought not to be a binary division between intellection and life.

This renewed thirst in *this* generation of evangelicals for the study of the history, tradition, and faith of the church does not function anymore as a private calculus. Modern evangelicals yearn to explore the rootedness of their faith and approach modernity with great ambivalence. Yet, as many recent works, discussions, and conferences (including the 2007 "Ancient Faith for the Church's Future," conference at Wheaton College) have made evident, it is unquestionable that the gyroscope at the center of this rising generation is being reoriented and postmodernity's ambivalence towards claims of authority and objectivity are quickly being replaced by a generational yearning for faithfulness and re-rootedness in doctrine and creed and practice, in life and sacrament.

As we move forward, teaching Christianity in any academic institution (even more so in a Christian academic institution) demands a commanding new topography of "respect from within" and a dialectical necessity of fellowship that notices the *other* as such.

---

17. Hauerwas, "Foreword," x.

Bibliography

Books

Allen, Joel Stevens. *The Despoliation of Egypt in Pre-Rabbinic, Rabbinic, and Patristic Traditions.* Supplements to Vigiliae Christianae 92. Leiden, 2008.

Athanasius. *St. Athanasius On the Incarnation: The Treatise De incarnatione verbi Dei.* Crestwood, NY: St. Vladimir's Seminary Press, 1982.

Bacq, Philippe. *De l'ancienne à la nouvelle Alliance selon S. Irénée: Unité du livre IV de l'adversus haereses.* Bibliothèque de la Faculté de Philosophie et letters des Facultés universitaires Notre-Dame de la Paix 58. Paris: Lithielleux, 1978.

Baker, Frank. *John Wesley and the Church of England.* Nashville: Abingdon, 1970.

Bainton, Roland H. *Christian Attitudes toward War and Peace: A Historical Survey and Critical Re-Evaluation.* New York: Abingdon, 1960.

Baltzell, E. Digby. *Philadelphia Gentlemen: The Making of a National Upper Class.* Englewood Cliffs, NJ: Prentice Hall, 1958.

Barrett, David B., George T. Kurian, and Todd M. Johnson. *World Christian Encyclopedia: A Comparative Survey of Churches and Religions in the Modern World.* 2 vols. 2nd ed. Oxford: Oxford University Press, 2001.

Bebbington, D. W. *The Dominance of Evangelicalism: The Age of Spurgeon and Moody.* A History of Evangelicalism 3. Downers Grove, IL: InterVarsity, 2005.

Bingham, D. Jeffrey. *Irenaeus' Use of Matthew's Gospel in Adversus Haereses.* Traditio exegetica Graeca 7. Leuven: Peeters, 1998.

Bowerstock, G. W., Peter Brown, and Oleg Grabar, editors. *Late Antiquity: A Guide to the Postclassical World.* Harvard University Press Reference Library. Cambridge, MA: Belknap, 1999.

Bozeman, Adda B. *Politics and Culture in International History: From the Ancient Near East to the Opening of the Modern Age.* 2nd ed. New Brunswick, NJ: Transaction, 1994.

Bozeman, Theodore Dwight. *To Live Ancient Lives: The Primitivist Dimension in Puritanism.* Chapel Hill: University of North Carolina Press, 1988.

Briggs, Charles A. *A Critical and Exegetical Commentary on the Book of Psalms.* 2 vols. International Critical Commentary. New York, 1906–1907.

Cadoux, Cecil John. *The Early Christian Attitude to War: A Contribution to the History of Christian Ethics.* Christian Revolution Series 3. London: Headley Bros., 1919.

Campbell, Ted. *The Gospel in Christian Traditions.* New York: Oxford, 2009.

————. *John Wesley and Christian Antiquity: Religious Vision and Cultural Change.* Nashville: Kingswood, 1991.

Casey, Michael. *A Guide to Living in the Truth: St. Benedict's Teaching on Humility.* Liguori, MO: Liguori/Triumph, 1999.

————. *Sacred Reading: The Ancient Art of Lectio Divina.* Ligouri, MO: Triumph, 1995.

Chafer, Lewis Sperry. *Systematic Theology.* 8 vols. Dallas: Dallas Seminary Press, 1947.

Collins, John J. *Does the Bible Justify Violence?* Minneapolis: Fortress, 2004.

Collins, Kenneth J. *The Theology of John Wesley: Holy Love and the Shape of Grace.* Nashville: Abingdon, 2007.

Cox, Harvey Gallagher. *Turning East: The Promise and Peril of the New Orientalism.* New York: Simon and Schuster, 1977.

Daniélou, Jean. *From Shadows to Reality: Studies in Biblical Typology of the of the Fathers.* Translated by Wulstan Hibbert. London: Burns & Oats, 1960.

Dickey, Eleanor. *Ancient Greek Scholarship.* American Philological Association Classical Resources Series 7. Oxford: Oxford University Press, 2007.

Engels, Donald W. *Roman Corinth: An Alternative Model for the Classical City.* Chicago: University of Chicago Press, 1990.

Fantino, Jacques. *La théologie d'Irénée: lecture des Ecritures en réponse à l'exégèse gnostique: une approche trinitaire.* Cogitatio fidei 180. Paris: Cerf, 1994.

Fee, Gordon D. *The First Epistle to the Corinthians.* NICNT. Grand Rapids: Eerdmans, 1987.

Galen. *Claudii Galeni Opera Omnia.* Translated edited by Carolus Gottlob Kühn. 20 vols. Medicorum Graecorum opera *quae* exstant 1–20. Leipzig: C. Cnobloch, 1821–1833; reprint, Hildesheim: Olms, 1965.

———. *On Prognosis.* Translated and edited by Vivian Nutton. Corpus medicorum Graecorum 5.8.1. Berlin: Akademie-Verlag, 1979.

Gamble, Harry Y. *Books and Readers in the Early Church: A History of Early Christian Texts.* New Haven, CT: Yale University Press, 1995.

Gerrish, B. A. *Tradition and the Modern World: Reformed Theology in the Nineteenth Century.* Andrew C. Zenos Memorial Lectures, 1977. Chicago: University of Chicago Press, 1978.

González, Justo L. *Mañana: Christian Theology from a Hispanic Perspective.* Nashville: Abingdon, 1990.

Graham, Stephen R. *Cosmos in the Chaos: Philip Schaff's Interpretation of Nineteenth-Century American Religion.* Grand Rapids: Eerdmans, 1995.

Grant, Robert M. *Irenaeus of Lyons.* Early Church Fathers. New York: Routledge, 1997.

Graves, Michael. *Jerome's Hebrew Philology: A Study Based on His Commentary on Jeremiah.* Supplements to Vigiliae christainae 90. Leiden: Brill, 2007.

Green, Richard. *The Works of John and Charles Wesley: A Bibliography.* 2nd ed. London: Methodist, 1906; reprint, New York: AMS, 1976.

Greenman Jeffrey P., and George Kalantzis, editors. *Life in the Spirit: Spiritual Formation in Theological Perspective.* Downers Grove, IL: InterVarsity, 2010.

Gregory I, Pope. *Morals on the Book of Job.* Translated and annotated. 3 vols. in 4. Library of Fathers of the Holy Catholic Church 18, 21, 23, 31. Oxford: J. H. Parker, 1844–1850.

———. *S. Gregorii Magni Moraba in Job.* Edited by Marci Adriaen. Corpus Christianorum, Series Latina 143, 143a, 143b. Turnhout: Brepols, 1979–1985.

Gregory of Nyssa. *The Lord's Prayer. The Beatitudes.* Translated by Hilda Graef. Ancient Christian Writers 18. New York: Newman, 1954.

Gunnemann, Louis H. *The Shaping of the United Church of Christ: An Essay in the History of American Christianity.* New York: United Church Press, 1977.

Hall, Christopher A. *Reading Scripture with the Church Fathers.* Downers Grove, IL: InterVarsity, 1998.

Hall, Christopher A., and John Sanders. *Does God Have a Future?: A Debate on Divine Providence.* Grand Rapids: Baker, 2003.

Hanson, R. P. C. *Tradition in the Early Church*. Philadelphia: Westminster, 1963.

Hart, D. G. *John Williamson Nevin: High Church Calvinist*. American Reformed Bibliographies 2. Phillipsburg, NJ: P&R, 2005.

Hatch, Nathan O. *The Democratization of American Christianity*. New Haven, CT: Yale University Press, 1989.

Haykin, Michael A. G., Kenneth J. Stewart, and Timothy George. *The Advent of Evangelicalism: Exploring Historical Continuities*. Nashville: B&H, 2008.

Heitzenrater, Richard P. *Wesley and the People Called Methodists*. Nashville: Abingdon, 1995.

Hempton, David. *Methodism: Empire of the Spirit*. New Haven, CT: Yale University Press, 2005.

Horneck, Anthony. *The Happy Ascetick, or, The Best Exercise*. 3rd ed. London: printed for Henry Mortlock, 1693.

Hurtado, Larry W. *Lord Jesus Christ: Devotion to Jesus in Earliest Christianity*. Grand Rapids: Eerdmans, 2003.

Husbands, Mark, and Jeffrey P. Greenman, editors. *Ancient Faith for the Church's Future*. Downers Grove, IL: InterVarsity, 2008.

Im, Seung-An. "John Wesley's Theological Anthropology: A Dialectic Tension between the Latin Western Patristic Tradition (Augustine) and the Greek Eastern Patristic Tradition (Gregory of Nyssa)." PhD diss., Drew University, 1994.

Irenaeus. *Against Heresies, Books 1–5 and Fragments*. Translated by A. Roberts and W. H. Rambaut. In *Ante-Nicene Fathers*, vol. 1 (*The Apostolic Fathers, Justin Martyr, Irenaeus*), edited by Alexander Roberts, James Donaldson, and A. Cleveland Coxe, 315–578. Peabody, MA: Hendrickson, 1994.

———. *Contre les hérésies*. Edited, translated, and annotated by A. Rousseau, L. Doutreleau, B Hemmerdinger, and C. Mercier. 10 vols. Sources chrétiennes 100, 152, 153, 210, 211, 263, 264, 293, 294. Paris: Cerf, 1965–1982.

———. *The Proof of the Apostolic Preaching, with Seven Fragments*. Armenian version edited and translated by Karapet ter Mekerttshian and S. G. Wilson with the cooperation of H. R. H. Prince Maxe of Saxony. Patrologia Orientalis 12.5. Tournhout: Brepols, 1989.

Jaeger, Werner. *Two Rediscovered Works of Ancient Christian Literature: Gregory of Nyssa and Macarius*. Leiden: Brill, 1954.

Johnson, Luke Timothy. *The Creed: What Christians Believe and Why It Matters*. New York: Doubleday, 2003.

Gunter, W. Stephen, et al. *Wesley and the Quadrilateral: Renewing the Conversation*. Nashville: Abingdon, 1997.

Kimbrough Jr., S. T., editor. *Orthodox and Wesleyan Scriptural Understanding and Practice*. Crestwood, NY: St. Vladimir's Seminary Press, 2000.

———, editor. *Orthodox and Wesleyan Spirituality*. Crestwood: St. Vladimir's Seminary Press, 2007.

Kuklick, Bruce. *Churchmen and Philosophers: From Jonathan Edwards to John Dewey*. New Haven, CT: Yale University Press, 1985.

Larsen, Timothy, and Daniel J. Treier. *The Cambridge Companion to Evangelical Theology*. Cambridge Companions to Religion. Cambridge: Cambridge University Press, 2007.

Le Boulluec, Alain. *La notion d'hérésie dans la littérature grecque, IIe—IIIe siècles*. 2 vols. Paris: Études Augustiniennes, 1985.

Lindsay, D. Michael. *Faith in the Halls of Power: How Evangelicals Joined the American Elite*. New York: Oxford University Press, 2008.

Long, D. Stephen. *John Wesley's Moral Theology: The Quest for God and Goodness.* Nashville: Kingswood, 2005.

———. *Living the Discipline: United Methodist Theological Reflections on War, Civilization, and Holiness.* Grand Rapids: Eerdmans, 1992.

Luther, Martin. *The Bondage of the Will.* In *Martin Luther's Basic Theological Writings,* edited by Timothy F. Lull. Minneapolis: Fortress, 1989.

Mosheim, Johann Lorenz. *A Concise Ecclesiastical History, from the Birth of Christ, to the Beginning of the Present Century.* Translated by Archibald Maclaine. 4 vols. London: J. Paramore, 1781.

MacMullen, R. *Roman Social Relations, 50 B.C. to A.D. 284.* New Haven, CT: Yale University, 1974.

Maddox, Randy L. *Responsible Grace: John Wesley's Practical Theology.* Nashville: Kingswood, 1994.

Marrou, Henri-Irénée. *Saint Augustin et la fin de la culture antique.* 4th ed. Paris: E. de Boccard, 1958.

Maxwell, Jack Martin. "The Liturgical Lessons of Mercersburg: An Examination of the Issues which Emerged during the Mercersburg Liturgical Controversy with a View toward Establishing Procedural and Theoretical Principles for Liturgical Committees in the Reformed Tradition." PhD diss., Princeton Theological Seminary, 1969.

McGinn, Bernard. *The Foundations of Mysticism: Origins to the Fifth Century.* The Presence of God: A History of Western Christian Mysticism 1. New York: Crossroad, 1991.

McGrath, Alister E. *The Christian Theology Reader.* 3rd ed. Oxford: Blackwell, 2007.

McKnight, Scot, and Hauna Ondrey. *Finding Faith, Losing Faith: Stories of Conversion and Apostasy.* Waco, TX: Baylor University Press, 2008.

McLaren, Brian D. *Reinventing Your Church.* Grand Rapids: Zondervan, 1998.

Meredith, Anthony. *Gregory of Nyssa.* The Early Church Fathers. New York: Routledge, 1999.

Middleton, Conyers. *A Free Inquiry into the Miraculous Powers, which Are Supposed to Have Subsisted in the Christian Church, from the Earliest Ages through Several Successive Centuries.* London: R. Manby and H. S. Cox, 1749.

Mitchell, Margaret Mary. The Heavenly Trumpet: John Chrysostom and the Art of Pauline Interpretation. Louisville: Westminster John Knox, 2002.

Monk, Robert C. *John Wesley: His Puritan Heritage.* 2nd ed. Pietist and Wesleyan Studies 11. Lanham, MD: Scarecrow, 1999.

Mosheim, Johann Lorenz. A Concise Ecclesiastical History, from the Birth of Christ, to the Beginning of the Present Century. 4 vols. London: J. Paramore, 1781.

Mullin, Robert Bruce. Episcopal Vision/American Reality: High Church Theology and Social Thought in Evangelical America. New Haven, CT: Yale University Press, 1986.

Nautin, Pierre. *Lettres et* écrivains *chrétiens des IIe et IIIe siècles.* His Patristica 2. Paris: Cerf 1961.

Neufeld, Vernon H. *The Earliest Christian Confessions.* New Testament Tools and Studies 5. Grand Rapids: Eerdmans, 1963.

Neuschäfer, Bernhard. *Origenes als Philologe.* 2 vols. Schweizerische Beiträge zur Altertumswissenschaft 18.1–2. Basel: F. Rienhardt 1987.

Nevin, John Williamson. *The Anxious Bench.* Chambersburg, PA: Publication Office of the German Reformed Church, 1843.

———. *Vindication of the Revised Liturgy*. Philadelphia: J. B. Rodgers, 1867.

Nichols, James Hastings. *Romanticism in American Theology: Nevin and Schaff at Mercersburg*. Chicago: University of Chicago Press, 1961.

Noll, Mark A. *America's God: From Jonathan Edwards to Abraham Lincoln*. New York: Oxford University Press, 2002.

———. *The New Shape of World Christianity: How American Experience Reflects Global Faith*. Downers Grove, IL: InterVarsity, 2009.

———. *The Scandal of the Evangelical Mind*. Grand Rapids: Eerdmans, 1994.

Ochagavia, Juan. *Visibile Patris Filius: A Study of Irenaeus' Teaching on Revelation and Tradition*. Orientalia Christiana analecta 171. Rome: Pont. Institutum Orientalium Studiorum, 1964.

Orbe, Antonio. *Parábolas Evangélicas en San Ireneo*. 2 vols. Biblioteca de autores cristianos 331, 332. Madrid: La Editorial Católica, 1979.

Osborn, Eric Francis. *Irenaeus of Lyons*. Cambridge: Cambridge University Press, 2001.

Owens, E. J. *The City in the Roman World*. New York: Routledge, 1991.

Pelikan, Jaroslav. *Interpreting the Bible and the Constitution*. Yale University Press, 2004.

Pew Forum on Religion & Public Life. *U.S. Religious Landscape Survey. Religious Affiliation: Diverse and Dynamic*. Washington, DC: Pew Research Center, February 2008. Online: http://religions.pewforum.org/pdf/report-religious-land scape-study-full.pdf.

Pfeiffer, Rudolph. *History of Classical Scholarship: From the Beginning to the Hellenistic Age*. Oxford: Clarendon, 1968.

Ramm, Bernard L. *The Evangelical Heritage: A Study in Historical Theology*. Grand Rapids: Baker, 2000.

Richardson, Cyril C., editor and translator. *Early Christian Fathers*. Library of Christian Classics 1. Philadelphia: Westminster, 1953.

Roberts, Alexander, James Donaldson, and Cleveland Coxe. *The Ante-Nicene Fathers*. 10 vols. Rev. ed. Edinburgh: T. & T. Clark, 1867–1873; reprint, Peabody, MA: Hendrickson, 1994.

Rudolph, Kurt. *Gnosis: The Nature and History of Gnosticism*. Translated and edited by R. McL. Wilson. New York: Harper & Row, 1983.

Runia, David T. *Philo in Early Christian Literature: A Survey*. Compendia rerum Iudaicarum ad Novum Testamentum, Section 3: Jewish traditions in Early Christian Literature 3. Minneapolis: Fortress, 1993.

Sack, Daniel. *Whitebread Protestants: Food and Religion in American Culture*. New York: Palgrave, 2000.

Sandys, John Edwin. *A History of Classical Scholarship*. 3rd ed. Cambridge: Cambridge University Press, 1921.

Santayana, George. *The Life of Reason*. Vol. 1: *Introduction, and Reason in Common Sense*. New York: Scribner, 1905.

Schaff, Philip. *The Principle of Protestantism: What Is Church History?* American Religious Thought of the 18th and 19th Centuries. New York: Garland, 1987.

Schäublin, Christoph. *Untersuchungen zu Methode und Herkunft der antiochenischen Exegese*. Theophaneia, Beiträge zur Religions- und Kirchengeschichte des Altertums 23. Köln: P. Hanstein, 1974.

Shriver, George H. *Philip Schaff: Christian Scholar and Ecumenical Prophet*. Macon, GA: Mercer University Press, 1987.

Stambaugh, John E. *The Ancient Roman City*. Ancient Society and History. Baltimore: John Hopkins University Press, 1988.

Starr, Chester G. *The Roman Empire, 27 B.C.–A.D. 476: A Study in Survival*. New York: Oxford University Press, 1982.

Steer, Roger. *Basic Christian: The Inside Story of John Stott*. Downers Grove, IL: InterVarsity, 2009.

Tacitus. *The Complete Works of Tacitus*. Translated by Alfred John Church and William Jackson Brodribb, edited by Moses Hadas. The Modern Library of the World's Best Books. New York: Modern Library, 1942.

Theodore of Mopsuestia. *Commentary on Psalms 1–81*. Translated by Robert C. Hill. Writings from the Greco-Roman World 5. Atlanta: SBL, 2006.

Thomas, W. H. Griffith. *The Catholic Faith: A Manual of Instruction for Members of the Church of England*. New York: Longmans, Green, 1920.

Thompson, John L. *Reading the Bible with the Dead: What You Can Learn from the History of Exegesis That You Can't Learn from Exegesis Alone*. Grand Rapids: Eerdmans, 2007.

Tracy, David. *Blessed Rage for Order: The New Pluralism in Theology*. New York: Seabury, 1975.

Treier, Daniel J., and David Lauber, editors. *Trinitarian Theology for the Church: Scripture, Community, Worship*. Downers Grove, IL: InterVarsity, 2009.

Tertullian. *Contre Marcion*. Edited and translated by René Braun. 5 vols. Sources chrétiennes 368, 368, 399, 456, 483. Paris: Cerf, 1990–2004.

Turcan, Robert. *The Cults of the Roman Empire*. Translated by Antonia Nevill. The Ancient World. Cambridge, MA: Blackwell, 1996.

Wacker, Grant. *Augustus H. Strong and the Dilemma of Historical Consciousness*. Macon, GA: Mercer University Press, 1985.

Walker, Andrew, and Luke Bretherton, editors. *Remembering Our Future: Explorations in Deep Church*. Deep Church. Colorado Springs, CO: Paternoster, 2007.

Webber, Robert. *Ancient-Future Faith: Rethinking Evangelicalism for a Postmodern World*. Grand Rapids: Baker, 1999.

———. *Common Roots: The Original Call to an Ancient-Future Faith*. Grand Rapids: Zondervan, 2009.

———. *The Divine Embrace: Recovering the Passionate Spiritual Life*. Ancient-Future Series. Grand Rapids: Baker, 2006.

———. *Evangelicals on the Canterbury Trail: Why Evangelicals Are Attracted to the Liturgical Church*. Harrisburg, PA: Morehouse, 1985.

———. *The Younger Evangelicals: Facing the Challenges of the New World*. Grand Rapids: Baker, 2002.

Webber, Robert, and Donald G. Bloesch, editors. *The Orthodox Evangelicals: Who They Are and What They Are Saying*. Nashville: T. Nelson, 1978.

Wells, David F. *Above All Earthly Pow'rs: Christ in a Postmodern World*. Grand Rapids: Eerdmans, 2005.

———. *No Place for Truth, or, Whatever Happened to Evangelical Theology?* Grand Rapids: Eerdmans, 1993.

Wesley, John. *A Christian Library: Consisting of Extracts from, and Abridgements of, the Choicest Pieces of Practical Divinity Which Have Been Published in the English Tongue*. 50 vols. Bristol: Felix Farley, 1749–55.

———. *A Concise History of England: From the Earliest Times, to the Death of George II*. 4 vols. London: Printed by R. Hawes, 1776.

———. *The Works of John Wesley.* CD-ROM. Franklin, TN: Providence House, 1995.

———. *The Works of John Wesley.* Edited by Albert C. Outler. 26 vols. Bicentennial edition. Nashville: Abingdon, 1984–.

———. *The Works of the Reverend John Wesley, A. M.* 14 vols. London: Wesleyan Conference Office, printed by W. Nichols, 1872.

———. *The Works of the Reverend John Wesley, A. M.* Edited by John Emory. 7 vols. New York: J. Emory and B. Waugh for the Methodist Episcopal Church, printed by J. Collard, 1831.

Wicker, Christine. *The Fall of the Evangelical Nation: The Surprising Crisis Inside the Church.* New York: HarperCollins, 2008.

Wilken, Robert Louis, with Angela Russel Christman and Michael J. Hollerrich, translators and editors. *Isaiah Interpreted by Early Christian and Medieval Commentators.* Church's Bible. Grand Rapids: Eerdmans, 2007.

Williams, Daniel H. *Evangelicals and Tradition: The Formative Influence of the Early Church.* The Evangelical Ressourcement. Grand Rapids: Baker, 2005.

Wuthnow, Robert. *The Restructuring of American Religion: Society and Faith since World War II.* Studies in Church and State. Princeton, NJ: Princeton University Press, 1988.

Yrigoyen, Charles, and George H. Bricker, editors. *Catholic and Reformed: Selected Writings of John Williamson Nevin.* Pittsburgh: Pickwick, 1978.

Articles and Essays

Alford, Robert. "Why Do Historians Write about Race, Class & Gender?" History News Network. http://hnn.us/articles/3520.html.

Audet, T. "Orientations Théologiques chéz Saint Irénée," *Traditio* 1 (1943) 33–39.

Bloom, Allan David. "The Study of Texts." In *Giants and Dwarfs: Essays 1960–1990,* 295–314. New York: Simon and Schuster, 1990.

Brown, Harold O. J. "Proclamation and Preservation: The Necessity and Temptations of Church Tradition." In *Reclaiming the Great Tradition: Evangelicals, Catholics and Orthodox in Dialogue,* edited by James S. Cutsinger, 69–87. Downers Grove, IL: InterVarsity, 1997.

Brox, N. "Rom und 'jede Kirche' im 2. Jahrhundert: Zu Irenäus, adv. haer. III 3.2." *Annuarium Historiae Conciliorum* 7 (1975) 42–78.

Bundy, David. "Christian Virtue: John Wesley and the Alexandrian Tradition." *Wesleyan Theological Journal* 26.1 (1991) 139–63.

Campbell, Ted A. "Albert C. Outler and the Heart of the Christian Tradition." *Methodist History* 48.2 (2010) 113–24.

———. "John Wesley and Conyers Middleton on Divine Intervention in History." *Church History* 55.1 (1986) 39–49.

———. "Scripture and Tradition in the Wesleyan Tradition." In *Orthodox and Wesleyan Scriptural Understanding and Practice,* edited by S. T. Kimbrough Jr., 159–69. Crestwood, NY: St. Vladimir's Seminary Press, 2005.

———. "Wesley's Use of the Church Fathers." *Asbury Theological Journal* 50.2/51.1 (1995/96) 57–70.

Carter, Kelly D. "The High Church Roots of John Wesley's Appeal to Primitive Christianity." *Restoration Quarterly* 37.2 (1995) 65–79.

"The Chicago Call: An Appeal to Evangelicals." *Christianity Today,* 17 June 1977, 28–29.

"The Chicago Call—Collection 33." Billy Graham Center Archives. Online: http://www.wheaton.edu/bgc/archives/GUIDES/033.htm.

Christensen, Michael J. "Theosis and Sanctification: John Wesley's Reformulation of a Patristic Doctrine." *Wesleyan Theological Journal* 31.1 (1996) 71–94.

Clarke, G. W. "Irenaeus *Adv. haer.* 4.30.I." *Harvard Theological Review* 59.1 (1966) 95–97.

Collins, Kenneth J. "The State of Wesley Studies in North America: A Theological Journey." *Wesleyan Theological Journal* 44.2 (2009) 7–38.

Davies, Rupert E. "Introduction." In Wesley, *The Works of John Wesley*, edited by Albert C. Outler, 9:20–23. Bicentennial edition. Nashville: Abingdon, 1984–,

Donovan, M. A. "Irenaeus in Recent Scholarship." *Second Century* 4.4 (1984) 219–241.

Douthat, Ross. "Mass-Market Epiphany." *New York Times*, 8 March 2010, op-ed. Online: http://www.nytimes.com/2010/03/08/opinion/08douthat.html?scp=1&sq=Mass-Market%20Epiphany&st=cse.

Duffy, Eamon. "Primitive Christianity Revived: Religious Renewal in Augustan England." In *Renaissance and Renewal in Church History: Papers Read at the Fifteenth Summer Meeting and the Sixteenth Winter Meeting of the Ecclesiastical History Society*, edited by Derek Baker, 287–300. Studies in Church History 14. Oxford: Blackwell, 1977.

English, John C. "References to St. Augustine in the Works of John Wesley." *Asbury Theological Journal* 60.2 (2005) 5–24.

Escoula, L. "Saint Irénée et la connaissance naturelle de Dieu." *Revue des sciences religieuses* 20.3–4 (1940) 252–70.

Fowden, Garth. "Religious Communities." In *Late Antiquity: A Guide to the Postclassical World*, edited by G. W. Bowersock, Peter Brown, and Oleg Grabar, 82–106. Harvard University Press Reference Library. Cambridge, MA: Belknap, 1999.

Gallo, Michael F. "*The Chicago Call* Ten Years Later." *Touchstone*, Winter 1988. Online: http://www.touchstonemag.com/archives/article.php?id=02-02-007-f.

Goalen, Martin. "The Idea of the City and the Excavations at Pompeii." In *Urban Society in Roman Italy*, edited by Tim Cornell and Kathryn Lomas, 181–202. New York: Routledge, 1995.

Greer, R. A. "The Dog and the Mushrooms: Irenaeus's View of the Valentinians Assessed." In *The Rediscovery of Gnosticism*, vol. 1 (*The School of Valentinus*), edited by Bentley Layton, 1:146–75. Studies in the History of Religions 41. Leiden: Brill, 1980.

Gregory of Nazianzus. "The First Theological Oration." In *Christology of the Later Fathers*, edited by Edward Rochie Hardy. Library of Christian Classics 3. Philadelphia: Westminster, 1954.

Hammond, Geordan. "John Wesley's Mindset at the Commencement of His Georgia Sojourn: Suffering and the Introduction of Primitive Christianity to the Indians." *Methodist History* 47.1 (2008) 16–25.

Hart, David Bentley. "The Mirror of the Infinite: Gregory of Nyssa on the Vestigia Trinitatis." *Modern Theology* 18.4 (4 October 2002) 541–61.

Hauerwas, Stanley. "Foreword." In *Heresies and How to Avoid Them: Why It Matters What Christians Believe*, edited by Ben Quash and Michael Ward, ix–xi. Peabody, MA: Hendrickson, 2007.

Hefner, P. "Theological Methodology and St. Irenaeus." *Journal of Religion* 44.4 (1964) 294–309.

Heitzenrater, Richard P. "John Wesley's *A Christian Library,* Then and Now." *American Theological Library Association Summary of Proceedings* 55 (2001) 133–46.

———. "John Wesley's Reading of and References to the Early Church Fathers." In *Orthodox and Wesleyan Spirituality,* edited by S. T. Kimbrough Jr., 25–32. Crestwood, NY: St. Vladimir's Seminary Press, 2002.

Holifield, E. Brooks. "On Teaching the History of Christianity: Traditions and Presuppositions." *Church History* 72.2 (June 2003) 237–50.

Jackson, R. "The Role of Doctors in the City." In *Roman Working Lives and Urban Living,* edited by A. MacMahon and J. Price, 202–21. Oxford: Oxbow, 2005.

Keefer, Luke L., Jr. "John Wesley: Disciple of Early Christianity." *Wesleyan Theological Journal* 19.1 (1984) 23–32.

Keresztes, P. "A Favourable Aspect of the Emperor Commodus' Rule." In *Hommages* à *Marcel Renard,* edited by Jacqueline Bibauw, 2:368–77. Collection Latomus 102. Brusselles: Latomus Revue d'Études Latines, 1969.

Lee, Hoo-Jung. "John Wesley and Early Eastern Spirituality." In *Religious Pluralism and Korean Theology.* Seoul: Korean Institute of Theology Press, 1992.

———. "Experiencing the Spirit in Wesley and Macarius." In *Rethinking Wesley's Theology for Contemporary Methodism,* edited by Randy Maddox, 197–212. Nashville: Kingswood, 1998.

Lim, Richard. "Christian Triumph and Controversy." In *Late Antiquity: A Guide to the Postclassical World,* edited by G. W. Bowersock, Peter Brown, and Oleg Grabar, 196–218. Harvard University Press Reference Library. Cambridge, MA: Belknap, 1999.

Lindsell, Harold. "Religious Roots: A Call to Dig." *Christianity Today,* 17 June 1977, 27.

Litfin, Bryan M. "The Rule of Faith in Augustine." *Pro Ecclesia* 14.1 (2005) 85–101.

MacMillan, Ken. "John Wesley and the Enlightened Historians." *Methodist History* 38.2 (2000) 121–32.

Maddox, Randy L. "John Wesley and Eastern Orthodoxy: Influences, Convergences, and Differences." *Asbury Theological Journal* 45.2 (1990) 29–53.

McCormick, K. Steve. "Theosis in Chrysostom and Wesley: An Eastern Paradigm on Faith and Love." *Wesleyan Theological Journal* 26.1 (1991) 38–103.

McKnight, Scot. "The Ironic Faith of Emergents." *Christianity Today,* September 2008, 62–63.

Mead, Richard T. "A Dissenting Opinion about Respect for Context in Old Testament Quotations." *New Testament Studies* 10.2 (1963–64) 279–89.

Middleton, Robert G. "The Bosford Declaration." *The Christian Century,* 18–25 August 1976, 704–8.

Nevin, John Williamson. "The Apostles' Creed—II. Its Inward Constitution and Form." *Mercersburg Review* 1.3 (May 1849) 201–21.

———. "Cyprian (Second Article)." *Mercersburg Review* 4.4 (1852) 335–87.

———. "Cyprian (Third Article)." *Mercersburg Review* 4.5 (1852) 417–52.

———. "Cyprian (Fourth and Last Article)." *Mercersburg Review* 4.6 (1852) 513–63.

———. "Early Christianity (Second Article)." *Mercersburg Review* 3.6 (November 1851) 513–62. Reprinted in *Catholic and Reformed: Selected Writings of John Williamson Nevin,* edited by Charles Yrigoyen and George H. Bricker. Pittsburgh: Pickwick, 1978.

———. "Modern Civilization." *Mercersburg Review* 3.2 (March 1851) 165–208.

———. "Puritanism and the Creed." *Mercersburg Review* 1.6 (November 1849) 585–603.

————. "Theology of the New Liturgy." *Mercersburg Review* 14 (January 1867) 23–66.

Noble, Thomas A. "East and West in the Theology of John Wesley." *Bulletin of the John Rylands University Library of Manchester* 85 (2003) 359–72.

Noll, Mark A. "Evangelicals on the Canterbury Trail." *Eternity* 29 (March 1978) 14–19.

Norris, Richard A. "The Transcendence and Freedom of God: Irenaeus, the Greek Tradition and Gnosticism." In *Early Christian Literature and the Classical Intellectual Tradition: In Honorem Robert M. Grant*, edited by William R. Schoedel and Robert L. Wilken, 87–100. Théologie historique 54. Paris: Éditiones Beauchesne, 1979.

North, J. A. "Religion and Rusticity." In *Urban Society in Roman Italy*, edited by T. J. Cornell and K. Lomas, 135–50. New York: Routledge, 1995.

Outler, Albert C. "Introduction." In *John Wesley*, edited by Outler, 3–34. Oxford: Oxford University Press, 1964.

Porter, James I. "Hermeneutical Lines and Circles: Aristarchus and Crates on the Exegesis of Homer." in *Homer's Ancient Readers: The Hermeneutics of Greek Epic's Earliest Exegetes*, edited by Robert Lamberton and John J. Keany, 73–77. Princeton, NJ: Princeton University Press, 1992.

Schoedel, William R. "Enclosing, Not Enclosed: The Early Christian Doctrine of God." In *Early Christian Literature and the Classical Intellectual Tradition: In Honorem Robert M. Grant*, edited by William R. Schoedel and Robert L. Wilken, 75–100. Théologie historique 54. Paris: Éditiones Beauchesne, 1979.

Seaborn, Joseph William, Jr. "Wesley's Views on the Uses of History." *Wesleyan Theological Journal* 21.1–2 (1986) 129–36.

Simonetti, Manlio. "Theodore of Mopsuestia (CA. 350–429)." In *Handbook of Patristic Exegesis: The Bible in Ancient Christianity*, edited by Charles Kannengiesser, 2:799–828. Leiden: Brill, 2004.

Smith, J. Warren. "John Wesley's Growth in Grace and Gregory of Nyssa's Epectasy: A Conversion in Dynamic Perfection." *Bulletin of the John Rylands University Library of Manchester* 85 (2003) 347–58.

Spencer, Michael. "The Coming Evangelical Collapse." *Christian Science Monitor*, 10 March 2009. Online: http://www.csmonitor.com/Commentary/Opinion/2009/0310/p09s01-coop.html.

Sly, Randy. "Special Report: Evangelicals Discover Treasures Old and New." Catholic Online. http://www.catholic.org/national/national_story.php?id=27157.

Steward, Kenneth J. "Evangelicals and Patristic Christianity: 1517 to the Present." *Evangelical Quarterly* 80.4 (2008) 308.

Stroumsa, G. G. "The Christian Hermeneutical Revolution and Its Double Helix." in *The Use of Sacred Books in the Ancient World*, edited by L. V. Rutgers et al., 9–28. Contributions to Biblical Exegesis and Theology 22. Leuven: Peeters, 1998.

Thompson, J. Earl, Jr. "Church History Comes to Andover: The Persecution of James Murdock." *Andover Newton Quarterly* 15.4 (March 1985) 213–27.

Tolar Burton, Vicki. "Appendix B: John Wesley's Book Inventory, Compiled at the Time of His Death." In *Spiritual Literacy in John Wesley's Methodism: Reading, Writing, and Speaking to Believe*, 315–39. Studies in Rhetoric and Religion 6. Waco, TX: Baylor University Press, 2008.

Webber, W. "The Antonines: (7) The Accession and Reign of Commodus." In *The Cambridge Ancient History*, vol. 11 (*The Imperial Peace: A.D. 70–192*), edited by S. A. Cook et al. Cambridge: Cambridge University Press, 1936.

Woodward, Kenneth L., with Frank Maier. "Roots for Evangelicals." *Newsweek*, 23 May 1977, 76.

Scripture Index

Name and Subject Index

Wesley, John, 2, 52–76, 78–84, 245
   Christian Library, 67–69, 72, 75, 78, 84
   Electicism, 53
   fascination with early Church, 53, 63
   historical methodology, 62, 71
Wesleyanism, 57, 75
Westminster Confession, 155
Wheaton College, 5, 15, 112, 124, 125, 127, 137, 210, 211, 242, 251
The Wheaton Center for Early Christian Studies, The, 1, 2, 15, 23, 43, 50, 131, 135, 138, 247, 250

Whitefield, George, 6
Wicker, Christine, 159, 160
Wilken, Robert Louis, 2, 7, 13, 116, 132, 136, 250
Williams, Daniel H., 245, 246
Williams, George, 132
Worship, 109
   liturgical, 128
Wright, Tom, 145, 153, 157
Wuthnow, Robert, 115

Young, Francis, 245

Zwingli, Huldrych, 230